Edited by Jill Scott

TRANSDISCOURSE 3

WOMEN IN ART, SCIENCE AND BODY POLITICS

Transdisciplinary Studies: Exploring the dynamic intersections of discovery, creativity and inclusive futures from the arts and the sciences

DE GRUYTER

CONTEXTUALISATIONS

PERSONAL REFLECTIONS

EXHIBITIONS

CONVERSATIONS

INVESTIGATIONS

BIOGRAPHIES

FOREWORD

RETHINKING CREATIVITY

Silvie Cuperus, *Life Science Zurich, University of Zurich & ETH Zurich*

Creativity is becoming increasingly essential to address the most pressing challenges of our time, such as climate change, global health crises, inequality, political polarisation and technological disruption. These complex, interconnected challenges require trans- and interdisciplinary cooperations to be tackled effectively. In this book *Rethinking Creativity* is about the fusion of discovery with creativity from a female perspective. It can be a powerful and necessary step in addressing these issues. This approach may lead to stronger transdisciplinary collaborations, transcend the conventional metrics of efficiency and foster innovative, empathetic, and sustainable solutions. Women in the arts and sciences are increasingly breaking down disciplinary boundaries to utilise a variety of inspiring processes that might address these issues. Because cultural analysis incorporates life, sociology and philosophy, visual artists, curators and art historians are open to work with scientists, not only for inspiration but to discuss these controversies from new perspectives and explore the potentials of emotional and metaphorical communication to the public. What creative approaches and themes do women in these fields share? How can creativity rather than efficiency become the basic theme that leads us to work together?

Transdiscourse 3: Women in Art, Science and Body Politics showcases the ways in which researchers and artists engage with cutting-edge transdisciplinary research, exchange ideas and collaborate on projects that integrate art, science and technology. Focusing on research by women encourages critical reflection on inclusivity, diversity, and the ethical responsibility, recognising the interconnectedness of these issues to meet today's challenges.

Key explorations include:

- How female artists and scientists are reshaping creative processes, using both conscious and unconscious thought.
- How the creative processes of research, preparation, incubation, illumination, evaluation, and implementation can create a space for new dialogues.
- How transdisciplinary dialogue in science and art can challenge traditional boundaries and envision original solutions for our planet.
- How the relevance of themes such as eco-feminism, biomimicry, and degrowth are being reflected in both artistic and scientific practices.

Therefore, this book aims to inspire women to forge meaningful connections and to encourage a dialogue between researchers in science, art, and technology. To this end, *Transdiscourse 3: Women in Art, Science and Body Politics* can facilitate the discussion of paradigm shifts in scientific research, the implementation of new technologies and novel developments for gender studies, with a focus on women.

INTRODUCTION

WOMEN IN ART, SCIENCE AND BODY POLITICS

Jill Scott

Women in Art, Science and Body Politics unites international women from the arts to explore dynamic intersections of science, body politics, and inclusive futures. Through creative approaches and collaboration with scientists, they reflect on the ethics of care and urgent social and environmental issues. Divided into five themes (*Contextualisations, Personal Reflections, Exhibitions, Conversations* and *Investigations*), the authors explore how the rethinking of creativity and body politics might affect human rights, sustainability, bodily representations and personal expressions. *Transdiscourse 3* is a unique space for dialogue and a vital transdisciplinary resource, designed to inspire and encourage others to engage with creativity, discovery and change.

Feminism in both art and science often references the intersection of gender, knowledge, and power dynamics. While some authors in this book examine how societal norms and biases have influenced artistic and scientific processes, others reflect on the role of social and cultural factors in art and scientific research for knowledge production, or work on projects that explore the representation of the female body and gender equality. Therefore, in this book, we have taken a more contextualised and intersectional approach. It seems that cultural, political, and historical forces shape gendered experiences, and these forces tend to manifest differently across race, class, ability, and time. Personal reflections can only deepen this understanding, providing an insight into the lived realities and emotional landscapes often absent from traditional scholarship. Such narratives challenge dominant power structures and offer alternative ways of knowing: linking personal histories with broader struggles for representation and justice. In this book, we focus on the artist's perspective and exploration of identity through visual media. These accounts illuminate the complexity and resilience of women navigating layered systems of power that exist in both worlds: art and science.

As a background to this relationship between feminism, visual art and science, it may be interesting to trace some "her-stories" of literature, performance art and video art where women have explored their own sexuality and the need to break away from the male gaze. In the art world of the 1970s, women artists reclaimed their bodies, identities, and voices under the banners of human rights. In science as well, pioneers emerged like Rachel Carson (1962), whose conservation legacy was a vital influence on the growth of the ecofeminism movement and US Environmental Protection Policy.

In the arts, women joined the resistance against art as commodity and rather opted for ephemeral and intangible quest for creative alternatives that could give them a stronger voice. For example, pioneering figures such as Carolee Schneemann, Yvonne Rainer, and Valie Export pushed the boundaries of art by using their own bodies in performances as living materials and valuing the process as more important than the art product. These revolutionaries confronted issues like objectification, gender inequality, and violence against women. Their work often combined media, movement, and protest to challenge how the female body was viewed in both, art and society. By doing so, they redefined what art could be, and for whom it was made. Across Europe, artists like Ulrike Rosenbach, Marina Abramović and Rebecca Horn explored themes of femininity, identity, and power. Rosenbach (Figure 1) used video and ritualistic actions to critique patriarchal art history, while Horn's fantastic body extensions transformed the human form into a symbol of struggle, resilience, and transformation. These women turned their physical presence into a statement of defiance - resisting how the female form had historically been portrayed and asserting their own narratives. Their work still resonates today, under the umbrella of body politics, urging us to consider how women's identities can be self-defined, rather than shaped by external norms.

Other influential voices like Louise Bourgeois from France and Suzanne Lacy and Judy Chicago from the U.S. made significant contributions by mixing visual art with deeply personal and political themes. Bourgeois' haunting sculptures explored the complexities of family, trauma, and sexuality, while Lacy and Chicago created large-scale social practice works that involved communities and addressed topics such as female genitals, aging, and domestic violence. Their collective legacy reminds us that art is not just something to be viewed - it's something that can transform how we see ourselves and society (Goldberg, 2004). By the mid 1970s, a global network of feminist artists had emerged, from Australia's Philippa Cullen, who used movement-sensitive floors and Theremins in her dance, to collectives that met to reimagine women's roles in art, science, and ecology. At the same time, I was working as an artist in San Francisco - my body was taped to the city's walls and bridges with masking tape. (Taped 1975). All in all, these 70s reactionaries seemed to lay the groundwork for future generations and it was followed by an unprecedented era of academic freedom in universities during the 80s and the formation of many departments for gender studies. Women quickly realised that a culture that does not question itself can become toxic over time!

By the 80s and in relation to the increase in the use of digital technology as a tool to emphasise our voices, theorists like Donna Haraway (1991) opened provocative discourses that might challenge traditional boundaries, suggesting that the cyborg, a hybrid for organism and machine can offer a powerful metaphor to understand complex notions about the self and the other. Such theorists influenced media artists to engage more deeply in the senses and interactive technology, encouraging them to blur the boundaries between the organic body and computer interaction. I was also interested in this discussion and made an interactive media project called *Frontiers of Utopia* (Scott, 1995) (Figure 2), exploring idealism and women from different generations.

Later in the 90s, gender theorists like Judith Butler, suggested that we focus in gender studies on the incorporation of action, theory and women's history, because such contexts allow for more structured approaches to human rights. It seems that language itself can influence biases toward gendered thinking as well as change societal expectations regarding equal representation, the value of performativity and queer identification. When I recently attended the Frauen Strike* in Bern, Switzerland this year, I remembered how the above groups of artists and writers often asked provocative questions. Certainly, today's young feminists and non-binary creatives continue to speak out, act out, and challenge the norms. Women continue to be critical antennas of society. Whether through performance, video, or activism, the energy of the 70s, 80s and 90s lives on, embodied in every woman who dares to take up space and shape her own story (National Women's History Museum).

To explore some of these spaces and influences in a more contemporary light, my copy editor Karen Wong-Dorall and I have divided the essays in this book into five categories or practices, all ending with the letters "ions": *Contextualisations, Personal Reflections, Exhibitions, Conversations and Investigations.* In physics, an ion is an atom or molecule with a net electric charge due to the loss or gain of one or more electrons, and it plays a crucial role in the energy cycle, particularly in photosynthesis and cellular respiration. Additionally, ions also play crucial roles in the human body, acting as messengers and workers within cells to facilitate essential processes and maintain overall health.

It is hoped that this book serves as a "working messenger": an electrical charge to shift focus and re-reflect on body politics and feminism. While *Contextualisations, Conversations, and Investigations* provide fertile ground for engaging with these dynamics, *exhibitions* of women artists not only challenge the myth of the male artistic genius but also recover and reassert the significance of forgotten voices, feminist perspectives, and art as activism.

Similarly, in the section titled *Conversations*, cross-disciplinary exchange allows for expanded understanding, revealing how gender inequalities manifest differently in science labs, studios, and academic fields, while also uncovering shared strategies and goals, particularly about our current environmental issues. Artistic research and science communication through creative practice push the boundaries of how knowledge is produced and shared, bridging emotional insight with intellectual inquiry. Together, these practices promote not only visibility and representation, but also foster critical dialogue and collective transformation in how we perceive women's roles in shaping both artistic and scientific "future worlds."

In the section titled *Contextualisations*, the role of context in women's studies is emphasised as crucial to understand the complexities of women's experiences and the structures that shape them. Because knowledge is often situated in physical spaces, such engagement can provide a framework for understanding how social, political, economic, and cultural contexts influence gender roles, power dynamics, and the lived realities of women across different groups and historical periods.

In the first essay, Alexandra Krawiec talks about how, at the start of the 21st century, women faced new challenges amid technological advances and cultural shifts. As she suggests, despite progress, gender inequality still affects the recognition of women's achievements, while persistent discrimination limits education access, undervalues contributions, and enables political manipulation. Some leaders use gender issues politically, restricting women's agency and cutting funding in female-dominated groups like art and biology, causing deep systemic marginalisation. She asks: How can technology and socio-political instability reshape the roles of women artists and scientists? What new and exciting opportunities for creative women exist in our current technophilic world?

In the second essay, I collaborated with authors, Rewa Wright and Clarissa Ribero, to explore how women in arts, sciences, and indigenous communities could collaborate around mediated environments, body politics, natural science, and an "ethics of care". We begin with an analysis of, and the lasting impact of, activist movements like Degrowth, Ecofeminism and Biomimicry. We aim to contextualise some of our own current artistic research on human-nature connections, thereby fostering engagement with ways to enable collective action to care for nature more responsibly. We authors also highlight how initiatives like co-creative workshops might raise public reflection, education, and equality, as well as encourage collaboration for actions to rewild our local landscapes. We argue that hands-on experience on-site and embodiment are more likely to lead to sustainable community action.

In the final section of *Contextualisation*, art historian Marìa Fernández explores how posthumanism, in the context of climate change and ecological crises, highlights the interdependence of all lifeforms. She examines how scientific, social, and political systems shape our understanding of bodies and knowledge. Focusing on artists Sonya Bäumel and Anna Dumitriu, who use bacteria in their work, the essay discusses how their art reveals hidden aspects of the body and challenges ideas of human wholeness and autonomy. By blending domestic objects, craft, and microbiology, they disrupt boundaries between private and public, science and art, questioning power, legitimacy, and the invisibility of women's contributions in science.

The next section titled *Personal Reflections*, explores how artists can offer valuable insights from their own lived experiences, challenging dominant narratives and providing a nuanced understanding of gender, identity, and social inequalities. In this section, the intersectionality of gender with other disciplinary practices, like technology and biology can illuminate the power of shared struggles and the interconnectedness of women and natural systems.

In a project entitled: *The Absence of Alice* (AOA), Svenja Kratz explore life's transformative potential through the science of biotechnology. This five-part exhibition responded to culturing Saos-2 cancer cells from an 11-year-old girl, examining the liminality of living tissue, life, death, and identity. The project raised ethical questions about using human biological material and linking this material to the history of cell lines. The author challenges some posthuman ideas around the future impact of biotechnology. This issue, not only allows for speculation but can also provoke discussion on ethics, reproduction, and the roles of women in science.

Another bio-artist, Tarsh Bates, is interested in the challenges of coorporation on the microscale. She describes the moment when she realised that her own human body is 90% microbial, and how this fact is a metaphor for pluralism in gender identification. Drawing on biotechnology, microbiology, and art, she becomes "them" to explore bodies as queer ecologies and reflect on the care for non-human lifeforms. Influenced by artists like Ionet Zurr, she/they explore human-microbe relations and microbial agency. Can our bodies' microbes be reconsidered as a vital, co-creative relationship and kinship that sustains all life?

Tarsh, began "their" journeys with biology studies. In the next essay, Austrian media artist, Christa Sommerer also first studied botany and anthropology with a fascination for plant morphology, taxonomy, and botanical illustration. Here, she discovered *Phyllologia*: a speculative botanical art system that later influenced many of her art projects. Her blending of biology and technology into interactive art, encourages reflection and addresses the challenges of empathetic communication between nature and us. She also considers women's roles in media arts and her equal collaboration with Laurent Mignonneau on interactive plant projects for exhibitions.

The third section titled *Exhibitions* features women artists who combine art, life science, and technology, offering several learning opportunities. These artists not only challenge traditional narratives and foster a more inclusive understanding of the relations between art, culture and nature, through hands-on interactions, but they promote discussions about gender equality in both science and art contexts - raising issues that combine creativity and discovery.

In 2014, Rachael Parsons, Lubi Thomas and Trish Adams curated a unique international exhibition that is featured here in this book. Titled *Femel_ Fissions*, it showcased how discoveries by prominent women in science have inspired contemporary women artists. This exhibition aimed to highlight women's historical impact on science through newly commissioned works by international artists. Therefore, the curators selected women scientists from disciplines such as neurology, biology, cytogenetics, psychology, primatology, and anatomy. Scientists like Rita Levi-Montalcini (the Italian neurobiologist who discovered how cells and nerves cooperate) and evolutionary biologist Lynn Margulis, (who proposed the theory of endosymbiosis), were offered as inspirational characters (Thomas, 2014). The participating artists were Trish Adams, Tarsh Bates, Gina Czarnecki, Svenja Kratz, Rachel Mayeri, Helen Pynor and Jill Scott.

In another exhibition, *Feminist Climate Change*: Beyond the Binary from Ars Electronica in 2017, curator and media artist Victoria Vesna explored the intersecting crises of gender, ecology, and technology. The exhibition focused on Iranian designer Maryam Razi's journey from transnational collaborator to climate-displaced artist, highlighting women's growing precarity. Set against the backdrop of the #MeToo movement and Greta Thunberg's activism, the exhibition served as both a critical intervention and an archive of feminist climate justice. Vesna's accompanying essay advocates the re-imagining of institutional and ecological systems grounded in care, ecofeminism, interdependence, and radical transformation. Participating young artists included Phoebe Hui, Olivia Osborne, Noa Kaplan, Silvia Rigon, Xin Xin, Mary Magic Tsang, Rita Blaik, John Brumley, and Anne Niemetz. A panel discussion complemented the exhibition, serving as a method to open further dialogue on art, technology and ongoing conversations about these critical themes (Ars Electronica, 2017).

In the fourth section entitled *Conversations*, dialogues between women from different disciplines can offer a powerful tool for cross-disciplinary learning and analysis. While this section of the book is just a starting point, such conversations can expand perspectives and encourage people to think beyond their disciplinary boxes. Indeed, they can help move both art and science beyond narrow boundaries, allowing us to identify common threads, reveal shared challenges and experiences, and construct novel strategies for addressing gender inequality.

For years, conversations have been a central component of residency projects for artists in science labs. For example, the *Artist-in-labs* program in Zurich (*Artist-in-labs*, n.d.) or *SymbioticA* in Perth (SymbioticA, n.d.) have enabled many artists to be engaged with laboratories in technology and the life sciences. Currently, we conduct Leonardo LASER-ZURICHTalks, which bring together artists and scientists to exchange ideas on themes that are socially relevant and open up public debate (LASER-ZURICH, n.d.).

The first conversation in this book originated at one of these *LASER Talks* in Zurich between artist Helen Pynor and psychologist Bigna Lenggenhager. In their discussion, they explore how art and science share creative processes involving uncertainty, intuition, and serendipity – despite differing methodologies and criteria for success. While both may investigate similar subjects, such as living entities, they approach knowledge and critique differently, often borrowing from one another in asymmetric ways. The conversation reflects the perspectives of an artist trained in science and a scientist studying phenomena that extend beyond traditional scientific frameworks. How can their interdisciplinary backgrounds shape their practices and break down disciplinary borders?

In another conversation between Margaret Tan (artist) and Kathleen Ditzig (curator), the borders of art-as-research and technology are challenged. Margaret's evolution as a cyberfeminist artist is closely linked to the rise of feminist theory and technology in Singapore's art scene. Influenced by scholars and curators, she developed interdisciplinary, feminist, and new media art rooted in performance. Tan's work critiques cybernetic technologies and neoliberalism, and she has gained recognition for pioneering virtual reality art. The interview highlights her engagement with feminism, technology, globalisation, and her impact on Singapore's cyberfeminist movement.

In the fifth section titled *Investigations*, the authors delve into how art-based inquiry can provide fresh perspectives on complex issues, combining creativity with scientific exploration. Investigations in art and research like these offer distinct but potentially intertwined benefits. While experiencing art may enhance well-being, stimulate emotional responses, and improve cognitive skills, artistic research - can lead to new forms of knowledge and understanding through exploration and experimentation. Science communication often relies on analogies to communicate complex discoveries to the public. In contrast, art researchers draw on semiotics, multimodal sensory perception, aesthetics, emotional impact and more performative forms of expression, thus offering post-reflective insights into well-being, uncertainty, and potential solutions.

The first essay in this section, *Art as Evidence*, is by Inês Montalvão, who traces how research in the arts can offer hope in these times of uncertainty. In relation to the themes of climate change for example, the challenge is to combat denialism - an emotion driven by fake media, vested interests and capitalist ideology. Its consequences are severe: extreme weather events, ecosystem collapse, displacement, and rising death tolls. She suggests that by confronting denialism, artists and scientists can help build a world in which environmental care and social equity thrive - an investigation that is essential to the health and well-being of our planet.

By engaging in art and research related to the redesign of our digital systems and behaviour, we might also foster a deeper understanding of stimulation of our senses. In the second essay in this section of *Investigations*, Claudia Schnugg, Daniela Brill and Christian Stary explore the body's role in sensemaking during digital transformation, especially with scientists who are involved with cyber-physical systems (CPS) research. Within the science of communications and engineering, sensemaking involves jointly creating shared understanding beyond mere information gathering, emphasising embodiment, temporality, and sensory engagement. Here, a team of two female researchers introduce art, science, and feminist approaches into a male-dominated scientific institute, fostering collaboration through performances aligned with their scientific questions. This interdisciplinary effort highlights the body's importance in CPS sensemaking, promoting diversity, accessibility, and offers some new feminist perspectives on digital research and body politics.

In another investigation about the body and the ethics of care, Jane Prophet, Afton Hassett, and Rahbel Rahman-Tahir explore how interdisciplinary collaborations in art and design research can be combined with medicine and social work. In their example, a large team of twenty-one researchers explore chronic pain and health inequities, particularly for women of colour. Here, creative methods and community engagement challenge extractive research norms and their findings emphasise the need to share differences, build trust, and value lived experience as expertise. The authors argue that large cross-disciplinary groups of people can foster inclusive, patient-centred research, promoting equity and broader institutional transformation in health research.

In conclusion, the categorisations in this book hope to offer researchers some tangible ways to identify with gender and related research themes across art and science disciplines. Although the valuable history of women in science would constitute another whole book, it is hoped that this resource is stimulating for art researchers who wish to explore the subjects of science and gender in the future. Consequently, Karen Ann Wong-Dorall and I decided to include the start of an ongoing supplementary section in the back of *Transdiscourse 3* called *Current Resources of Herstorical Significance.* Such initiatives are important to find support sites and spaces for women - especially for women who are historically marginalised - working at the intersection of art and science. This effort aimed to create online and in-person spaces to engage with ethics of care and explore transdisciplinary practices. Rooted in feminist perspectives, they focus to promote equality through collaboration, experimentation, and dialogue, addressing gender inequality and representation in science and art. Key organisations and platforms provide community-building, interviews, and resources, fostering inclusive environments. These networks empower women to thrive, collaborate, and drive meaningful change, welcoming all who share these goals to advance more inclusive narratives in both art and science fields. We hope you, the reader, can and will add to this list.

Transdiscourse 3: *Women in Art, Science and Body Politics* is a starting point to enhance critical thinking skills: to engage with different perspectives and approaches to study and to allow for a more nuanced understanding of gender in transdisciplinary research and practice. By bringing visibility to these authors, curators and artists, our aim is to provide a unique glimpse into the worldviews, experiences, and artistic styles of women artists who are interested in the life sciences and technology. Here, *Contextualisations, Personal Reflections, Exhibitions, Conversations* and *Investigations* can be considered as "working messengers" to challenge dominant ideologies and make visible society's marginalised communities, encouraging audiences to discuss the impact of gender on society and the culture/nature divide.

References

- Ars Electronica, 2017. Feminist Climate Change: Beyond the Binary. [online] Available at: https://ars.electronica.art/aeblog/en/2017/09/05/feminist-climate-change/ [Accessed 20 June 2025].
- Artists-in-Labs, n.d. Artists-in-Labs. [online] Available at: https://www.artistsinlabs.ch [Accessed 20 June 2025].
- Butler, J., 2024. Who's Afraid of Gender? New York: Farrar, Straus and Giroux.
- Carson, R., 1962. Silent Spring. Boston: Houghton Mifflin.
- Goldberg, R.L., 2004. Performance: Live Art Since the 60s. [online] Available at: https://monoskop.org/images/a/ab/Goldberg_RoseLee_Performance_Live_Art_Since_the_60s_2004.pdf [Accessed 20 June 2025].
- Haraway, D., 1985. A cyborg manifesto: Science, technology, and socialist feminism in the late twentieth century. In: Simians, Cyborgs and Women: The Reinvention of Nature. New York: Routledge, pp.149-181.
- LASERZURICH, n.d. Laser Zurich. [online] Available at: https://www.laserzurich.com [Accessed 20 June 2025].
- National Women's History Museum, n.d. Feminism: The Third Wave. [online] Available at: https://www.womenshistory.org/exhibits/feminism-third-wave [Accessed 20 June 2025].
- Scott, J., 1995. Frontiers of Utopia. [online] Available at: https://www.jillscott.org/artworks/archived/frontiers-of-utopia-1995/ [Accessed 20 June 2025].
- Thomas, D., 2014. Femel Fissions at the QUT Industries Precinct. [pdf] Available at: http://davisthomas.com.au/sites/default/files/uploads/pdf/femelfissions_floorbrochure.pdf [Accessed 20 June 2025].
- Wikipedia, n.d. Feminist performance art. [online] Available at: https://en.wikipedia.org/wiki/Feminist_performance_art [Accessed 20 June 2025].
- Wikipedia, n.d. SymbioticA. [online] Available at: https://en.wikipedia.org/wiki/SymbioticA [Accessed 20 June 2025].
- www.feministischer-streik-bern.ch [Accessed 20 June 2025].

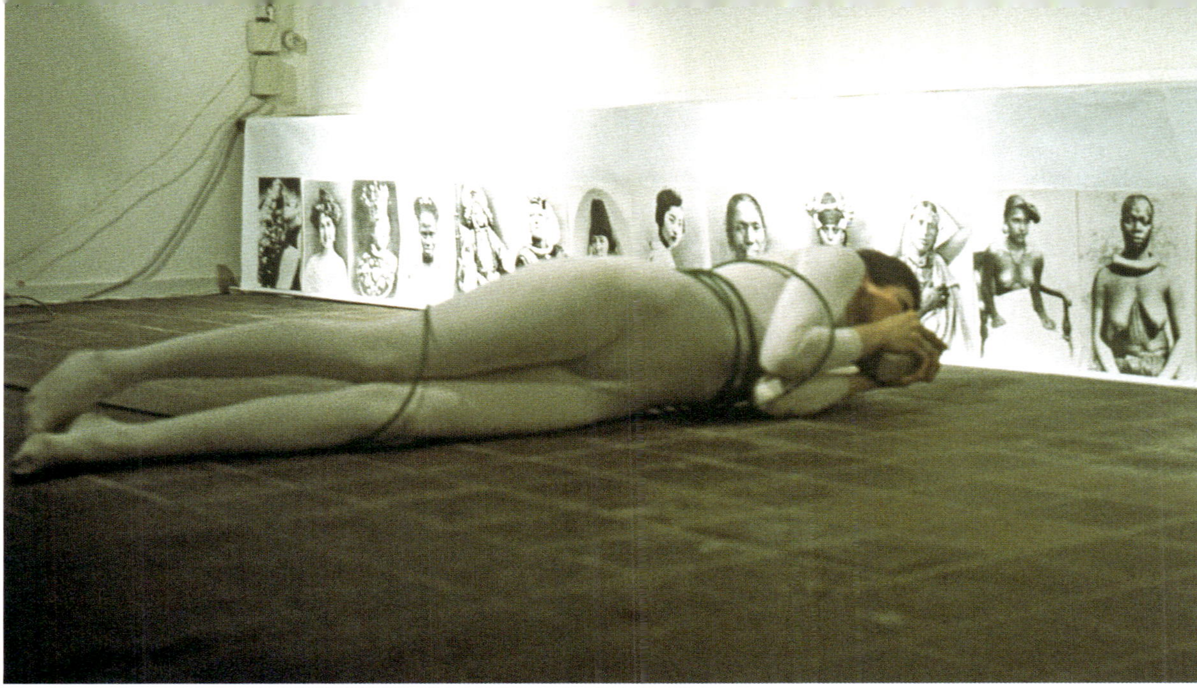

Figure 1: *Frauenkultur Kontaktversuch*. Rosenbach, U. (1977). Rotation Performance/Video.
The artist rolled along the floor to capture images from the history of women with a live video camera.
https//www.ulrike-rosenbach.de

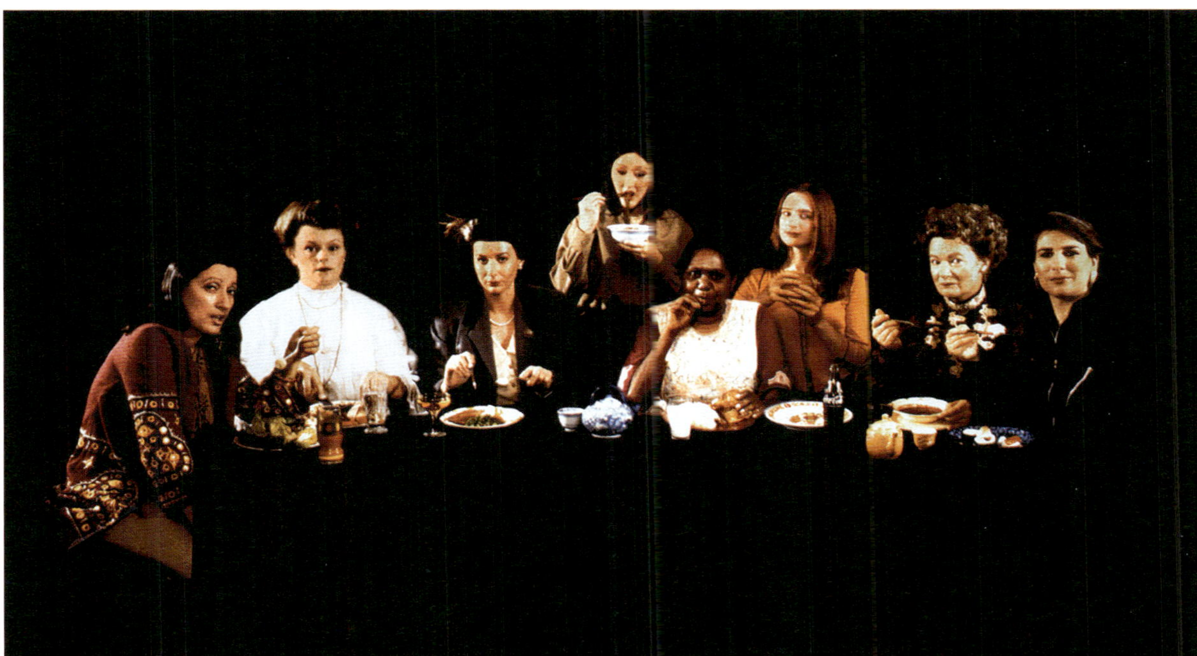

Figure 2: *Frontiers of Utopia*, Scott, J. (1995). Interactive Dinner Party. Characters: from left to right:
Maria (Hippy, Yugoslavia, 1960), Mary (Migrant, Paraguay, 1900), Margaret (Designer, New York, 1930), Ki (Physicist, China, 1990, Pearl (First Nation Poet, Darwin, 1930), Gillian (Student Activist, Melbourne 1970), Emma (Suffragette, Moscow NY, 1900) and Zira (Programmer, Sydney, 1994). https://www.jillscott.org

CONTEXTUALISATIONS

THE IMPACT OF EMERGENT CHALLENGES ON WOMEN IN THE ARTS AND SCIENCES

Alexandra Krawiec

At the turbulent start of the 21st century, women encountered new challenges shaped by technological advancements and shifting cultural paradigms. Despite significant strides towards gender equality, it remains a determining factor in the recognition and valuation of women's achievements. The enduring legacy of women's discrimination - marked by limited access to education, unrecognised contributions, and political manipulation - continues to shape the present. In recent years, in some parts of the world, decision-makers have sought to reinstate exclusionary practices by advancing interests that restrict women's access to positions of agency, often engaging in the political commodification of women's issues - treating gender as a bargaining tool or rhetorical device to further their own agendas. Funding cuts in women-dominated fields also exemplify this persistent trend, not as isolated incidents but as reflections of deeply ingrained systemic patterns that marginalise women's contributions, particularly in the arts and sciences - professions demanding rigorous training and creativity. By recognising the interplay between rapidly advancing technologies and socio-political instability, the author examines aspects of the evolving roles of women artists and scientists in an increasingly technophilic world.

A good designer has a lot in common with a good researcher. Both hunt for excellence and perfection.
Moser, 2014

Throughout most of history, women were a marginalised minority in privileged environments. They entered social arenas decades ago, but achieving equal footing with men required significant societal change. To better understand the current perception of women and their access to opportunities, we must recognise that many of the critical advancements in women's rights are relatively recent. In Europe and the U.S., it took decades to grant women even the basic right to vote. Switzerland lagged until as late as 1971 (Bredbenner, 1998), and in other countries, voting rights were restricted to women of certain backgrounds, often excluding women of color. The 19th Amendment to the U.S. Constitution, passed in 1920, prohibited the denial of voting rights based on sex. However, individual state constitutions continued to disenfranchise minority women. Despite being a global superpower, the U.S. saw some states delay ratification of the amendment for decades. For instance, Mississippi did not ratify it until 1984 (McCammon et al., 2018).

In 1971, the same year Switzerland finally granted women the right to vote, art historian Linda Nochlin (2017) published her provocatively titled essay *Why Are There No Great Women Artists?* In it, she analysed the structural barriers that hindered women's success in the arts, arguing that power dynamics within the art world were fundamentally unfavorable to women (Nochlin, 2017).

According to data analysis published by the National Museum of Women in the Arts (NMWA), in 2018, 87% of works exhibited in 19 major US museums were by male artists (Topaz et al., 2019). When it comes to acquisitions of women's art, 89% of artworks acquired by 26 of the U.S.A's major museums were by male artists. At major auctions, no women are in the top 0.03% of the market, where 41% of the profit is concentrated. Another interesting statistic provided by NMWA, which can be posited to have a causal link to the others, is the disproportion between exhibitions by male and female artists: 86% of exhibits were dedicated to male artists, with the remaining 14% presented to women's art (Halperin and Burns, 2019). As recent studies show, female artists are still less likely to be given opportunities to showcase their work and establish a name for themselves in the art world (Han et al., 2024). This same disparity extends to women musicians (Nokes et al., 2024).

Barriers for women in the sciences, meanwhile, can differ from those for women in the arts. One of the reasons for this is different approach to work evaluation. While in the arts, assessment can largely be based on subjective opinions, professional connections, and public reputation, the evaluation of scientific work is often measurable and more objective. For this and other reasons, women in the sciences have made noticeable progress in terms of representation. UNESCO reports (2024) that, as of 2024, women made up 31.7% of researchers in the sciences globally, a continuation of an upward trend consistent since data gathering began in 1996. In Central Asia, this figure is as high as 49.6% - near parity - and estimates are also above 40% in Latin America, the Caribbean, and the Arab states.

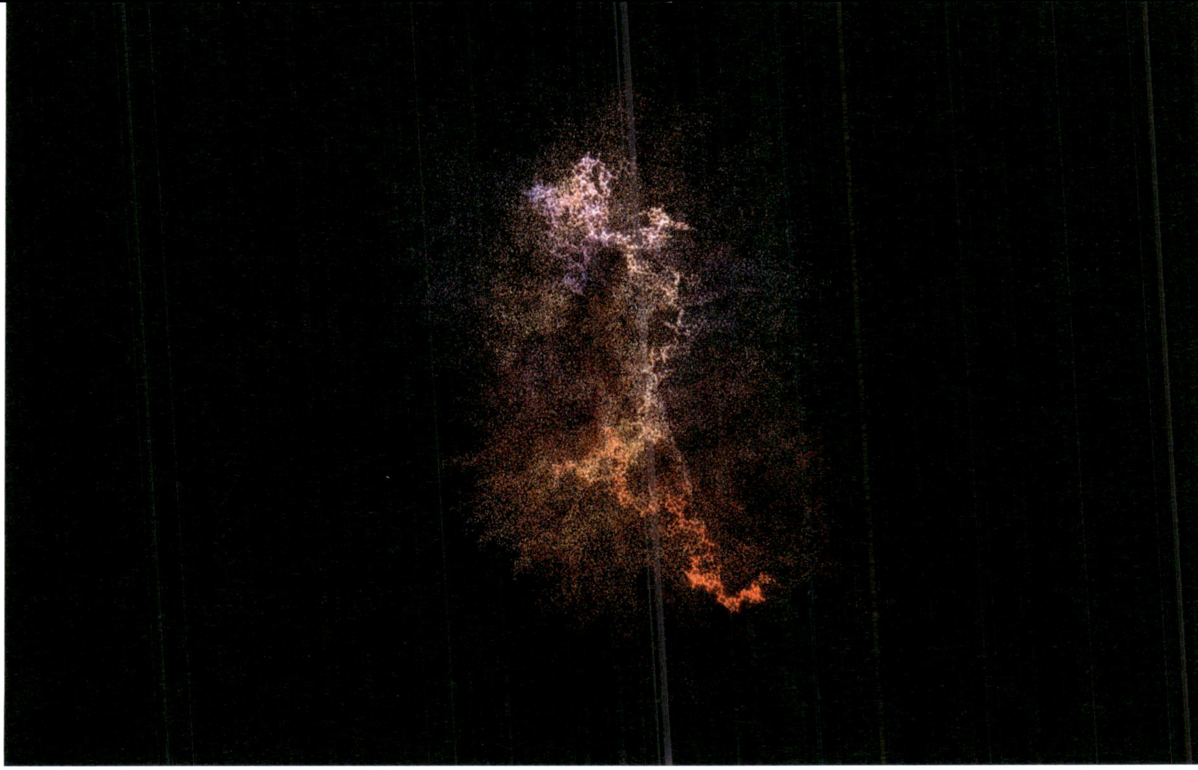

Figure 1: *Vitruvian Woman*. Hoffmann, J. (2019).
Interactive installation, in which Leonardo's drawing of Vetruvian Man is transformed into a dynamic multidimensional geometry of the RNA molecule. A viewer can use his or her breath to transform molecular states and move through various pathways of the poetic labyrinth to shift their identities. Collaborator: Prof. Janusz Bujnicki's Lab, International Centre for Molecular and Cell Biology Warsaw. https://www.johoffmann.com

It cannot be denied that women tend to do well in STEM degrees at the undergraduate level. The National Science Foundation (2019) reports that although only 38.6% of enrolled STEM undergraduates in 2019 were women, 50.1% of bachelor degrees across these fields were awarded to women. That does not mean that women in the sciences do not experience challenges that are not gender-neutral. As analysed by Amartya Sen (2022), the Nobel Prize-winning economist, during the 2020-22 pandemic, women in science experienced gender bias that limited the recognition of their work. He argued that the "information trap" - which can be interpreted as the manipulation of information, impacts the recognition of women who are "much less acknowledged than they should be" (Sen, 2022).

It is, however, clear that women continue to choose long-term careers in the sciences at lower rates than men. Many posit that the source of this discrepancy lies in our continued reliance on women's unpaid labour in the home and the high demands on those pursuing scientific careers. In societies that do not provide adequate social support, those women who wish to have families and personal lives are often unable to meet these expectations and leave their careers before they reach senior positions, contributing to the "leaky pipeline" phenomenon. The National Science Foundation (2019) reports that in 2019, women in STEM represented 41% of doctoral degree holders, 36% of postdoctoral fellows, and only 28.2% of tenured faculty. These statistics vary greatly by field, with areas such as mathematics having as few as 11% female full professors in 2021 (American Mathematical Society, 2022).

Perceived Values - Excellence and Perfection

To better understand the situation of women in the arts and sciences, we must consider the socio-economic factors influencing their status and the potential effects of technological advancement on their future roles. May-Britt Moser, a 2014 Nobel Prize winner in Physiology or Medicine, stated: "A good designer has a lot in common with a good researcher. Both hunt for excellence and perfection" (Midling, 2014).

Excellence is often viewed as the key to success in both art and science, achieved only through repeated failure. For women in these fields, like Moser, numerous setbacks are common before they are deemed "good enough" to join the ranks of excellence. In the art world, perfection is often equated with idealised female beauty - a concept rarely neutral (Nochlin, 2017). Men, in contrast, have often been celebrated for their flaws and failures - complexities that rarely apply to women, who are typically portrayed as either flawless or evil. Today, this binary portrayal is further exacerbated by social media's impact on women's self-esteem (Smith et al., 2024).

It wasn't until the late 20th century that women began to assert themselves as experts in science, the arts and other fields (Krawiec, 2016). According to the UNESCO Science Report (2021), while women constitute 33.3% of researchers globally, only 11% hold senior positions. Their underrepresentation stems from self-doubt, impostor syndrome, systemic biases, and lack of institutional support. Another factor is the Glass Cliff Hypothesis, which suggests women are often offered prestigious roles only in times of crisis (Ryan & Haslam, 2005).

The Glass Ceiling and Glass Cliff Hypothesis have been studied in relation to managerial and leader ship roles, including museum directors and art curators (Bruckmüller et al., 2014). However, these phenomena are relevant at all career stages. Laia Anguix-Vilches (2022) highlights the persistence of gender inequality in decision-making roles in European cultural institutions, while Aspegren (2021) notes that male artists are often given more exhibition space than women. Unsurprisingly, in fields that confer financial or institutional advantages women remain marginalised.

Recent plans to close many humanities departments - many of which are female-dominated - reflect a devaluation of fields as they become more female-oriented (Royal Historical Society, 2023). Disciplines with higher female participation are often seen as less challenging or valuable, a trend that risks dismantling women's career paths (Nussbaum, 2016). In the U.S., high education costs and living expenses make this situation particularly difficult for women (Moran, 2022). Many have already abandoned ambitious projects due to work overload, lack of recognition, and job dissatisfaction (Eagly & Steffen, 1984).

Today, we may only hope that imagination and creativity will eventually be valued equally to pragmatic skills. For scientists like Moser, excellence is grounded in systematic work and persistence, both of which require access to knowledge and resources. However, despite progress, the notion of an "excellent female scientist" remains nearly nonexistent in countries like Afghanistan, where women are still fighting for basic rights. The centuries-old indoctrination that has elevated men over women continues to shape some societal structures, and with the rise of modern technology, these inequalities risk being deepened if biases in data and algorithms replicate old patterns (Smith et al., 2024).

Anna Kobusinska, a computer science professor at Poznań University of Technology, Poland, was interviewed for this essay. She argues that increasing women's access to scientific disciplines foster more intuitive, flexible, and creative problem-solving. These perspectives enrich research without compromising quality, proving that excellence can stem from unconventional yet effective methods. Kobusinska shared that about two decades ago, as a young student, she faced a situation that nearly ended her career. A professor promised her and two male students, who attained high scores and perfect attendance, they would be excused from the final exam. While the two men received their exemption, Kobusinska was told there was still space in the auditorium and that she should take the exam. Shocked and unprepared, she failed the exam and considered quitting. A decade later, now a new mother with a PhD, she ran into the same professor, who congratulated her on motherhood but dismissed her academic achievement, suggesting that her baby, not her doctorate, was her 'true accomplishment.' While motherhood holds immense personal significance, it should not overshadow the importance of a woman's career, which is a significant accomplishment in its own right.

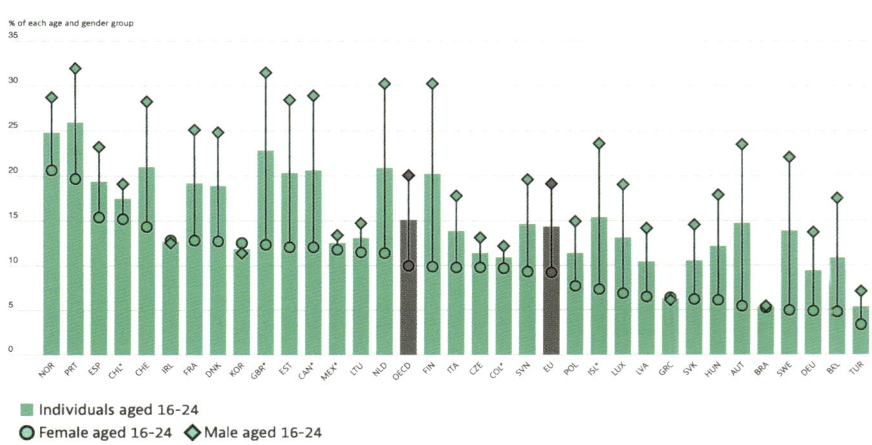

Figure 2:
The *OECD Going Digital Toolkit*, based on the *OECD ICT Access and Usage by Households and Individuals Database* (as of 2023).
The indicator measures women as a share of all 16-24 year-olds who can program, a skill in which gender bias has the potential to shape key general purpose technologies.

As Professor Kobusinska acknowledges: although such incidents are not uncommon, even one negative experience can deeply undermine a woman's confidence.

The value of women's achievements, both in the sciences and the arts, is often measured by the pragmatic impact of their work, overlooking the vital role of imagination and creativity in driving their contributions (Nussbaum, 2016). Professor Joanna Hoffmann, an artist and a professor at Magdalena Abakanowicz University of the Arts in Poznań, Poland, was interviewed for this essay. She posited that the primary goal of modern art is to ask questions and to question established patterns and paradigms.

In the modern world, Hoffmann proposes art plays a crucial role in democratising knowledge, fostering open communication, and creating collaborative networks. She advocates for a systems-based approach to interpreting reality, suggesting that we should perceive it as "a network of relationships and interactions, a dynamic and self-organising system" rather than a mechanistic structure. As she points out, attempts to analyse complexity through simplistic causal links often lead to oversights and oversimplifications. Artists, with their ability to think imaginatively and draw from diverse skill sets, are exceptionally well-positioned to contribute to our understanding of reality - especially in an era where sophisticated technologies enable them to bring their ideas to life. Their creative abilities allow them to perceive interconnectedness, embrace ambiguity, and navigate multifaceted challenges - qualities essential for engaging with complexity. Hoffmann has demonstrated this approach in numerous projects that foster collaboration between scientists and artists. Her work with biologists, as well as her other projects incorporating fieldwork, underscores the importance of a systems-based perspective in translating scientific concepts into meaningful artistic expressions. These collaborations make complex ideas more accessible through engaging imagery and music while also empowering women to build cultural bridges and promote the democratisation of progress. Hoffmann emphasises that the value of art extends beyond mere utility. Rather than serving as a tool to illustrate science, art activates the cultural dimensions of research, connects diverse perspectives, expands interpretations, and fosters imagination, intuition, and a passion for knowledge.

Women in the arts and sciences have driven such efforts to expand interpretive frameworks, fostering a more inclusive and dynamic discourse - one that increasingly includes men who are open to collaboration and support. Hoffmann's long career exemplifies this evolving landscape (Hoffman, 2021). Having worked extensively with both women and men, she reflects on her experiences in a way that challenges common narratives about gender-based barriers. She asserts that she has neither faced discrimination nor received advantages due to her gender, and that, in her view, success in both professional and private contexts is shaped more by personality rather than by gender.

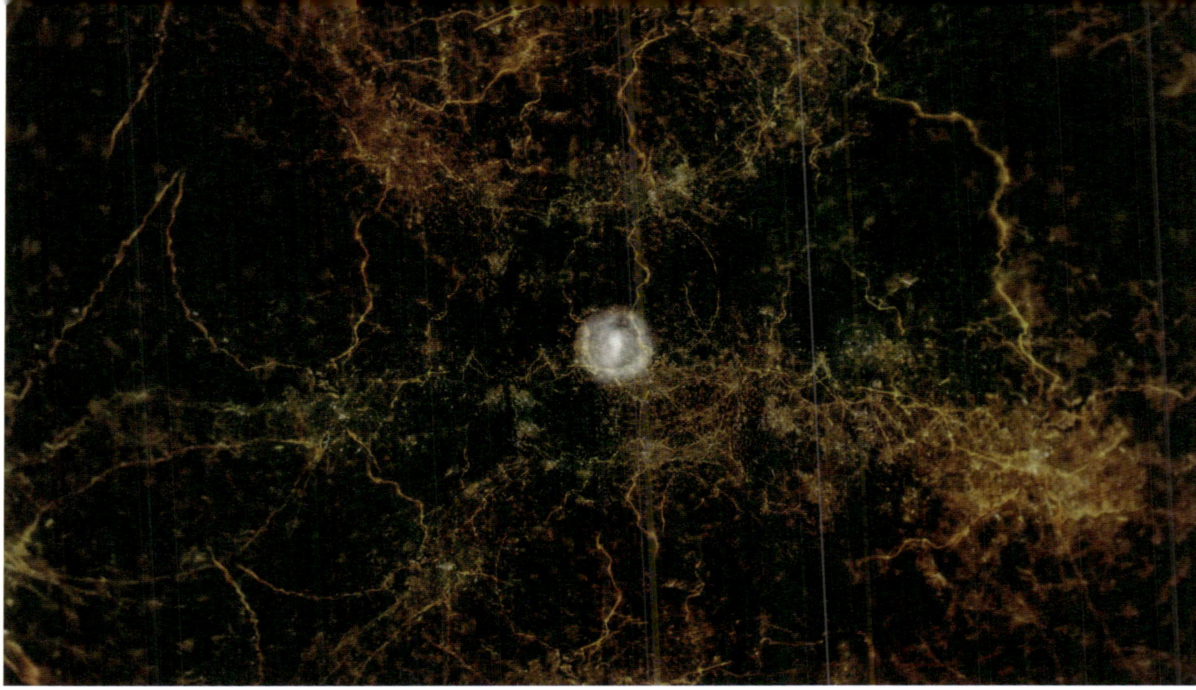

Figure 3: *RhiZone Papilla*. Hofmann, J. (2021). Media: VR narrative, 3DS, projection, AR app.
A series of multimedia artworks with VR & AR narratives inspired by research into the vast networks of the rhizosphere - symbiotic relationships between plant roots, fungi and micro-organisms. Based on symbiosis, diversity, and interdependence, these networks have evolved over millions of years securing their evolutionary success as well as sustainable growth and survival of all stakeholders.

Emergent challenges

Sadly, the majority of women artists and scientists have not been so fortunate. Studies show that many still work in environments where their contributions are undervalued and gender remains a disadvantage. Female researchers tend to have shorter, less well-paid careers, are under-represented in high-profile journals, and are often passed over for promotion (UNESCO, 2021). Moreover, numerous studies confirm that women professionals - whether in the arts or sciences - have frequently faced setbacks from men in authority who trivialised their success or attributed it to luck rather than competence (Sonnert and Holton, 1996).

Regardless of the progress we made, gender inequality is deeply entrenched in many parts of the world, with Afghanistan standing out as one of the most oppressive environments for women today. Under the current regime, women face severe restrictions on education, making careers in science or the arts unattainable and effectively erasing their professional opportunities (Cuthbert, 2024). While technological advancements have the potential to expand access to knowledge, cultural barriers and hostile socio-political conditions often render such progress nearly impossible.

In conclusion, a key factor of gender bias is defined as "a strong, often unfair preference for one group over another" (Oxford Learner's Dictionaries, 1995).

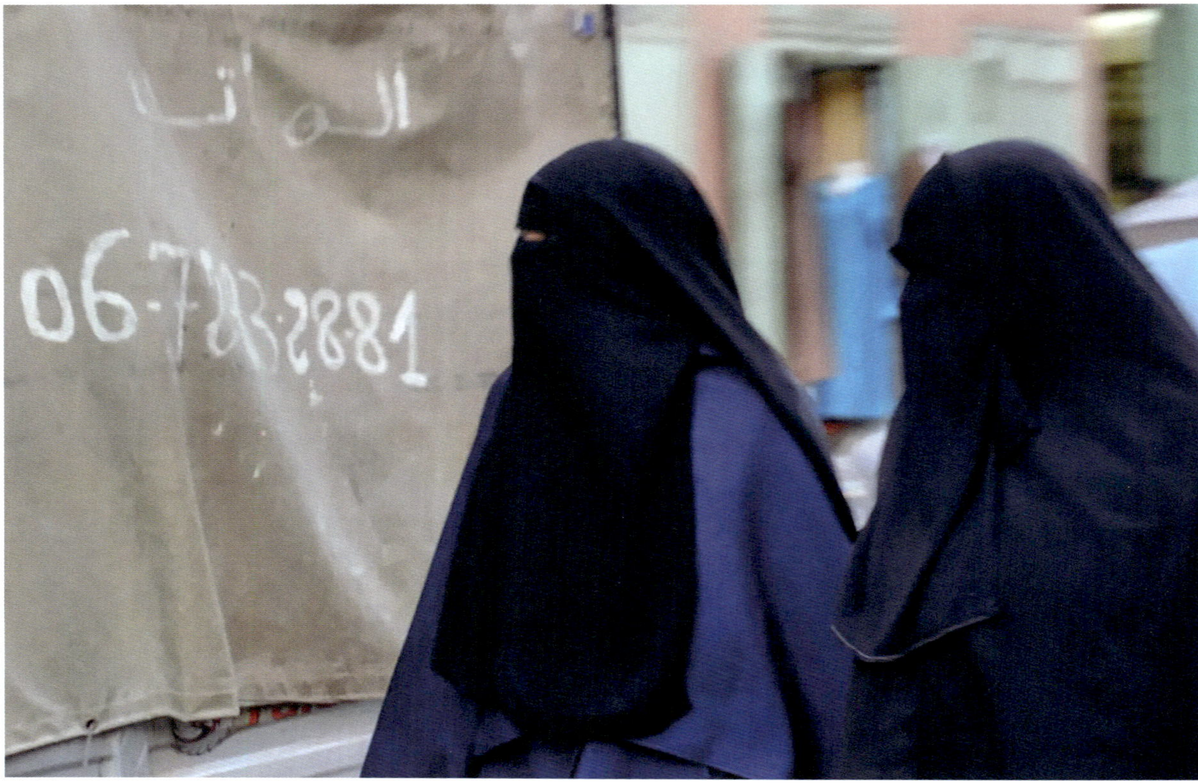

Figure 4: *Invisible Faces*. Krawiec, A. (2014). Photo: Krawiec, A. in Marocco.

Bias can manifest in implicit forms, where women's work is unconsciously undervalued, or explicit forms, where discriminatory beliefs actively restrict access to opportunities (Greenwald and Banaji, 1995). Cultural and social norms perpetuate these inequalities, and while modern technology can improve access to knowledge, digital spaces often reinforce harmful stereotypes. The recent rise of hyper-masuline leaders, violent, often misogynistic online contents, and gender stereotypes hightlight the urgent need for women to take an active role in shaping emerging technophilic societies (Smith et al., 2024).

In countries where power imbalances favour male-dominated perspectives, challenging gender biases is particularly difficult (Régner et al., 2019), though not impossible. While technological advancements have provided unprecedented access to information and connectivity, they have also introduced new obstacles, such as the digital divide and the spread of misinformation. Despite all negative challenges, there are some promising developments of recent decades. One of this is the increasing level of collaboration across disciplines which also creates new opportunities for women in the arts and sciences. This has not only expanded the scope of creativity and innovation but also fostered a more inclusive approach to problem-solving and discovery (Scott, 2006).

As discussed, women have played a pivotal role in reshaping traditional interpretive frameworks, transforming obstacles into opportunities, and advancing a more dynamic, multidimensional discourse. The challenges are evident, and we must not shy away from them. Technological disruptions have heightened competition, disproportionately affecting women, particularly in the arts and sciences. However, as with any upheaval, new possibilities await those who seek them. Solidarity and mutual support among women remain just as crucial in the Fourth Industrial Revolution as they were in the early 20th-century feminist movement.

Conclusion

Modern women are reshaping our understanding of the world and breaking new ground in the sciences and the arts. Yet, as numerous studies confirm, despite their success, gender remains a non-neutral factor that often works to their disadvantage. As discussed herein, the emergent properties of technological progress introduce challenges through disruption and uncertainty, which, combined with the legacy of discrimination, can disproportionately impact women in creative fields. At the same time, it must be acknowledged that these difficulties can also create exciting opportunities - an important topic, to explore and discuss for future analyses.

There may not be perfect solutions to women's challenges, as perfection is rare in both nature and human-made realities. But, as Moser - whose quote served as inspiration for parts of this essay - would likely agree, the pursuit of excellence has always propelled humanity forward. In turbulent times, women in the sciences and arts have a particularly important role to play as educators, mentors, science communicators, and pioneers of new scientific and artistic approaches. Women must try to engage decision-makers to secure support for their endeavours utilising legislation, well designed education systems, and compelling incentives. These measures will not only help women enter the fields of science and the arts but also enable them to remain, advance, and thrive in their careers, in retirement and in the future.

References

- American Mathematical Society, 2022. Conference Board of Mathematical Sciences 2020-2022 Surveys. Available at: https://www.ams.org/learning-careers/data/cbms-survey/cbms-survey. Accessed 9 September 2024.
- Anguix-Vilches, L. 2022, 'Women in museums: An interdisciplinary approach to the history of the first female administrators in European cultural institutions', Journal of Art Historiography, December 2022, available at: https://arthistoriography.wordpress.com/27s-dec22/. Accessed: 11 September 2024.
- Aspegren, A. 2021, 'Representation of women in art museums: How can we improve gender balance in exhibition practice?', European Journal of Cultural Management and Policy, 11(1), pp. 56-70.
- Bredbenner, C.L. 1998, A nationality of her own: Women, marriage, and the law of citizenship, University of California Press.
- Bruckmüller, S., Ryan, M.K., Rink, F. & Haslam, S.A. 2014, 'Beyond the glass ceiling: The glass cliff and its lessons for organizational policy', Social Issues and Policy Review, 8(1), pp. 202-232.

References

- Cuthbert, O. 2024, 'Another blow for female artists in Afghanistan', Ideas Beyond Borders, 15 November, available at: https://ideasbeyondborders.org/another-blow-for-female-artists-in-afghanistan [Accessed 2 April 2025].
- Eagly, A.H. & Steffen, V.J. 1984, 'Gender stereotypes stem from the distribution of women and men into social roles', Journal of Personality and Social Psychology, 46(4), p. 735.
- Goldin, C. & Rouse, C. 2000, 'Orchestrating impartiality: The impact of "blind" auditions on female musicians', American Economic Review, 90(4), pp. 715-741.
- Greenwald, A.G. & Banaji, M.R. 1995, 'Implicit social cognition: Attitudes, self-esteem, and stereotypes', Psychological Review, 102(1), p. 4.
- Halperin, J. & Burns, C. 2019, 'Museums claim they're paying more attention to female artists. That's an illusion', Artnet News, 19 September, available at: https://news.artnet.com/womens-place-in-the-art-world/womens-place-art-world-museums-1654714 [Accessed 12 July 2024].
- Han, J., Greve, H.R. & Shipilov, A. 2024, 'The liability of gender? Constraints and enablers of foreign market entry for female artists', Journal of International Business Studies, available at: https://doi.org/10.1057/s41267-023-00680-5.
- Hoffman, J. 2021, 'Interactive art projects', Art & Science Node, Berlin, available at: https://artscience-node.com/art-science-node-ar-joanna-hoffmann/ [Accessed: 3 April 2025].
- Krawiec, A.E. 2016, 'Socio-economic implications of female inclusion in organizational structures and in leadership positions', International Journal of Management and Economics, 49(1), pp. 106-134.
- McCammon, H.J., Hearne, B.N., McGrath, A.R. & Moon, M. 2018, 'Legal mobilization and analogical legal framing: Feminist litigators' use of race-gender analogies', Law & Policy, 40(1), pp. 57-78.
- Midling, A.S. 2014, 'Gala dress with grid cell glitter', Norwegian SciTech News, December, available at: https://norwegianscitechnews.com/2014/12/gala-dress-with-grid-cell-glitter/ [Accessed 22 September 2024].
- Moran, J. 2022, 'The humanities and the university: A brief history of the present crisis', Critical Quarterly, 64(3), pp. 5-28.
- National Science Foundation 2019, Women, Minorities, and Persons with Disabilities in Science and Engineering, National Center for Science and Engineering Statistics (NSF NCSES), NSF 19-304, 8 March, available at: https://ncses.nsf.gov/pubs/nsf19304/data [Accessed 19 September 2024].
- Nochlin, L. 2017, 'Why are there no great women artists?', in Goldblatt, D., Brown, L.B. & Partridge, S. (eds.), Aesthetics, pp. 46-51, Routledge.
- Nokes, C. et al. (Women and Equalities Committee, House of Commons, UK) 2024, Misogyny in music, Second Report of Session 2023-24, available at: https://publications.parliament.uk/pa/cm5804/cmselect/cmwomeq/129/report.html [Accessed 3 April 2025].
- Nussbaum, M.C. 2016, Not for profit: Why democracy needs the humanities, Updated edition, Princeton University Press.
- Oxford Learner's Dictionaries 2024, Oxford University Press, available at: https://www.oxfordlearnersdictionaries.com/definition/english/bias_1 [Accessed: 22 August 2024].
- Régner, I., Thinus-Blanc, C., Netter, A., Schmader, T. & Huguet, P. 2019, 'Committees with implicit biases promote fewer women when they do not believe gender bias exists', Nature Human Behaviour, 3(11), pp. 1171-1179.
- Robinson, K. & Aronica, L. 2016, Creative schools: The grassroots revolution that's transforming education, Penguin Books.
- Royal Historical Society 2023, History in UK Higher Education: A Statement from the Royal Historical Society, 13 June, available at: https://royalhistsoc.org/policy/history-in-uk-higher-education-a-statement-from-the-royal-historical-society/ [Accessed 16 September 2024].
- Ryan, M.K. & Haslam, S.A. 2005, 'The glass cliff: Evidence that women are over represented in precarious leadership positions', British Journal of Management, 16(2), pp. 81-90.
- Scott, J. 2006, 'Suggested transdisciplinary discourses for more art_sci collaborations', in Scott, J. (ed.), Artists-in-labs processes of inquiry, pp. 24-35, Springer, Vienna.
- Sen, A. 2022, 'Women scientists and pandemics', Economia Politica, 39, pp. 7-14, available at: https://link.springer.com/article/10.1007/s40888-021-00244-6.
- Smith, O.E., Mills, J.S. & Samson, L. 2024, 'Out of the loop: Taking a one-week break from social media leads to better self-esteem and body image among young women', Body Image, 49, p. 101715.
- Sonnert, G. & Holton, G. 1996, 'Career patterns of women and men in the sciences', American Scientist, 84(1), pp. 63-71.
- Topaz, C.M., Klingenberg, B., Turek, D., Heggeseth, B., Harris, P.E., Blackwood, J.C., Chavoya, C.O., Nelson, S. & Murphy, K.M. 2019, 'Diversity of artists in major US museums', PloS One, 14(3), p. e0212852.
- Townsend, R.B. & Bradburn, N. 2022, 'The state of the humanities circa 2022', Daedalus, 151(3), pp. 11-18.
- UNESCO 2021, UNESCO Science Report: the Race Against Time for Smarter Development, S. Schneegans, T. Straza & J. Lewis (eds.), UNESCO Publishing: Paris, available at: https://www.unesco.org/reports/science/2021/en [Accessed 20 August 2024].
- UNESCO For Women in Science team 2024, The gender gap in science: Status and trends, February, NSF NCSES 2019, SC-PBS-STIP/2024/FWIS/2, available at: https://unesdoc.unesco.org/ark:/48223/pf0000388805 [Accessed September 2024].

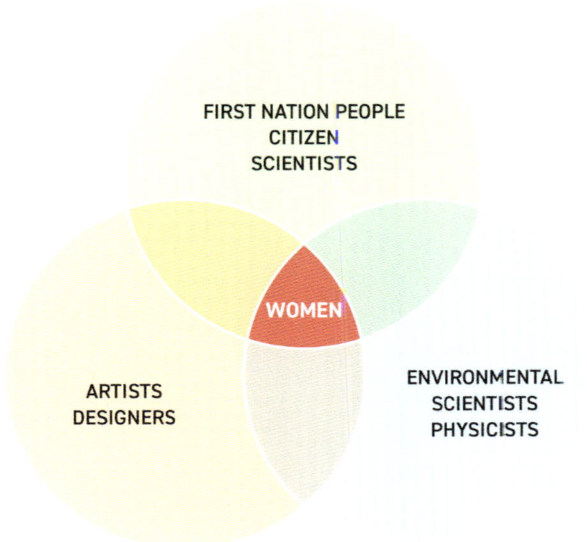

Figure 5: *The Need for Women Centered Transdiscourse.*
Scott, J. and Jankovski, N. (2023). Diagram.

WOMEN WHO CARE: DEGROWTH, ECO-FEMINISM, BIOMIMICRY

Jill Scott, Rewa Wright and Clarissa Ribeiro

In this chapter, we explore how women in the arts, sciences and communities can collaborate within the themes of mediated environments, body politics and natural science, and share a moral framework of reasoning called "an ethics of care" (Gilligan 1982). We begin with an analysis of similar levels of idealism across three feminist movements: Degrowth, Ecofeminism and Biomimicry. Each author contextualises her research and motivations for exploring the human/nature interface through these feminist ideals and perspectives. Clarissa Ribeiro references her artwork "Talking Through Tubes: Molecular Ecologies of Place", which aims to help us reconnect with nature, while Rewa Wright analyses of her project "He Koiora o te Wa: A Biology of Time", contextualises it within the neocolonialism of Mãori culture. Jill Scott describes her sci/art and citizen science collaboration "Water Stories", which may nurture unique levels of community engagement towards a healthier future. With backgrounds in architecture, animation and media art, the authors write in the third person here for clarity. They collaborated on a workshop at the International Symposia on Electronic Art (ISEA) in Brisbane in 2024 and presented an analysis of the results through two exercises: "Breaking the 4th Wall and Rich Picture Storytelling". Today, as women in transdisciplinary media art practice, we use art to engage the public in reflection – to rethink body politics, education, and promote an "ethics of care" for a better environment.

Introduction

The movements of Degrowth, Ecofeminism and Biomimicry all originated in the 1970s, at a time when young people were contemplating changing the relationship between capitalism and democracy in the future. Today, with the political changes and the rise of the right in politics, it is evident that young women, men and non-binary individuals of today still share some common themes with this earlier generation. Originally, Degrowth (Gortz, 1972), with its connections to Green Growth Earth Days (Earth Day, 1970), was a transformative idea nurtured by both men and women who care about our future and the future of nature. While this student-led *Green Growth* movement was policy oriented, with practical potentials, Degrowth has become a more theory-driven-movement based on human-nature interrelationships. Ecofeminism, a term first coined by feminist Françoise d'Eaubonne (1920-2005) in 1974, is still used by women activists as a critique of the patriarchal system that exploits human relationships, the environment and its resources. Meanwhile, Biomimetics, a name coined by Otto Schmitt in the 1950s (Learn Biomimicry, n.d) for the transfer of ideas and analogues from biology to technology, became a movement known as Biomimicry, focused on the design of our future. The term was later popularised by American environmental scientist Janine Benyus (Benyus, 1997).

All three movements addressed similar issues of sustainability, equality in the workforce, gender representation, migration and diaspora, as well as equal representation and equal economies. The women in these movements hoped for a new society: one that could learn from nature rather than attempt to dominate it. These movements can still encourage us to develop solutions to our planetary problems. They are not anti-technology but are mindful of resources and their depletion. For more specific correlations to the problems of today, we will examine the ideals of each movement more closely and connect them to some current art and design examples and workshops.

Degrowth

Degrowth began as a new left movement in the early 70s in Europe, describing the need to transform and radicalise economic and ecological criticism for civil society. By 2000, Jason Hickel (Hickel, 2000), an economic anthropologist and a member of the Extinction Rebellion, had proclaimed that limitless growth can "never be green" and wrote a seminal book about the subject called *Less is More.* More recently, a young German feminist cultural anthropologist, Andrea Vetter (Vetter, 2022), and her sociology colleagues applied the notion of Degrowth to focus on women, labour equality and the "ethics of care". Vetter claimed that there are five issues regarding the status of women in our society that need to be considered under the concept of Degrowth: ecosystems, bio-economic problems, anthropological problems, democratic issues, and spiritual knowledge. She aligns herself with this movement because all these issues effect ecological analysis and counter the primacy of nature. Here, nature is seen as the main bio-economic source, which accepts the limits of economic growth and criticises the Wests' reliance on cheap labour, particularly from poorer countries.

Indeed, the Degrowth movement deeply questions the dominance of neo-colonial materialism and the uniformisation of the world under global trade. She uses the example of technology we use every day - the iPhone or the Android phone. Each phone is loaded with minerals from the global south: copper, tin, nickel and iron, and the labour used to produce it is cheap labor (EHNE, n.d.). (Available at: https://ehne.fr/en/encyclopedia/themes/material-civilization). Furthermore, 95 % of other rare earth components in these phones come from China, and the biggest lithium reserves for their batteries are found in countries like Chile, Ukraine and Australia. In fact, the new lithium trade is a real indicator of the senselessness of trying to mitigate climate change at the expense of both nature and indigenous communities. Therefore, as members of the Degrowth movement, we are concerned about the social as well as the economic implications of the extensive extraction of these resources on local communities.

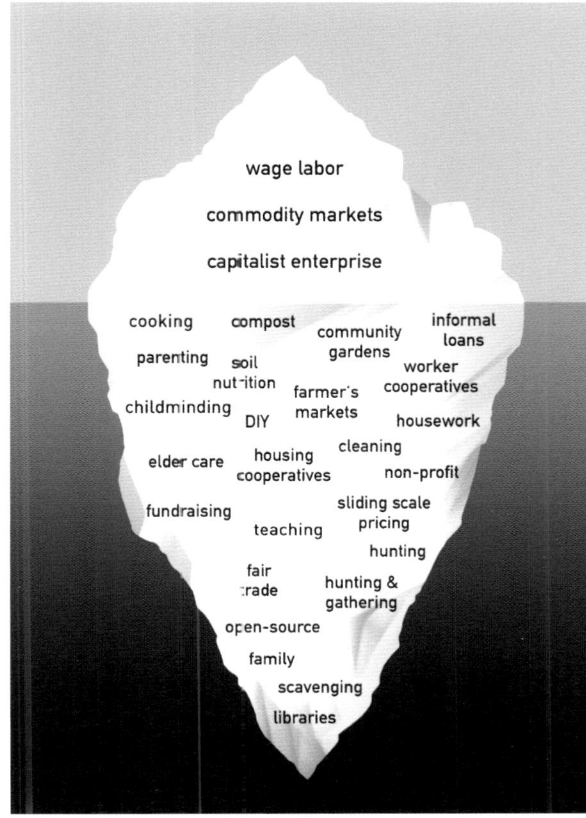

Figure 1: *The Iceberg Model of the GDP system.*
Modified from Source: EHNE, n.d. (referencing The Future is Degrowth by Schmelzer et al., 2022). Women play a big role in unpaid labour.

As feminists in the Degrowth movement currently posit, this planet's economic system is also not gender neutral. In fact, the entire model of the capitalist economy is based on an "Iceberg model of the GDP system" (Figure 1), in which almost 30 percent of the economy is propped up by women through their unpaid labour, such as cooking, cleaning and caring for children and husbands. The iceberg is a metaphor, representing the fact that in a sociotechnical system, most of what drives, shapes and perpetuates that system is hidden from view. (Available at: https://www.mechanical-orchard.com/insights/the-iceberg-model-towards-unraveling-our-patriarchal-legacy).

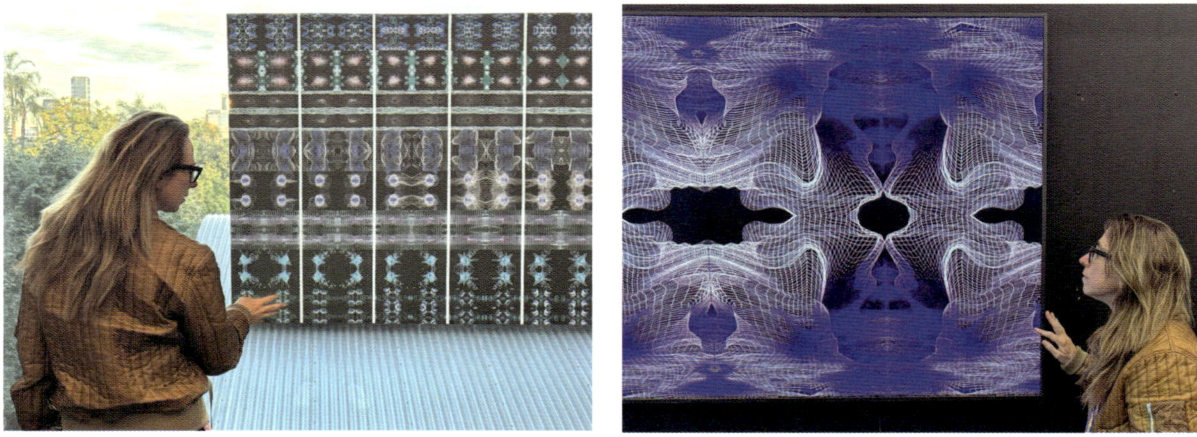

Figure 2: *He Koiora o te Wa.* Wright, R. (2024). A computer-generated image about the biology of time.

Degrowth feminists also question older anthropological sources and advocate for society to help them reinvestigate and re-legitimise the relationship between democracy, money, and public debate. Currently, the main aim of the Degrowth movement is the democratisation of technology and energy, based on care: the care and need to organise our own workload and activities at a shared and equal community level. Only then can we overcome the sense of alienation from these fruits of women's labour. This "overcoming" they claim, would result in a shared sense of responsibility for the preservation of natural systems on this planet. However, one prerequisite might be a recognition of indigenous knowledge or the spiritual respect for nature that Indigenous Australians call "care-for-country". In other words, "if you look after country, country will look after you" (AIATSIS, 2022). This may require educational initiatives and access to the relevant activities that sustain our lives, including how to deal with these technical resources from the Global South. It may also require new artistic initiatives that may help rethink our relationship to natural resources in general.

Currently, some artists are aiming to create wake-up calls for the public about some of these issues. It seems that new mediated tools may need to be adapted for transmission and collective public discussion based on activities that might mitigate changes in our thinking. In *He Koiora o te Wa: A Biology of Time* (Figure 2), New Zealand / Māori artist Rewa Wright combines bio-electrical data, real-time animations, and living plants in a poetic and sophisticated experience for a participatory audience.

Here, her aim was to reveal the hidden signals produced by living plants, through sonification and data visualisation, to help humans understand that plants are not simple "passive machines", but that they communicate through energy and life force. *He Koiora o te Wa* can be translated in the ancestral language of te reo Māori as the "biology of time". She believes we need to look beyond the lens of Western epistemology and the scientific discourse on plant biology and examine the complex interrelationships between humans and plants. Drawing on the indigenous knowledge system of Rewa's culture, mātauranga Māori (Māori epistemology), plant-human relations can be approached from the perspective of genealogical connections, embedded in bloodlines that co-mingle earth, sea, sky, and water with human and plant-kin. Like humans, plants are considered to have mauri (energy) and wairua (life force). This plant rhythm is phenological and traces processes such as photosynthesis and osmosis as plants pursue circadian patterns of growth, seeding and decay. In this work, the public can reflect on the different temporality or chronobiology of how plants vest interest in seasonal shifts, temperature, water, and light. As Australian evolutionary ecologist Monica Gagliano (Gagliano, 2023) has noted, the signals that plants emit are akin to intentional communication and sentience, and this communication is now recognised as solid area of scientific study.

By making the electrical signals manifest as sonic frequencies, Rewa Wright allows the audience to touch the plants and shift the frequencies so that people can gain an understanding of the hidden operations of plants and how we can communicate with them through a sharing of bioelectrical signal energy transduced as aural and visual data. She hopes that through cultural representation, high tech and inclusion, humble respect for sustainable systems might emerge.

Similar intentions can be found in the Paris group of artists that call themselves Disnovation (http://disnovation.org). They believe that "growth" is actually a big illusion which struggles to sustain itself, and if everyone in society seeks to technically rise above all other species and all natural resources, we are travelling down the wrong pathway. They believe that individual artists may have to reassess their priorities, to set goals and to work more collaboratively, plan works and events that address the needs of the audiences and involve them to respect the environment. They also talk about how the colonisation of the atmosphere or "pollution by carbon of less developed countries as a form of colonisation" is being produced by the limitless growth ideology of the most developed countries.

Indeed, this may be yet another factor to address under the climate change agenda. Consequently, some women artists are currently thinking about the challenges of media art and carbon footprints and couple up with geographers, atmospheric scientists and technologists who already have monitoring systems that measure the carbon limitations of pollution. In CoP21, the artist Andrea Polli showed a project entitled *Particle Falls*, which used a nephelometer from atmospheric science to measure the smallest and most dangerous pollution particle for human health - PM2.5 (Science History Institute, n.d.).

Here, she linked a projection of a waterfall on the side of a building to the fluctuation of carbon particles in the street monitored by this nephelometer. The less pollution, the more the volume of the water in the waterfalls increased. In this way, she developed a direct wake-up call for the public about the effects of fossil fuel on our urban environment and our need to develop an "art-of-caring." Art examples like this can also challenge other women artists and designers to think of themselves as custodians of this planet and to revisit ecofeminism as an idealistic concept.

Ecofeminism

As French Feminist Françoise d'Eaubonne (1974) once suggested, the correlations between the ethics of care and the health of the environment needs to be rethought. Today, the movement is divided into two trends: one based on academic research, and another based on community activism, although they may work together on tasks. By 1997, UK academic Karen J. Warren (Warren, 1997) became interested in exploring how ecofeminists' real life concerns could be an essential part of women's studies at the University level. At this same time, the interest in post-human discourse was being discussed alongside the globalisation potentials and criticisms of the internet and robotic research. However, Dutch theorist Rosi Braidotti (n.d) later claimed that mainstream post-human scholarship had neglected feminist theory. Feminism has always specifically criticised the idea that "man" is the central figure who imagines "a post- human body." They highlighted the ways in which man sits at the center of Western thinking, especially in his attempts to dominate natural systems.

Here, women artists have joined in to comment on how women have a very large role to play in this nature and nurture experience; one that can be reenforced by the presence of their own bodies and their voices. In an artwork entitled *Talking Through Tubes: Molecular Ecologies of Place* (2023) by Brazilian artist, Clarissa Ribeiro, she explores and interprets these layered ecologies, considering the interactions of human, non-human, and technological actors in shaping sustainable and interconnected places in the digital age. Here, a flexible tube hose or "prosthesis", a flexible PVC pipe, Arduino, a dust sensor and LCDs are attached to a tree branch. This "tube" is both an object and a concept, related to the breath of the body. The audience is invited to play with the tube, holding and moving it freely, blowing air through the tube or sucking on it, therefore promoting microbial exchange between humans and the microbiota interior of the tree. The aim is to mimic biotic conversations in an anthropogenic context. This physical action of breathing uncovers hidden molecular and microscopic stories and attempts to amplify these voices inside our own organism and an other species.

Here, Clarissa merges nature, technology, and the human body in a way that highlights the deeply entangled relationships between all life forms and breath. Breath becomes a powerful interface and metaphor for the symbiotic relationships that ecofeminism seeks to illuminate. In this context, the tree is not simply an object but a living participant, just as ecofeminism insists on seeing nature as a subject with agency rather than a resource to be exploited. The artwork disrupts the anthropocentric view and reenforces the ecofeminist idea that the domination of nature and the domination of women are interconnected under patriarchal structures.

In many Brazilian cultures, women are nurturers and caregivers, often at the forefront of environmental activism, advocating for sustainable

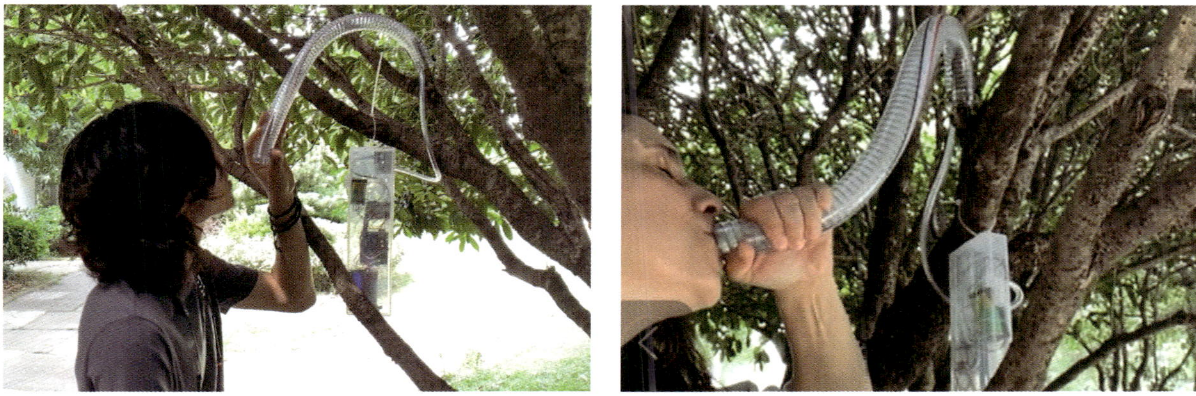

Figure 3: *Talking Through Tubes*. Ribeiro, C. (2023). Installation about molecular ecologies.

practices that respect both life and the planet. In the realm of Amazonian cosmologies, ecofeminism calls for relational thinking - moving beyond dualistic separations like man/woman and nature/culture, to a more holistic, interconnected understanding of existence.

Here, Clarissa refers to a seminal work from 1979 by English ethnographers: Stephen and Christine Hugh-Jones' (Hugh-Jones, 1975), whose perspectives reveal how indigenous worldviews often do not treat nature and culture as separate entities but as deeply intertwined and gendered principles of the cosmic order. These perspectives appeal to ecofeminist artists who believe that gender goes beyond binary divisions and seeks to dismantle the cultural logic that equates femininity with nature and weakness, and masculinity with culture and power.

In *The Palm and the Pleiades*, Stephen Hugh-Jones explores the fluidity of gender roles in Amazonian symbolism, focusing on balance and cosmic unity rather than appropriation. Ecofeminism critiques the gendered power structures that drive environmental exploitation, linking women's empowerment with environmental justice and opposition to patriarchal capitalism. *Talking Through Tubes* serves as an ecofeminist artistic intervention, amplifying the silenced voices of nature and marginalised women. The installation reflects ecofeminism's vision of interconnectedness, where the health of all beings is inseparable. This approach has influenced academia, leading to new workshops that intertwine women's empowerment, capitalist critique, and social science research, offering a way forward in challenging patriarchal systems.

Our Workshop at ISEA Brisbane in 2025, aimed to intertwine women's empowerment, capitalism growth, and performative data visualisation to explore a paradigm shift in leadership through theoretical discussions and interactive activities. The whole workshop sparked insightful conversations, linking practical and conceptual aspects of women's empowerment to capitalism, resources, and growth. On the first day, participants explored two exciting exercises. The first was a performative

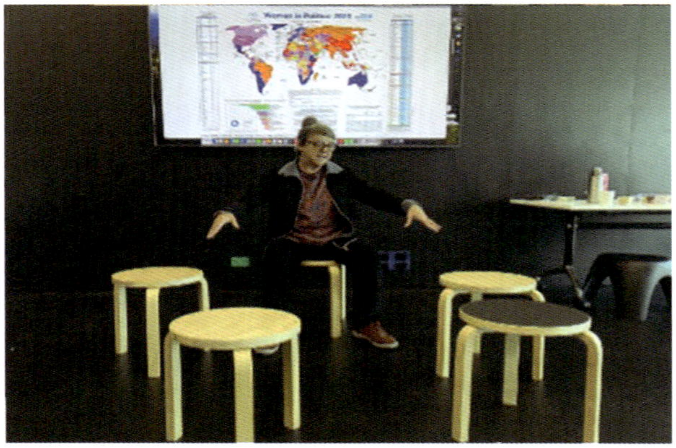

Figure 4: *Breaking the Fourth Wall.* From the workshop: Women Who Care: Degrowth, Eco-Feminism, Biomimicry at International Symposium on Electronic Art, Brisbane. (2024). Led by Clarissa Ribeiro.

data visualisation - through play - to express their visions for a self-aware, alternative growth society. The second was a sociology-based workshop that allowed participants to draw large mind maps with keywords to construct dynamic solutions. On the second morning, we opened a discussion on colonisation and degrowth. Overall, we aimed to create a space to dissect the interplay of women, politics, circular economies, leadership, and societal growth, and create a space where these past movements of degrowth and ecofeminism might converge in a thought-provoking and innovative future narrative.

In the first exercise, the metaphor of "Breaking the 4th Wall" (Wikipedia, 2025), was inspired by Bertolt Brecht's "alienation effect." (Brecht 1949; Britannica, 2025). It was framed by Clarissa Ribeiro as an exploration of performative "technoetics" by using five chairs as mediators for theatrical purposes, situating a performative data visualisation approach (Figure 4).

Here, the participants used interactive performance and data visualisation to explore power, gender, and societal structures, particularly focusing on women's empowerment and leadership. Participants were asked to rearrange chairs to symbolise gender roles in future societal scenarios, reflecting power imbalances, such as men being elevated over women in positions of authority. This exercise, along with Jill Scott's introductory performance depicting patriarchal control, sparked conversations on gendered oppression and the limitations it places on women's personal, familial, and societal status. The exercise resulted in six performances on the themes of inequality, empowerment, and the evolving dynamics of feminism in the modern world. From the first performance's powerful critique of patriarchal dominance to the second one on visual metaphors of systemic breakdown, each attendee invited us to reflect on how power is distributed and the roles that gender plays in maintaining or challenging these structures. The third performance added a deeply personal layer, demonstrating the oppressive forces within family dynamics and the inherited weight of societal expectations. The fourth performance, with its disengagement from patriarchal systems, illuminated the growing trend of resistance and disengagement from traditional power structures, while the fifth attendee's portrayal of wealth, gender, and economic disparity highlighted the critical importance of addressing structural inequalities at their root. Finally, the sixth performance brought a sense of optimism and empowerment, offering a counter-narrative that celebrated gender fluidity and the possibility of reimagining power dynamics through openness and inclusivity.

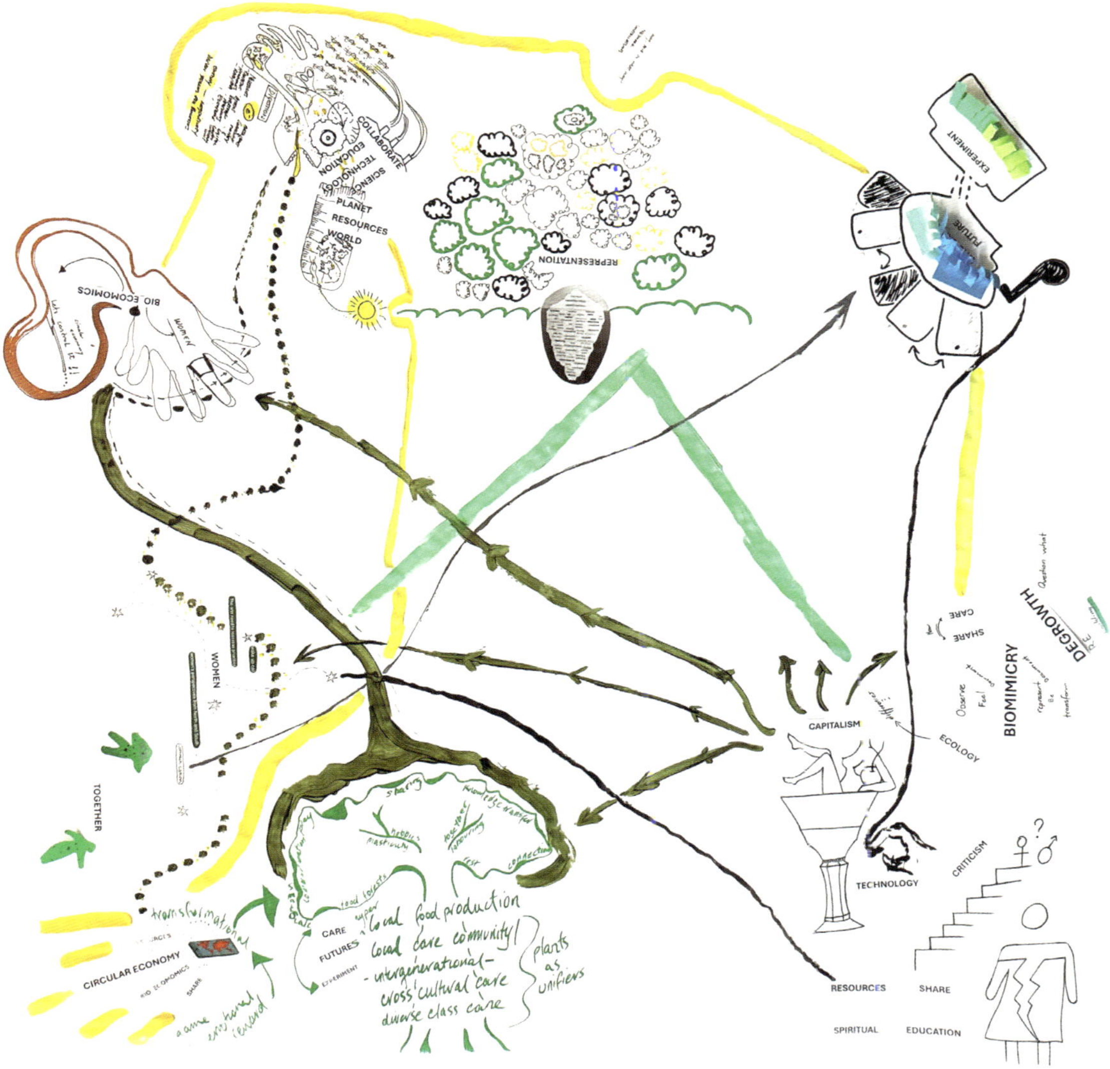

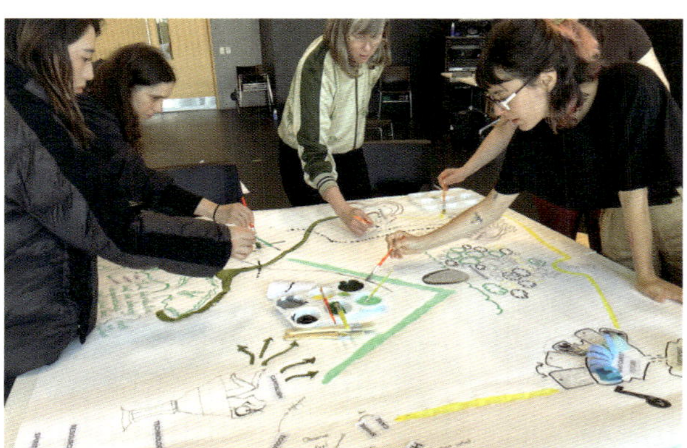

Figure 5 and 6: *Rich Pictures.*
From the workshop: *Women Who Care: Degrowth, Eco-Feminism, Biomimicry* at International Symposium on Electronic Art, Brisbane. (2024).
Led by Jill Scott.

Names of registered participants in the ISEA 24 Workshop were: Michele Barker, Laura Jade Hindes, Cat Jones, Melania Jack, Chang Liu, Sarah Neville, Lorenza Ramos, Louise Rollman, Samatha Siripol and Sarah Waterson.

The second exercise called *Rich Pictures Storytelling* is adapted from sociology (https://journals.sagepub.com/doi/full/10.1177/15344843221148044) and we started with a single challenging question: How can we explore ways to create local action and communicate concern? This exercise took a series of steps. After a lecture and discussion about eco-feminism, degrowth and biomimicry, the participants were asked to choose only three printed keywords that they felt that personally stimulated their imagination as solutions to social problems from the following list:

degrowth, eco-feminism, biomimicry, gender, women, migration, brainstorm, equal representation, circular economy, workforce, ethics, future, empowerment, together, nature, learning, solutions, collaborate, planet, technology, resources, depletion, world, capitalism, ecology, criticism, bio economics, ethics, democracy, spiritual, primacy, shared planet, global south, responsibility, global north, transmission, collective, environment science, recycle, sociology, technology regeneration, education, experimentation.

Next, on the same sheet of paper, they were asked to draw their own diagram or mind map that integrated these keywords onto a story (15 minutes duration). This part was conducted in silence to consolidate one's thoughts and attempt to represent them on paper. In the next step, each participant was asked to explain their own drawings to the others. Jill Scott then posed a question: How can we draw and link these ideas together with lines and references to make the connections visible and share the ideas? In the final step, the large drawing with connected stories was hung on the wall for discussion (See Fig 5). All the participants agreed that the method was a great mind mapping process to talk about eco solutions for the plants and society. This exercise provided a powerful commentary on the intricate entanglements between gender, power, and society, offering a diverse range of perspectives on how to navigate and challenge the deeply entrenched systems that define our world.

Both exercises opened a dialogue of resistance and activism, as well as encouraged participants to engage critically with degrowth, ecofeminism and biomimicry, prompting a deeper understanding of how performance and artistic expression can serve as tools for both reflection and action in the pursuit of a more equitable and inclusive future. Through these performances, the attendees not only broke the fourth wall but also challenged the societal walls that continue to shape our realities, leaving us with a call to reimagine and reconfigure the spaces we inhabit; physically, socially, and politically. The Rich Pictures workshops was directly related to the Ecofeminist movement and perspectives from North and South cultures on the problems of environmental deterioration.

This subject was extended on the following morning of the workshop, when we engaged a discussion about ecofeminism and the ethics of care in relation to cultural difference. We talked about the fact that in 1993, Marxist feminist scholar, Marie Miles and Indian scholar and environmental activist, Vandana Shiva wrote a book called *Ecofeminism* (Miles and Shiva, 1993) together. It focused on women and the rejection of the commodification of needs that included a commitment to a new ethics-of-care and the sharing of concerns about climate change and biodiversity across cultural differences. Their aims were to build a respectful relationship between the oppression and domination of all marginalised groups (women, people of color, children, the poor) and the oppression and domination of nature (animals, land, water, air, etc.). Today, ecofeminists are still interested in addressing the inherent inequalities in world structures which permit the North to dominate the South and to question colonialism and its effect on the development and treatment of women over time.

A pertinent example was given by Rewa Wright. Prior to European settlement of New Zealand, Mãori women had varied responsibilities as tribal leaders, military strategists, warriors, poets, composers and healers. Their roles were irrespective of their gender. According to *Te Whata*, a Mãori designed and owned data platform, identification and affiliation through tribal groupings is essential (Te Whata, 2025). Reasons are clear: iwi operate on principles of whanaunga (bloodline relations of care), providing support, connections, kindness and love, regardless of current government perspectives and policies, which can be extremely adverse. Many tribes or iwi are notably resource rich, with a range of kaupapa (philosophies) that increase opportunity, from Mãori business initiatives to support economic success, through to scholarship programs to encourage greater access to tertiary education. Affiliating through bloodlines with tribal groups has the follow-on effect of fuelling cultural strength and encouraging positive initiatives which expand participation in politics, economy and community. Education statistics are especially encouraging, with 14% of whanau holding a bachelor's level qualification in 2023. For example, in Rewas iwi, "Ngãpuhi", a very large number for the women, have adult tertiary qualifications (Te Whata, 2025).

Our final workshop discussion was about how women in these cultures had a very strong ethics about working together and many found empowerment through NGOS (CEEW, 2025). Perhaps some of them may also be interested in working together with artists and designers to share their environmental knowledge and enrich the lives of these women and their collaborators.

Biomimicry

Biomimicry is a movement that seeks to address these questions through new design and art as well as novel manufacturing processes. The main aim of Benyus and her friends at the biomimicry institute was to create a regenerative future through nature-inspired solutions and designs. "Life", she suggested, "should echo the behavior of nature" (Benyus, 1997). Nature creates its own conditions to live, so perhaps society could become nature's apprentice? Since then, the movement promotes an empathetic and interconnected understanding of how life works and ultimately where we fit in. Therefore, in the West we could cultivate a design practice that learns from and mimics the strategies of nature. This means that all our products, processes, and systems could attempt to solve our greatest design challenges of sustainability and care for the land. In biomimicry, the main question is: how is nature solving this problem? If design evolved around nature as a healer for the planet, then art and design might remain in balance with

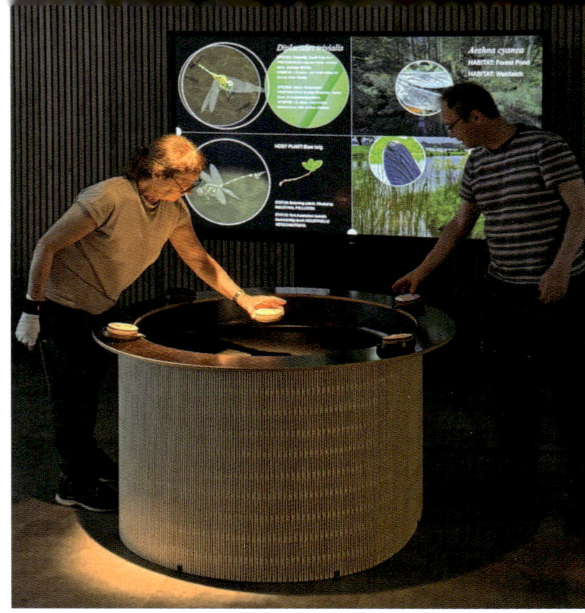

Figure 6a: *Worried Wings* in *Water Stories*. Scott, J. (2025). Interactive installation with female dragonfly sculptures. Papiliorama, Kerzers, Switzerland.

the biosphere and address potential concepts like circular economies and recycling.

Water is considered by many people to be a sacred gift that is critical to their identity and existence, as well as being economically important. In an exhibition called *Water Stories* by Jill Scott, she explores how biomimicry could be combined with interactive media art and citizen science workshops, to learn about local water issues like pollution and the importance of biodiversity. There were 2 parts to this exhibition, *Worried Wings* and *Biodiversity Lives Here*. In the mixed reality installation, *Worried Wings*, Jill Scott used 3D prints to bio-mimic the plight of four dragonflies that float in a pool inside the exhibition space. Through interaction, the viewers can discover why these dragonflies from four different countries are becoming extinct due to human impacts like industrial pollution, microplastics and changes to their environment (Figure 6a and 6c).

Biodiversity Lives Here hikers were asked to become citizen scientists led by sound artists, geographers, biologists and local guides. Together, they made observations of plants and animals as well as sound recordings in local ponds and soil sites. The participants also learned from the scientists how to sample environmental DNA (eDNA) without harming the environment. These were then analyzed by Simplex eDNA and the results of all species found in the ponds were hung on the wall as part of the exhibition. All the art and science samples collected in this workshop were incorporated into specially designed workbenches, at the same exhibition. The aim of *Biodiversity Lives Here* was to discuss water quality and quantity as well as how to take care of biodiversity in local ponds and rivers. Although these citizen science workshops where open to everybody, we noticed, that mostly women wanted to join them. In reports they said that by collecting water and biodiversity data, creating images from observations, using hydrophones for sound collections and making stories, that it may be best to “ask nature” to help us learn about recycling, rewilding or reconstruction so that polluted or degraded ponds can recover. In agreement, when art and design involve the mimicking of the behavior of biological micro organisms such as fungi, bacteria, yeast, and algae, then issues of waste and reuse, repair, or recycling of natural resources become much clearer. On an educational level, biodiversity workshops like ours and those of various STEAM groups offer particular significance for young girls. They encourage confidence, improve the quality of their life, help them recognise gender bias and reduce their hesi-

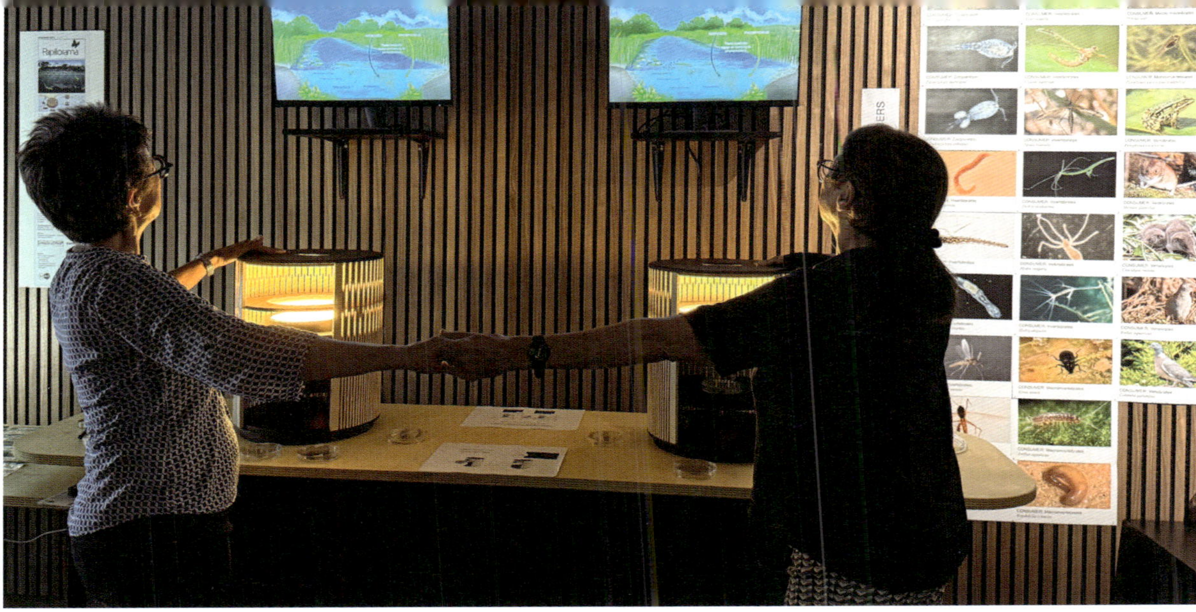

Figure 6b: *Biodiversity Lives Here* in *Water Stories*. Scott, J. (2025). Showing results from the workshop facilitated by SciArt and Ec(h)oart including samples from eDNA analysis. Viewers hold hands to trigger metaphors about human impacts and look at samples of biodiversity. (See page 137).

tation or apologetic tendencies. Today, we believe that young women need help identifying new role models and increase their knowledge of the options available to them. This, in turn, can affect their discussions about the need for climate justice and the ethics-of-care in the future.

Conclusion

As illustrated above in the three movements of Degrowth, Ecofeminism and Biomimicry, they share a common theme that includes the "ethics of care" and a sustainable future where producers, consumers and decomposers are all essential parts of a healthy ecosystem: a system that can influence artists, scientists, educators and workshop participants. By combining and working together inside these movements and expanding their ideologies in a transdisciplinary way, we hope to encourage women to gain access to different approaches and points of view about art, design, and environmental science research and how to bring it to the public. We could also think about education in a more transdisciplinary way - one that can share meaning and language more easily and learn from nature together. We hope to collaborate and instigate more discourses about the ethical and social side of our research in the future. We certainly need to brainstorm about ways to change our education and production so that art, design, environmental science and cultural studies can collaborate with a high level of gender representation. Rather than drown in so many doomsday dystopias, let's reach out to other groups and disciplines to join the idealistic dots and work together with nature and care for a better future!

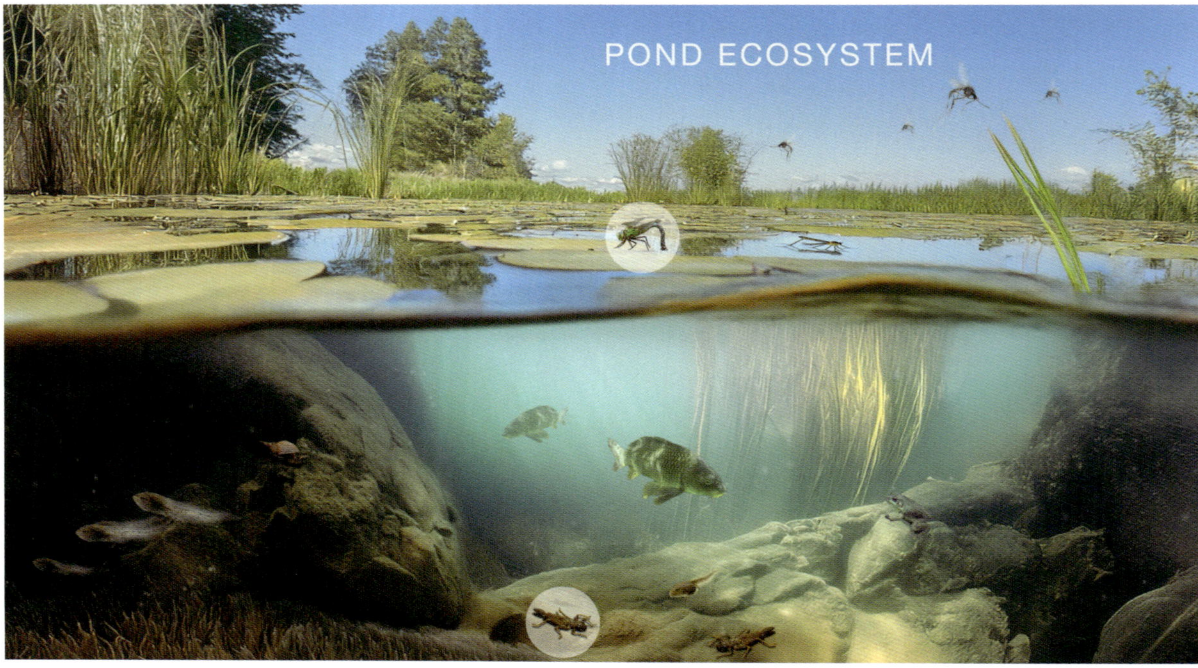

Figure 6c: *Worried Wings. (2025).* Pond Ecosystem by Jankovski, N.: Consists of (1) Producers: Algae, Hydrophytic Plants, (2) Consumers: Primary (Protozoa, Crustacea), Secondary (Insects Larve, Dragonfly nymphs), Tertiary (Fish, Dragonflies) and (3) Decomposers: Bacteria, Fungi, Microbes.

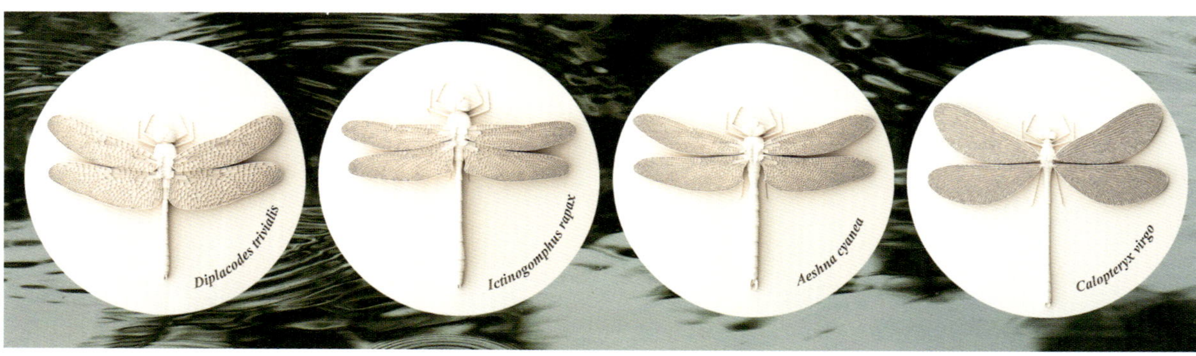

Figure 6d: *Worried Wings.* Scott, J., Jankovski, N., Chastonay, J., Giger, S. (2025). Four female dragonflies currently under the threat of extinction: Calopteryx virgo, Diplacodes trivialis, Aeshna cyanea and Ictinogomphus rapax. All essential for the survival of wet-land ecosystems both under and above water.

References

- AIATSIS, 2011. 'Benefits of Care-for-Country'. Available at: https://aiatsis.gov.au/sites/default/files/research_pub/benefits-cfc_0_3.pdf [Accessed 3 March 2025].
- Ask Nature, 2025. 'AskNature: Biomimicry Resources'. Available at: https://asknature.org [Accessed 10 March 2025].
- Benyus, J., 1997. Biomimicry: Innovation Inspired by Nature. New York: William Morrow.
- Biomimicry Institute, 2025. 'Biomimicry and its Organizations'. Available at: https://biomimicry.org [Accessed 10 March 2025].
- Braidotti, R., n.d. 'Publications'. Available at: https://rosibraidotti.com/publications/2239/ [Accessed 3 March 2025].
- Brecht, B., 1949. 'Alienation effect'. [online] Available at: https://www.britannica.com/art/alienation-effect [Accessed 10 March 2025].
- CEEW, 2025. 'How Rural Indian Women are Using Clean Energy DRE-Powered Appliances to Improve Incomes'. Available at: https://www.ceew.in/blogs/how-rural-indian-women-are-using-clean-energy-dre-powered-appliances-to-improve-incomes [Accessed 10 March 2025].
- Disnovation, 2025. 'Predictive Art Bot: Turning Female'. [online] Available at: http://disnovation.org [Accessed 10 March 2025].
- Earth Day, 2025. 'History of Earth Day'. [online] Available at: https://www.earthday.org/history/ [Accessed 3 April 2025].
- EHNE, n.d. 'Degrowth History and Idea'. Available at: https://ehne.fr/en/encyclopedia/themes/material-civilization/transnational-consumption-and-circulations/degrowth-history-idea [Accessed 15 January 2025].
- EHNE, n.d. 'Material Civilization'. Available at: https://ehne.fr/en/encyclopedia/themes/material-civilization [Accessed 15 January 2025].
- Flickr, 2025. 'Andrea Polli: Particle Falls'. Available at: https://www.flickr.com/photos/andreapolli/albums/72157624630451892/ [Accessed 10 March 2025].
- Gagliano, M., Ryan, J.C. and Vieira, P., 2023. 'Introduction: On Becoming Plant-Minded'. The Ethnobotanical Assembly, 9. Available at: https://www.tea-assembly.com/issues/9/on-becoming-plant-minded [Accessed 20 August 1994].
- Gilligan, C., 1982. 'In a Different Voice' referenced as the origin of the term 'the ethics of care' in Larrabee, M.J., 1993. An Ethics of Care: Feminist and Interdisciplinary Perspectives. Routledge.
- Gortz, A., 1972. 'Nouvel Observateur: Origin of the Term Degrowth'.
- Hickel, J., 2000. 'Less is More'. [online] Available at: https://www.jasonhickel.org [Accessed 10 March 2025].
- Hugh-Jones, C., 1975. From the Milk River. Cambridge: Cambridge University Press.
- Hugh-Jones, S. and Hugh-Jones, C., 1975. The Palm and the Pleiades: Initiation and Cosmology in Northwest Amazonia. Cambridge Studies in Social and Cultural Anthropology, Series Number 24. Cambridge: Cambridge University Press.
- Learn Biomimicry, 2025. 'History of Biomimicry'. Available at: https://www.learnbiomimicry.com/blog/history-of-biomimicry [Accessed 10 March 2025].
- Mies, M. and Shiva, V., 1993. Ecofeminism. London: Zed Books Ltd.
- Polli, A., 2025. 'Particle Falls'. [online] Available at: https://www.sciencehistory.org/sensing-change-particle-falls [Accessed 10 March 2025].
- RNZ, 2024. 'Statistics Reveal Big Changes to Iwi Populations'. Available at: https://www.rnz.co.nz/news/te-manu-korihi/529115/statistics-reveal-big-changes-to-iwi-populations [Accessed 23 October 2024].
- Science History Institute, n.d. 'Sensing Change: Particle Falls'. Available at: https://www.sciencehistory.org/sensing-change-particle-falls/ [Accessed 15 March 2025].
- ScienceDirect, 2023. 'Comparing Green Growth with Degrowth'. [online] Available at: https://www.sciencedirect.com/science/article/abs/pii/S0921800923003300#:~:text=Using%20a%20comparative%20analysis%20of,theory%2Ddriven%2C%20focuses%20on%20the [Accessed 3 April 2025].
- Schmelzer, M., Vetter, A. and Vansintjan, A., 2022. The Future is Degrowth: A Guide to a World Beyond Capitalism. London: Verso.
- Scott, J., 2025. 'Water Stories: Worried Wings and Biodiversity'. Available at: https://www.jillscottart.org [Accessed 13 March 2025].
- Simplex DNA, 2025. 'Environmental eDNA'. Available at: https://www.simplexdna.com [Accessed 10 March 2025].
- Te Whata, 2024. 'Ngāpuhi: Adult Qualifications'. Available at: https://tewhata.io/ngapuhi/social/education/adult-qualifications/ [Accessed 23 October 2024].
- Te Whata, 2024. 'Post-School Qualification Field of Study'. Available at: https://tewhata.io/all-maori/social/education/adult-qualifications/post-school-qualification-field-of-study [Accessed 23 October 2024].
- Te Whata, 2024. 'Te Whata Online Platform'. Available at: https://tewhata.io/ [Accessed 23 October 2024].
- Vetter, A., 2025. 'Rare Earth Minerals - Global South: Copper, Tin, Nickel, Iron, Lithium - IPHONE - Plus 90% Rare Earth Minerals Come from China'. [online] Available at: https://www.transcript-verlag.de/author/vetter-andrea-320006437/ [Accessed 15 January 2025].
- Warren, K.J., 1997. Ecofeminism: Women, Culture, Nature. Bloomington: Indiana University Press.
- Wikipedia, 2025. 'The Fourth Wall'. Available at: https://en.wikipedia.org/wiki/Fourth_wall [Accessed 10 March 2025].
- Zed Books Ltd., 1993. Ecofeminism by Mies and Shiva.

INVISIBLE INTIMACIES: SUBJECTS, GENDER, AND SCIENCE

María Fernández

Posthumanism, along with climate change, the ongoing reduction of resources, biological species, and the threat of human obliteration from the planet, contributes to disseminating recognition of the interdependence of the earth's life forms. The health of these entanglements cannot be separated from our scientific, technological, economic, social, political, and discursive practices. These intricate relations affect conventional ideas of both the human body and scientific knowledge. After briefly introducing posthumanism and recognising its compatibility with Indigenous philosophies, this essay centres on historically significant works by Sonya Bäumel (Austria) and Anna Dumitriu (UK), two artists who employ bacteria to make visible formerly invisible aspects of the body. Their art questions notions of the human based on wholeness, unity, and autonomy, and implicitly calls attention to other forms of invisibility, such as the achievements of women in scientific fields. Using crafts, quotidian objects, and sometimes bacteria from their own bodies, these artists disturb the boundaries between private and public, domestic and scientific. In so doing, they challenge traditional understandings of the self and the social assignations of power and legitimacy which circumscribe scientific knowledge. Bäumel questions the body, subjectivity, and fashion, whereas Dumitriu departs from the body's multiplicity to interrogate power and scientific knowledge. Their work invites consideration of human-nonhuman relationships, science, and the knowledge it occludes.

Posthumanism, along with climate change, the ongoing reduction of resources, biological species, and the threat of human obliteration from the planet contributes to increasing recognition of the interdependence of the earth's life forms. The health of these entanglements cannot be separated from our scientific, technological, economic, social, political, and discursive practices (Barad, 2007). These intricate interrelations and their effects on conventional ideas of the human body, gender, and scientific knowledge as they appear in select artworks, constitute the core of this essay. These works disturb the boundaries between scientific, domestic and personal, often gendered spaces. In so doing, they challenge traditional understandings of the self and the social assignations of power and legitimacy which circumscribe scientific knowledge.

Posthumanism defies humanist notions of rational progress, sovereign subjects and the powers of human reason to instead focus on interdependence, intersubjectivity, and relationality among humans and nonhumans. The latter include animals, microbes, machines, objects, and matter. The theorists Rosi Braidotti, Stacy Alaimo, Karen Barad, Diana Coole and Samatha Frost among others, integrate these theories to feminism (Barad, 2007; Coole and Frost, 2010, Braidotti, 2022). As some Native American scholars cogently argue, ideas central to posthumanism have been part of indigenous knowledge systems for millennia, yet these traditions remain excluded from both posthumanism and science (Bignall and Rigney 2019; Todd, 2016). The isolation of science from nonscience and rationality from belief bars recognition of these forms of knowledge. The artists Sonya Bäumel (Austria) and Anna Dumitriu (UK) challenge those boundaries even though they work within the West. Both artists use science to interrogate the constitution of bodies, subjects, knowledge, and agency and trouble conventional divisions between science and nonscience, science and art, public and private, craft and experimental technique, low and high culture.

For the last twenty years, Sonya Bäumel has collaborated with scientists, scholars, artists, and designers to make scientific research accessible to a wider public. Bäumel's works communicate scientific knowledge and assert themselves as visually arresting provocations in which the artist interrogates notions of the human body and, by extension, the stability of subjectivity and identity. Bäumel calls attention to the body's nonhuman components by making perceptible the microbial partnerships that constitute it.

Bäumel's work of 2011, *Textured Self*, commissioned by the Textielmuseum Tilburg, focuses on the vast populations of bacteria that live on our skin. The work was an offshoot of *Cartography of the Human Body*, a collaboration with the bacteriologist Erich Schopf, which mapped the bacteria on the artist's skin collected on 11 November 2010. They analysed, documented and bred these microorganisms for an eight-month period, feeding them to acquire specific colors. The artist then applied to her skin the bacteria with agar and imprinted her body image on a textile (Bäumel, 2008-2023 a).

The Textured Self presents a crocheted body silhouette, textiles and colored yarns, showing the amount, colour, and structure of the bacteria found on specific regions of her body as shown on the first day of the *Cartography*. She translates processes usually viewed under the microscope or in a computer screen into physical and tangible shapes. She expected that the objects would "confront people with the fact that a human being is not an individual person but a hybrid, a superorganism, which is only able to exist if the different forms of life in and on the body cooperate" (Bäumel, 2008-23 d). The multiple organisms appear here as differently coloured shapes on the crocheted body form (Figure 1).

Crocheted Membrane consisting of a series of crocheted garments, formed part of the *Invisible Membrane* Project, the artist's Master's Thesis. Here, Bäumel envisioned possible applications to clothing of the diverse communities of bacteria that reside in our skin and suggested that the bacteria, which normally are sensitive to environmental factors, could respond to their milieu as well as to the needs of the human bodies on which they reside (Bäumel, 2008-2023 b). Slime fungi could act as a kind of coating that in interaction with the bacteria and possibly plants, could adapt to climatic changes. The clothes would spontaneously develop in response to the needs of the user and environmental factors such as temperature or wind. These garments would be unique, depending on each individual microbiome (Bäumel, 2008-2023 c). Accordingly, some items look more like body decorations than clothing. In one instance, a patterned net covers the heels and the back of the ankles but not the rest of the feet or legs. What appears to be a pair of gloves fails to cover the hands and arms of the user because of the large voids between the crocheted patterns (Figure 2). The

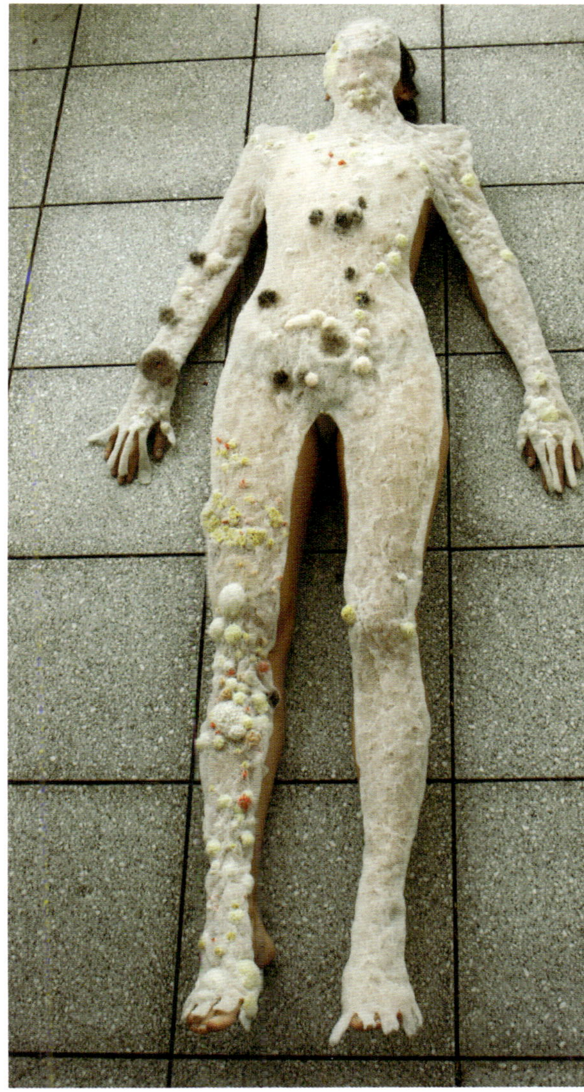

Figure 1: *The Textured Self.* Bäumel, S. (2010). Performance by the artist with interactive bacteria. https://sonjabaeume .at

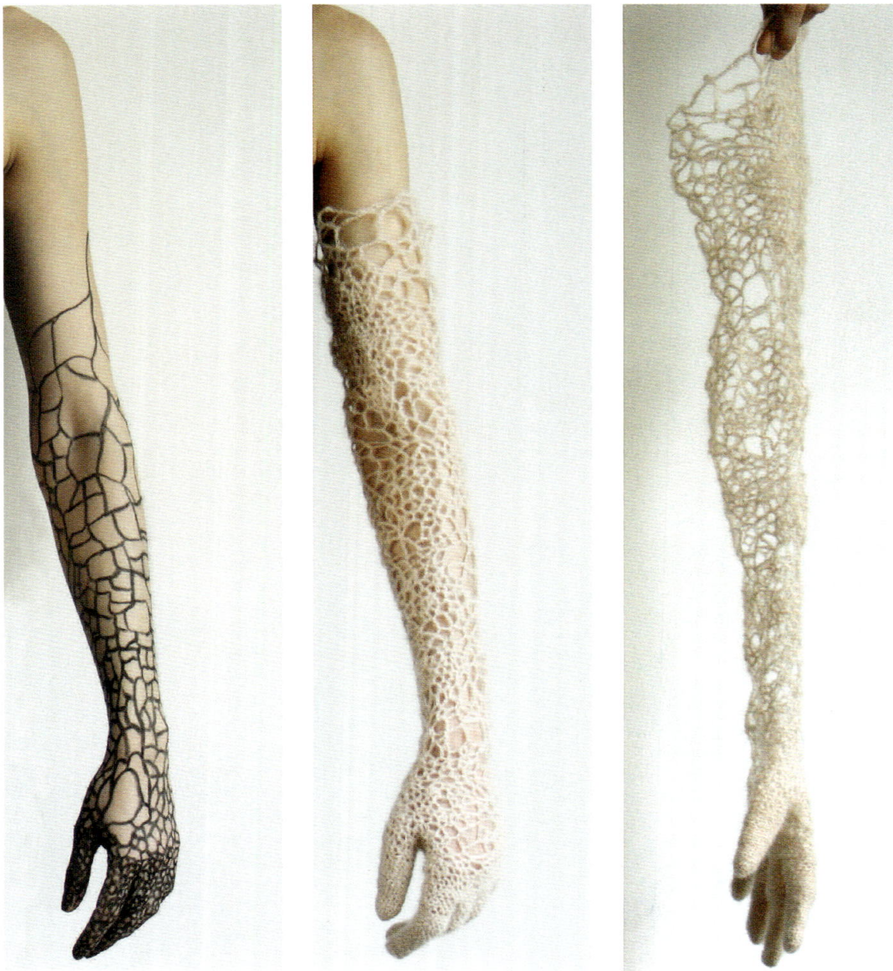

Figure 2 : *Crocheted Membrane.* Bäumel, S. (2008-2009). Performance by the artist. Photo: Wing Lam Kwok.

artist's declarations call attention to the illusion of the naked body, for humans, like other animals, are always already covered with microbes thriving on our skin. In these artworks, clothes are no longer a "second skin," but a third, artificial one (Felshin, 1995, p. 77). The artist's use of crochet reasserts a feminist artistic practice. This craft, traditionally associated with women, was excluded from art until the advent of feminist art in the 1970's.

In these historical works, Bäumel expanded on then-current microbiological research to question the singularity of the self, a concept foundational to classical humanism. The destabilisation of humanist ideals has a long history through Marxism, psychoanalysis, semiotics, the materialist philosophy of Deleuze and Guattari, and posthumanism (Braidotti, 2013; Deleuze and Guattari, 1987). In contrast, the idea of the self as bounded-

prevailed in medical sciences such as immunology until the late 20th century (Martin, 1994; Haraway, 1991; Rees, Bosch, and Douglas, 2018). Bäumel's work supported the philosophical proposition of manifold subjectivities with microbiology.

Like Bäumel, the British artist Anna Dumitriu collaborates with scientists to make art that involves bacteria. Some of her work incorporates art forms traditionally associated with crafts and hobbies, such as crochet and embroidery. Dumitriu has been the recipient of sponsorships by diverse scientific and public health institutions and has interned in multiple laboratories. She not only translates scientific research into forms comprehensible to a lay public, but also involves the audience in the making of the work. Her eclectic art practice includes microbiology, textiles, robotics, and digital media.

Many of her projects concern the inseparability of the history of science and socially constructed gender roles, which as multiple scholars have argued, affect the history of scientific knowledge (Keller, 1985; Haraway, 1989; Martin, 1991). Several works involve the history of lethal epidemic diseases which devastate populations and sometimes relate to sexual, cultural, and religious difference. These associations often result in unprovoked violence against specific groups. Her early works, however, concerned the ubiquity of bacteria in our daily environments without allusions to disease.

In *Normal Flora*, Dumitriu cultured bacteria, moulds, and yeasts residing in objects we routinely use, including chairs, blankets, clothes, clean cutlery, and food. Although people of all genders use these items, traditionally, they are associated with domestic spaces whose care and maintenance have been the responsibility of women. These common objects are grounds for the lives of microscopic multitudes that coexist with us. Dumitriu made images of the bacteria using electron microscope transmission (TEM), a method that employs an electron beam, electromagnetic converging lenses, a phosphorescent screen, and a digital camera to capture and magnify the image of a microscopic object in a vacuum environment (Central Microscopy Research Facility, University of Iowa, no date). Later, she and her collaborators interpreted the illustrations in other media. In *Bed and Chair Flora*, a work from this series, she carved bacterial patterns in a found chair and also decorated the upholstery with similar forms in needlepoint. Volunteers from the audience contributed to crochet a blanket that represented bacteria from the artist's bed. She has described this project in relation to intimacy because it displays her personal microbial imprints (Dumitriu, 2012) (Figure 3).

Similarly, in *Lab Coat Flora*, (Figure 4) embroidered patterns in a lab coat represent microbes cultured from it. Dumitriu's use of clothing and homemade textiles to interpret scientific images also speaks to other kinds of intimacy: the interpenetration of scientific, traditionally male domains, with objects associated with domestic spaces and primarily female activities. Literally, she imprints these objects with the tools and subject matter of scientific experimentation and in so doing, materially and symbolically confounds the boundaries of the scientific and the domestic. As the scientist and philosopher Isabel Stengers and the historian Julie des Jardins maintain, historically the separation of these realms has been zealously guarded. Des Jardins explains, "the very definition of professional science relies on its antithetical concept amateur science, defined in its methods and orientation as quintessentially domestic" (Des Jardins, 2010, p.6). This distinction, in addition to the association of scientific prestige to genius as well as masculine ideals of detachment, "objectivity," and single-mindedness, contributed to make women nearly as invisible as microbes in most of the history of science (Des Jardins 2010, p. 10; Stengers 2010, p. 21). According to the science historian Margaret Rossiter, in the 1950s and 1960s, women scientists "were at best invisible, and at worst an embarrassment" (Rossiter, 1995, p.xvi). Not only did they lack public recognition, but also, they were unknown to one another (Rossiter, 1995, p. 304). Most frequently, females occupied positions as assistants and technicians in science laboratories.

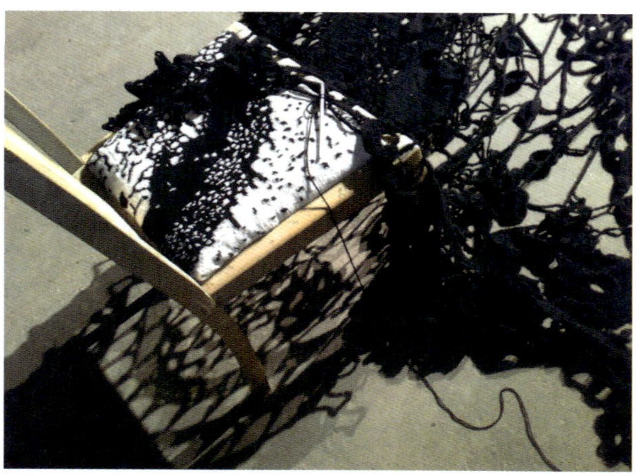

Figure 3: *Bed and Chair Flora.* Dumitriu, A. (2004-2005). Crochet installation.

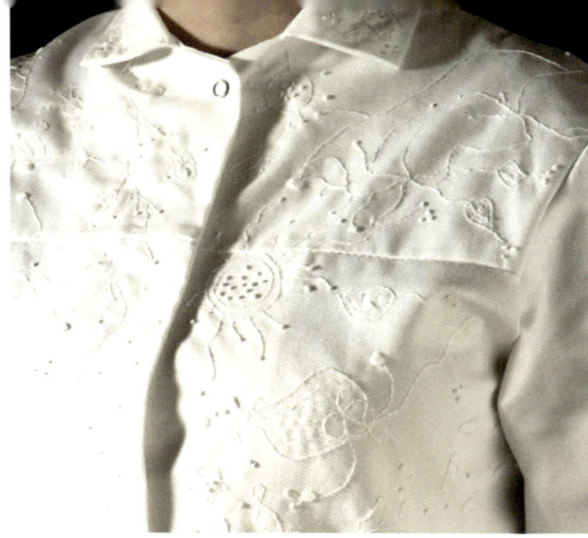

Figure 4: *Lab Coat Flora.* Dumitriu, A. (2004-2005). Wearable installation.

Labs are purified settings for the performance of rational procedures (Stengers, 2010). Interpenetrating the lab and the home, Dumitriu's work "pollutes" the sacred realm of science by transgressing its boundaries. As the anthropologist Mary Douglas once argued, "pollution only works in reference to a total structure of thought whose keystone, boundaries, margins, and internal lines are held in relation by rituals of separation" (Douglas, 2003, p. 51). Even if scientific research is diverse, numerous scholars portray it as a set of discourses and practices with universalising objectives, based on consensus (Stengers, 1997; De Sousa Santos, 2018). Without rejecting science, Dumitriu's works disturb its isolation.

Allusions to the two spaces in a single object suggest correspondences between traditional female labour and science. Crafts and scientific experiments share similarities. Both require specialised knowledge, attentiveness following sequential processes, diligence, and patience to achieve the desired results. Ultimately, the works suggest that despite having divergent cultural values, the two activities share similarities. Yet, while Western science is one of the most prestigious and powerful knowledge systems in the world, domestic work, which to this day is largely performed by women, remains undervalued (International Labour Office Geneva, 2013; Carpenter, 2018; Jurviste and Penas Dendariena, 2016). Dumitriu's later installations interweave related narratives.

At the *6th Guangzhou Triennial at Guangdong Museum of Art* (21 Dec 2018-10 March 2019), Dumitriu's *Plague Dress* confronted visitors with an unlikely visual juxtaposition and a familiar scent: An embroidered 17th century woman's dress, out of whose collar and sleeves, instead of a head and arms, emerged branches of fragrant lavender. One could take the work for one of the many recuperations of surrealism, known for its involvement with psychoanalysis and for its appeal to senses other than vision, most notably, smell (Verbeek, 2018). While indisputably this is one aspect of the pieces' heritage, the work does a lot more than stir the unconscious. The dress commemorates the third arrival of plague to London, in 1665. The selection of female attire is significant as recent research indicates that women were disproportionally affected by the plague.

Once more, Dumitriu integrated domestic crafts and science by dyeing the garment with walnut husks and decorating it with original 17th century embroidered appliqués imbued with the inactivated DNA of Yersinia pestis, the bacillus responsible for plague. Yesinia pestis lives in the bloodstream of rodents such as rats and marmots and spreads to humans from flees that feed on the blood of these

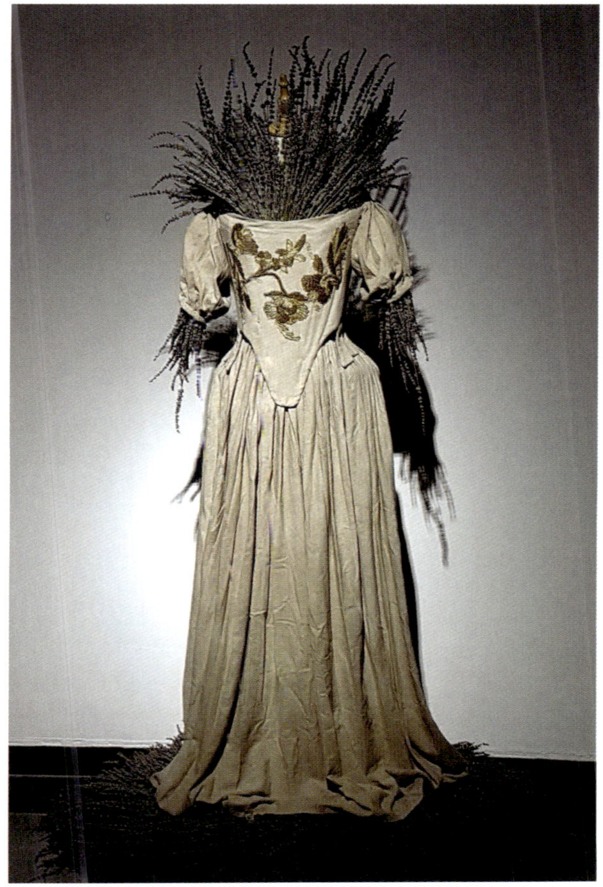

Figure 5: *Lab Coat Flora.* Dumitriu, A. (2004-2005). Dress from the time of the plague 1665. https://annadumitriu.co.uk

animals. The bacteria mutate through time; consequently, there are varieties of plague. Recent studies of the disease suggests that the vectors of transmission may be multiple, and the bacteria develop in response to environmental conditions, so much so, that the historian of medieval European medicine, Monica Green, proposes that it is best to think of plague, not as a single organism but as an "ecological package" (Green, 2015, p, xi). Today, many scholars accept the identification of the Black Death as plague based on recent DNA analysis of graves (Green, 2015; DeWitte, 2014; Ziegler, 2015). Although this pandemic is best known in association with medieval Europe, in the mid fourteenth century, it decimated 40-60% of the total population of Europe, the Middle East, and North Africa (Welford, 2018). Plague sporadically reemerges as it appears continuously to evolve.

In the Middle Ages in Europe, aromatic plants and herbs including rosemary and lavender were used to ward off plague in addition to other measures such as isolation of the sick. Although there were several explanations for the origin of the mysterious disease, the most prevalent one was that it was due to infestation of the air (Dumitriu, Plague Dress, no date; Martin, 2014). This understanding precluded neither the belief that plague was a divine punishment for humanity's sins nor the conviction that Jews caused its propagation. As a result of these associations, in the 14th century, Europe experienced the most violent persecutions of Jews before the Holocaust (Martin, 2014; Welford, 2018).

In England the plague epidemic of 1665 was one of the most virulent resurgences of the disease since the Black Death. In Dumitriu's work, the silk dress refers to the trade routes from which pandemics spread. Textiles are implicated in this story as some chroniclers believed that plague moved undetected in clothes (Dumitriu, no date; Shrewsbury, 1970). The expansion of English commercial and colonial power from the sixteenth century onwards accelerated its global dissemination. In the 17th century, the English competed with the Dutch for maritime commerce with the East. By 1684, England dominated the textile trade (Lemire and Riello, 2008).

As empire and commerce advanced, plague also extended its reach. In 1866, it reappeared in Yunan province in China and within decades, travelled east to the port city of Guangzhou (formerly Canton) which in 1894 lost at least 70,000 people to the disease. From there, it spread to Hong Kong and traveled the world in British ships. Some of the cities that fell to the bacterium included Macao, Singapore, Taiwan, Bombay, Kobe, Japan, San Francisco, Manila and Sydney, Australia (Welford, 2018).

Linking London and Guangzhou, the Plague Dress refers to human networks that facilitated the spread of the infection. Because of the two historical moments the work references, it involves the history of British colonialism. The seventeenth century witnessed the growth of British maritime power that sustained the British empire. *Plague Dress* is poignant considering the recent COVID-19 pandemic, which demonstrated the interdependence of nations, their shared vulnerability as well as the relationship of disease prevention and containment to economic power (Miguel and Mobarak, 2022). COVID-19 took its greatest death toll on marginalised populations, which as with the plague, sometimes were also scapegoated for the disease.

Dumitriu and Bäumel's use of textiles is compatible with, but differs in significant ways from the resurgence of crafts as "craftivism" (Wilson, 2019, p. 23). In contrast to these recent practices, these artists' works lack direct associations with leftist politics. But that does not mean they lack a politic. Seeing oneself as a multiplicity has implications for how we view humans and their position in the world: Anthropos as master of the world or inextricably entwined with it. Both artists index the body through its complements: microbes and clothes. Both accentuate the body's precariousness and open the possibility of its disappearance through signs of its absence - bodily bacterial imprints for Bäumel and empty dresses for Dumitriu.

These artists' selection of textiles is consistent with the border-crossing functions of the medium. As Julia Bryan-Wilson reminds us, "Cloth has the ability to traverse the line between public and private as it travels with us on our bodies as we shift from the domestic to the realm of the street" (Wilson, 2019, p. 34). In their art, both artists merge the private spaces of bodies, the home, the laboratory and the art gallery to different ends. Bäumel explores ideas of the body, subjectivity, fashion, and the future of clothing whereas Dumitriu departs from the body's multiplicity to interrogate power and scientific knowledge. She asks us to consider who produces knowledge? Who has credibility and authority? Who communicates knowledge and to what effects?

Informed by contemporary science, art, history, and theory, Bäumel and Dumitriu interrogate notions of subjectivity, relationality, interdependence, science, and knowledge production at this time of ecological crises. Their work does not solve problems but invites reflections about power, Western science, human entanglements, and our responsibilities to the earth and all its life forms.

References

- Barad, K., 2007. Meeting the Universe Halfway: Quantum Physics and the Entanglement of Matter and Meaning. Durham, NC: Duke University Press.
- Bäumel, S., 2008/2023a. 'Cartography of the Human Body.' Available at: http://www.sonjabaeumel.at/work/bacteria/cartography-of-the-human-body [Accessed 20 June 2019).
- Bäumel, S., 2008/2023b. 'Crocheted Membrane.' Available at: http://www.sonjabaeumel.at/work/bacteria/crocheted-membrane [Accessed 19 July 2017].
- Bäumel, S., 2008/2023c. '(In)visible Membrane.' Available at: http://www.sonjabaeumel.at/info/13-archive/8-invisible-membrane [Accessed 19 July 2017].
- Bäumel, S., 2008/2023d. 'Textured Self.' Available at: https://www.sonjabaeumel.at/work/textured+self/ [Accessed 3 January 2017].
- Bignall, S. and Rigney, D., 2019. 'Indigeneity, Posthumanism and Nomad Thought,' in Braidotti, R. (ed.) Posthuman Ecologies: Complexity and Process after Deleuze. New York: Rowman & Littlefield International, pp. 159–181.
- Braidotti, R., 2013. The Posthuman. Cambridge, UK: Polity.
- Braidotti, R., 2022. Posthuman Feminism. Cambridge, UK: Polity.
- Bryan-Wilson, J. (2017). Fray: Art and Textile Politics. Chicago: University of Chicago Press.
- Carpenter, J., 2018. CNN Business. 'Millennial Women Are Working More. But They're Still Doing Most of the Housework.' Available at: https://www.cnn.com/2018/12/26/success/millennial-women-income/index.html [Accessed 27 June 2019].
- Central Microscopy Research Facility, University of Iowa (no date). 'Transmission Electron Microscopy.' Available at: https://cmrf.research.uiowa.edu/transmission-electron-microscopy [Accessed 20 May 2019].
- Coole, D. and Frost, S., 2010. New Materialisms: Ontology, Agency, and Politics. Durham, NC: Duke University Press.
- De Sousa Santos, B. de S., 2018. The end of the cognitive empire: The coming of age of epistemologies of the South. Durham, NC: Duke University Press.
- Deleuze, G. and Guattari, F., 1987. A Thousand Plateaus, translated by B. Massumi. Minneapolis, MN: University of Minnesota Press.
- DeWitte, S., 2014. 'The Anthropology of Plague: Insights from Bioarchaeological Analysis of Epidemic Cemeteries,' The Medieval Globe, 1(1), pp. 5–21. Available at: https://scholarworks.wmich.edu/tmg/vol1/iss1/6/ [Accessed 15 June 2018].
- Douglas, M., 2003. Purity and Danger: An Analysis of the Concepts of Pollution and Taboo. New York: Routledge.
- Dumitriu, A., 2012. 'The Normal Flora Project: Intimate Revelations in Art and Science,' in Chatzichristodoulou, M. and Zerihan, R. (eds.) Intimacy Across Visceral and Digital Performance. New York: Palgrave, pp. 74–85.

- Dumitriu, A., (no date). 'Plague Dress.' Available at: http://annadumitriu.tumblr.com/plaguedress [Accessed 3 April 2019].
- Felshin, N., 1995. 'Women's Work: A Lineage, 1966-94, Art Journal, 54 (Spring), pp. 71-85.
- Keller, E. F., 1985. Reflections on gender and science. New Haven: Yale University Press, pp. 172-176.
- Green, M.H. (ed.), 2015. Pandemic Disease in the Medieval World. Kalamazoo, MI: Art Medieval Press.
- Haraway, D., 1991. Simians, Cyborgs and Women: The Reinvention of Nature. New York: Routledge.
- Haraway, D., 1989. Primate Visions. New York: Routledge.
- International Labour Office Geneva, 2013. Domestic Workers Across the World: Global and Regional Statistics and the Extent of Legal Protection. International Labour Office Geneva, International Labour Organization. Available at: http://www.ilo.org/wcmsp5/groups/public/---dgreports/---dcomm/---publ/documents/publication/wcms_173363.pdf [Accessed 27 June 2019].
- Des Jardins, J., 2010. The Madame Curie complex: The hidden history of women in science. New York: The Feminist Press at the City University of New York.
- Jurviste, U. and Penas Dendariena, I., 2016. 'Women and Domestic Work in the EU.' Available at: https://epthink-tank.eu/2016/02/25/women-and-domestic-work-in-the-eu/ [Accessed 27 June 2019].
- Lemire, B. and Riello, G., 2008. 'East and West: Textiles and Fashion in Early Modern Europe,' Journal of Social History, 41(4), pp. 887-1102 (Summer 2008).
- Martin, E., 1991. 'The Egg and the Sperm: How Science Has Constructed a Romance Based on Stereotypical Male-Female Roles,' Signs, 16(1), pp. 485-501 (Spring 1991).
- Martin, M., 1994. Flexible Bodies: Tracking Immunity in American Culture from the Days of Polio to the Age of AIDS. Boston: Beacon Press.
- Martin, S., 2014. The Black Death. Harpenden, UK: Oldcastle Books.
- Miguel, E. and Mushfiq Mobarak, A., 2023. 'The Economics of the COVID-19 Pandemic in Poor Countries,' Annual Review of Economics, 14 (August). Available at: https://doi.org/10.1146/annurev-economics-051520-025412 [Accessed 16 December 2023].
- Rees, T., Bosch, T., and Douglas, A., 2018. 'How the Microbiome Challenges Our Concept of Self,' PLoS Biology, 16(2). Available at: https://journals.plos.org/plosbiology/article?id=10.1371/journal.pbio.2005358 [Accessed 10 October 2018].
- Rossiter, M. W., 1995. Women Scientists in America: Before Affirmative Action, 1940-1972. Baltimore, MD: The Johns Hopkins University Press.
- Shrewsbury, J. F. D., 1970. A History of Bubonic Plague in the British Isles. Cambridge, UK: Cambridge University Press.
- Stengers, I., 1997. Power and Invention: Situating Science. Minneapolis, MN: University of Minnesota Press.
- Stengers, I., 2010. 'The Symbiosis Between Experiment and Techniques,' in Brower, J., Mulder, A., Spuybrock, L. (eds.) The Politics of the Impure. Rotterdam, V2_Publishing, pp. 16-45.
- Todd, Z., 2016. 'An Indigenous Feminist's Take on The Ontological Turn: 'Ontology' Is Just Another Word for Colonialism,' Journal of Historical Sociology, 29(1), pp. 4-22.
- Verbeek, C., 2016. 'Surreal Aroma's: (Re)constructing the Volatile Heritage of Marcel Duchamp,' Relief - Revue électronique de littérature française, 10 (June 2016), pp. 133-142.
- Welford, M., 2018. Geographies of Plague Pandemics: The Spatial Behavior of Plague to the Modern Day. New York: Routledge.
- Ziegler, M., 2015. 'The Black Death and the Future of the Plague,' in Green, M. (ed.) Pandemic Disease in the Medieval World. Kalamazoo, MI: Art Medieval Press, pp. 259-284.

PERSONAL REFLECTIONS

ON BEING A GENDERQUEER MICROBIOARTIST: ARTMAKING IN MICROBIOLOGY LABORATORIES

Tarsh Bates

I am a scavenger: a feminist, an artist, a scientist, a parent and a holobiont.[1] *In 2012, I learnt that the human body is 90% microbial. I was transformed - not becoming, but already a teeming, seething crowd; always already multiple, always already sympoietic.*[2] *The vertigo of this realisation brought not horror, but joy in the queer fecundity of my myriad body. Using my background in biotechnology, microbiology and contemporary art, I explore the aesthetics of caring for nonhuman organisms, and bodies as queer ecologies. My work is shaped by art/science pioneers like Ionat Zurr, Kira O'Reilly and Cat Jones. This paper traces my artistic research with microbes, investigating the gendered and biopolitical entanglements between humans and microorganisms. I explore microbial "Umwelten",*[3] *- traversing microbe-human-planetary scales and considering the agency and "response-ability" of the microbes in whose worlds we live. The work, of blending transdisciplinary methodologies and collaborations, is rarely smooth sailing. Like queers, microbes and microbiological art are often misread, miscast, marginalised. Flourishing, for the living and non-living alike, hinges on the stories we tell. Dominant narratives centre control and death, yet life is only possible through microbial "kinshipping", gestures, unlikely pairings and generative relations.*

Part I: Prehistory

I graduated from high school at the end of the twentieth century. The ozone layer had a hole in it and the greenhouse effect was warming the planet; we were emerging from the threat of global nuclear annihilation and Y2K was still a few years away; Rachel Carson's *Silent Spring* was only twenty years old, and Ben Elton's hilarious apocalyptic novel *Stark* was only one year old. But there was still time! Fresh-faced and ready to save the world, I enrolled in a course in environmental engineering, where I was one of four women out of a five hundred students. I lasted six months. Undeterred, I enrolled in a new degree in the emerging field of biotechnology. I learnt microbiology, industrial fermentation, biochemistry, immunology and genetic engineering. I infected rats and rabbits to create antibodies and wrote business plans for the economical manipulation of life. Ethics, philosophy and feminism were not required courses.

East became West, we survived the Y2K virus, the hole in the ozone layer disappeared because we stopped using CFCs, but mass extinctions and carbon emissions accelerated. As a passionate feminist and animal rights activist, I turned to large scale composting, convinced that my contribution to saving the planet was to get people to stop throwing organic matter into landfills and wasting vital carbon and nutrients which generate methane (a potent greenhouse gas) and pollute groundwater. Microbes are vital to both these processes: the slow underground anaerobic fermentation in landfills and the rapid aerobic conversion involved in industrial composting. At that time, the microbes were merely useful tools, "natural" conversion factories for keeping nutrient and carbon cycles balanced and sustainable. However, over time, I became disillusioned with the entanglements of politics, capitalism and scientific research and one day, sitting in a pitch meeting for a local council where I was the only woman in a room of 20 male engineers, I understood that an engineering solution would always win. I quit science the next day.

Part II: The Dark Ages

Seduced by textiles, string and glass making, and a luscious sculpture workshop, I embraced the affective and sensuous refuges of art and craft. I learnt about feminist artists like Ana Mendieta, Judy Chicago, Jill Orr, Maria Abramovic, Kira O'Reilly, The Guerrilla Girls, Yoko Ono, Kiki Smith, Janine Antoni, Carolee Schneeman, Fiona Foley and Destiny Deacon, who embodied the "the personal is political" (Hanisch, 1969). They literally used their bodies to explore, understand and increase awareness of domestic and female experiences, care, labour and knowledge. I became fascinated by multispecies feminist theorist Donna Haraway, cyberfeminist art collectives VNS Matrix and subRosa, and the intersections of feminism, sexuality and technology. I felt seen and at home: the art of these amazing women and my peers reflected my outrage and grief at my own experiences. Their vibrancy outlined the howling lacunae of women's experiences, knowledge and concerns in universalist and objective science, and I was happily convinced I had found my place as far from science as I could get.

Then I attended a killing ritual by performance artist Stelarc and pioneering bioartists from the

Tissue Culture & Art Project (TC&A). The artists had grown living mouse cells over a tiny sculpture of Stelarc's ear and the killing ritual involved removing the sculpture from the bioreactor which sustained the life of the cells and exposing the cells to non-sterile air and hands, thereby killing them. The artists talked of life manipulation, control and an aesthetics of care. The combination of art, biology, care, and the bioreactor as a technological uterus was revelatory. I was even more excited to learn that TC&A had been involved in setting up SymbioticA, an artistic research laboratory in the anatomy school at one of the universities in my own city, which enabled artists to work in tissue culture and biological research laboratories.

Then, I had a car accident. Stationary at a set of lights, I was rear-ended by a young woman texting on her mobile phone while driving.

My embodiment profoundly changed in moments. From being strong, fit, dynamic and "able," my body became alien, unpredictable and uncontrollable. I woke up and went to sleep with blinding headaches. I quit swimming and yoga because they aggravated my neck and shoulders. My muscles were constantly contracted and became inflamed at the slightest pressure or twist. I was only able to work part-time. Navigating a dismissive, sexist and heteronormative, fractured and siloed medical and allied health industry, was extraordinarily expensive, frustrating and bewildering. Over the next two years, I was repeatedly informed that whiplash injuries usually resolve themselves within 6-8 weeks. I was called a "naughty girl" by a physiotherapist for getting treatment before the insurance claim was resolved. For more than a decade, I was enraged with the system and my body and its inability to do what it used to be able to.

Two things helped me survive: I was "adopted" by my best friend, her partner and their twin babies, and SymbioticA started the world's first Master's programme in Art/Science. For the next four years, I travelled between Perth, Australia and Switzerland, learning the skills, behaviours and aesthetics of parenting and biological art. SymbioticA's interdisciplinary programme was run by Ionat Zurr of TC&A fame and enabled artists to study science courses, and scientists to study art courses. I immersed myself in gender and science and technology studies, philosophy, art history and posthumanism. With the invaluable support and advice of interdisciplinary artists such as Ionat, Svenja Kratz, Kathy High, Kira O'Reilly, Helen Pynor, Alicia King, Cat Jones, and Sue Hauri-Downing, who were working at the cutting edge of art and science, I explored the tensions and contradictions involved in life manipulations and biotechnologies, and expanded my understanding of reproductive politics to include the more-than-human.[5]

The feminist and queer bio and eco art practices of these artists were particularly inspirational for me because of the ways they used hope and despair, kindness and humour to provoke and shift understandings of our place in the world as artists and as humans. The work of Svenja and Helen is mentioned elsewhere in this book, so I won't discuss it here. In the mid-1990s, Ionat Zurr formed the Tissue Culture & Art Project[6] with her collaborator Oron Catts. Over the next decade, Ionat and Oron created iconic semi-living sculptures using tissue culture techniques, including *Pig Wings* (2001-2002) and *Victimless Leather, - A Prototype of Stitch-less Jacket grown in a Technoscientific 'Body'* (2004), and *Disembodied Cuisine* (2001-2003) with Guy Benary. They aimed to bring life manipulation technologies into popular discourse and provoke discussions about the ethics and aesthetics of such technologies. They are considered pioneers of biological art and continue to make provocative work. Kathy High[7] is a queer multi-media artist, whose work with rats and microbiomes is simultaneously kind and hilarious: *Rat Laughter* (2009-2019), produces "musical soundscapes" from the ultrasonic laughter of lab rats, in *Blood Wars* (2010-2011), she staged *in vivo* fights between white blood cells drawn from audience members. *Bank of Abject Objects* (2016) and *OkPoopid* (2017) are two of several recent works by Kathy which explore microbiomes, digestion and shit.

Eco-punk artist Cat Jones[8] explores intimate and fraught relations between plants and humans in healing practices. Her works are extraordinarily empathic, sensorial and corporeal. In *Empathic Limb Clinic* (2013) and *Somatic Drifts* (2015-2016), she activated touch, neurobiology and illusion to help visitors become plants. In *Century's Breath* (2015) and *Scent of Sydney* (2017), she co-created future olfactory landscapes imagined by audiences. Eco-artist and social worker Sue Hauri-Downing[9] explores collaborative arts of noticing and mourning for disappearing ecologies. *Sanctuary* (2005), *Wardian Case* (2011) and *Threatened, Rare - Extant* (2018-2023) provide gentle and evocative reminders of what's at stake in the ongoing practices of colonisation, extractivism and preservation, evoking the fragile tensions between care and loss.

Part III: The Enlightenment

While learning to care for my adoptive human family, I also learnt how to care for eight model species used in reproductive research (Figure 1). I was particularly interested in the aesthetics of care and the behaviours involved in caring for organisms that are pests or that don't have faces. In capitalist, colonial Western cultures, we seem to find it difficult enough to live ethically with charismatic megafauna and flora, so I wanted to understand how we might learn to care for those upon whom our knowledge of our own existence is built.

I cared for these critters for six months in the SymbioticA laboratory, learning scientific protocols for feeding and maintenance them for researchers who were passionate about their subjects and bemused by my interest. I immersed myself in the technoscientific manipulation of the lives of these critters, focused on the aesthetics of caring for them. The project finished with me living with them for three months in a gallery at the Perth Institute of Contemporary Art (Figure 2). Each species was housed in a separate glass "uterus." Despite my attempts, not all flourished. I just could not get the nematode (*C. elegans*), the hydra, or the cress (*A. thaliana*) to thrive.

One of the species, the human commensal yeast and opportunistic pathogen *Candida albicans*, required biohazard protocols and a protective display for public exhibition. Although many of my female friends have had lifelong issues with vaginal candida infections, I was surprised by the gendered responses of the audience to this critter: although almost every woman knew exactly what

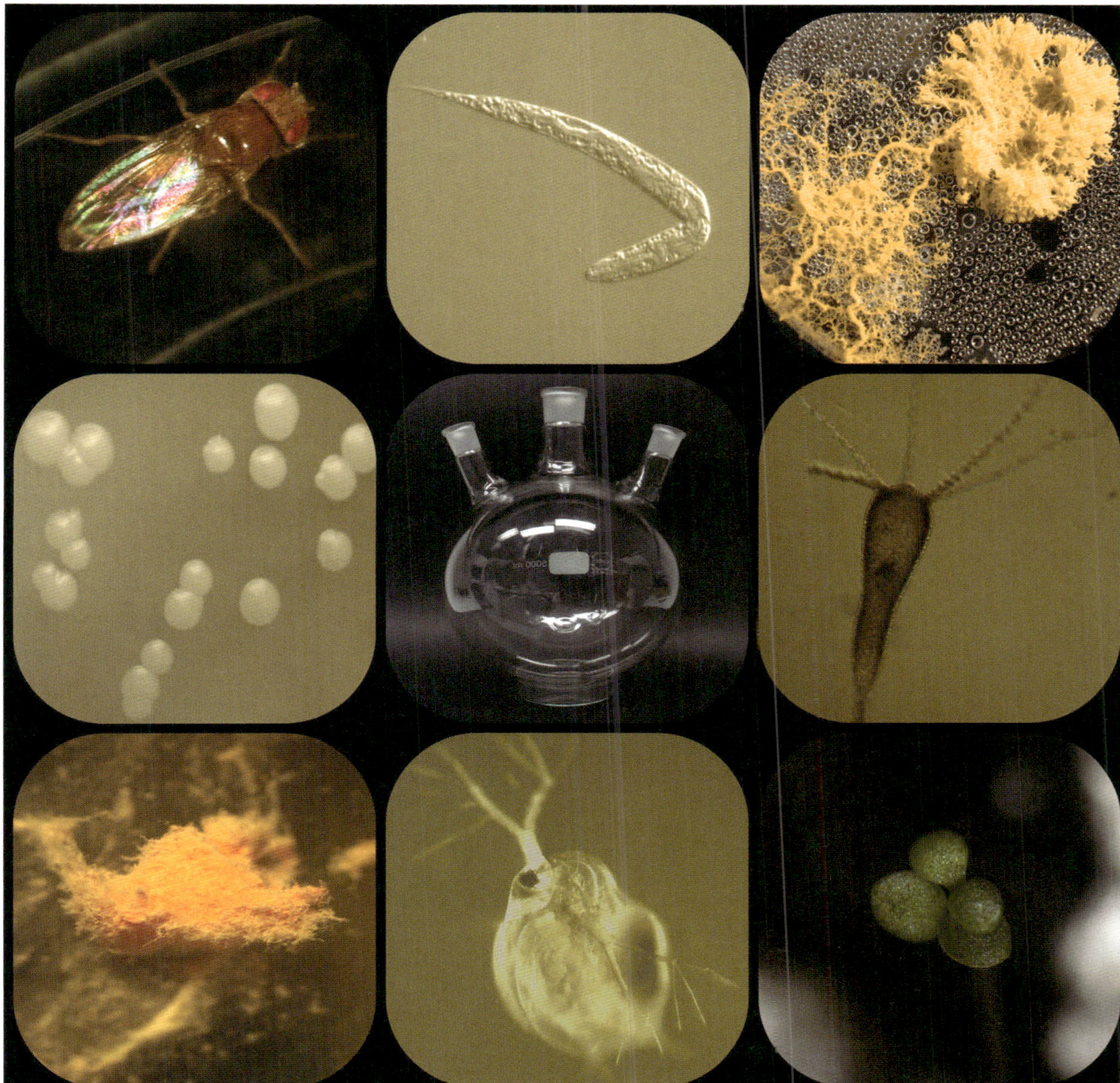

Figure 1: *In vitero logo.* Bates, T. (2011).
Critters clockwise from top left: *Drosophilia melanogaster* (fruit fly), *Caenorhabditis elegans* (nematode), *Physarum polycephalum* (slime mold), *Hydra vulgaris* (hydra), *Arabadopsis thaliana* (thale cress), *Daphnia pulex* (water fleas), *Neurospora crassa* (red bread mold), and *Candida albicans* (thrush). The central vessel represents the human as a model species in reproductive research.

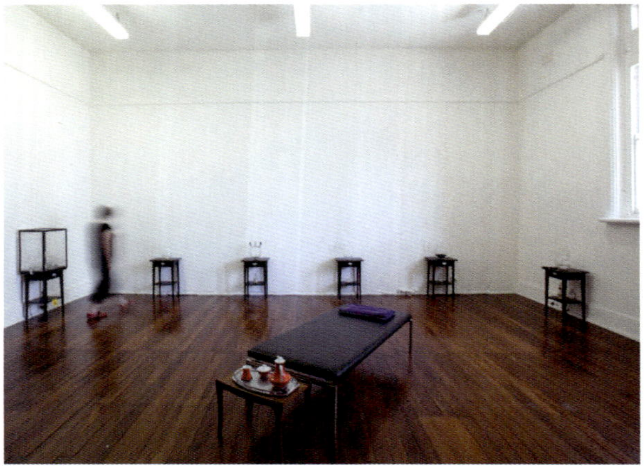

Figure 2: *In vitero*. Bates, T. (2011).
Performance and installation. Photo: Bo Wong.

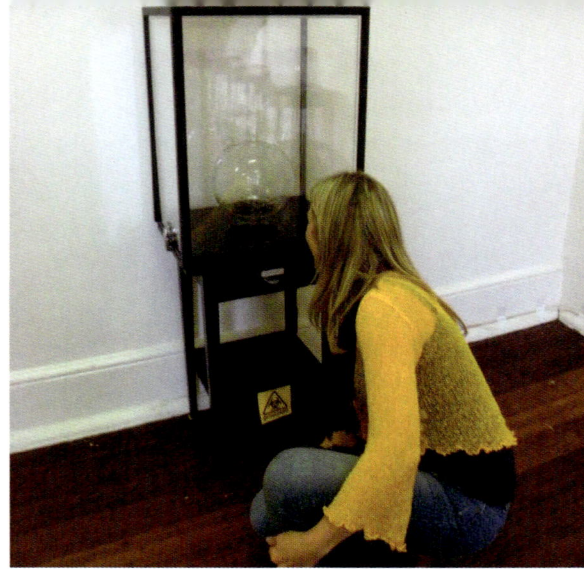

Figure 3: *Candida albicans*. Bates, T. (2011).
Installation still from *In vitero*. Photo: Megan Schlipalius.

candida was, very few men did. Even though many women responded with disgust, a few were fascinated and spent quite a lot of time in front of the display (Figure 3). Men who knew were excited and desperate to talk about their experiences. I was utterly stunned. The experience taught me how gendered our relationships with microbes can be, and how art can transform these relationships. The public exhibition of candida exposed a gendered dimension in human-microbial relations, and this revelation has changed my life.

I spent the next six years working to understand *Candida-Homo* ecologies.

Part IV: Candida-Homo ecologies

I began my relationship with candida and interest in the stories humans tell about it. This is "microbiopolitics" (Paxson, 2008, p. 17): the human systems of regulation and governance that work to control human-microbial relations. The different stories we tell - biological and artistic, evolutionary and ecological, medical and queer - have very material effects for the bodies involved. Lives and deaths hinge on these stories, which I untangled using an interdisciplinary methodology that encompasses theory and practice, discourse and being, knowledge and experience, art and science. I reached across and into microbiology, evolutionary ecology, queerness and aesthetics - disciplines through which we learn how bodies can be in the world.

Training in both scientific and artistic experimental practices, matters to me. Training in feminist, queer and environmental activism, aesthetics and philosophy, theory also matters to me. The materiality of theory and theories of materiality matter. This is the stuff of "being-in-the-world" (Heidegger, 1962), of "naturecultures,"[10] and of microbiopolitics. My artistic practice has become instinctively interdisciplinary, including practical laboratory and art-making experiments; material-semiotic scavenging from microbiology; art and craft; contemporary aesthetics; philosophy; pop culture; feminist and queer theory; anthropology; post-colonialism; race and crip theories; ecology; environmental biology; and humanities; speculative fiction: evolutionary biology and theory; biotechnology; sculpture; media archaeology and imaging practices.

I use a queer methodology that combines Haraway's analytical methods of "figurations" (1992, p. 86), *Cat's Cradle* (1994), and Karen Barad's (1998, p. 98) understanding of apparatuses to weave these disparate personae together. These methods map transitory convergences of bodies, concepts, technologies, economies and the un-objective political and material consequences of knowledge production, and are ideal for teasing out the tacit, implicit and unspoken. They enable rigorous exploration without foreclosure and demand self-reflection and diffraction.

Harawayan figurations reveal underlying assumptions, failures and contradictions. They also expose the material effects of such discourses: i.e., how "certain forms" emerge from the convergence of discourses – scientific, social, historical, physiological, genetic, economic, ethical, religious, spiritual, political, etc. that would not be possible singly. Like Haraway, Barad argues that there is no pre-existing, independent reality waiting to be discovered. Rather, materiality emerges from interactions and the apparatuses that generate them (Barad, 1998, p. 95, 2015, p. 407). An apparatus is the physical and/or sensual material and the theoretical or conceptual frameworks in which an intra-action emerges. Apparatuses materialise discursive cradles and the differential agencies of the partners in them. Matter at all scales has agency but, as Barad (2011, p. 128) argues, apparatuses recognise "practices of differentiating engaged in by nonhumans, whereby nonhumans differentiate themselves from their environments, from other nonhumans, and from humans, as well as from other others." They are an obligation to pay attention to what gets included and what gets excluded and why, and to the consequences. In this, apparatuses are like cat's cradles. However, they are not just tools for reconfiguring what counts as knowledge; they are intrinsic to its formation and consequences.

I also frame my practice through Michel Foucault's (1990) notions of *scientia sexualis* and *ars erotica*, by which he differentiates the mechanics of knowledge production from the pleasure of experience, and Yoko Ono's (2000) instruction painting, which separates practice from realisation and opens artworks to aleatory and collaborative production. Barad, Foucault and Ono all recognise the performativity of bodies and production through collaboration or relationality and critique, or reject reductionist claims to truth and determination to certain form. This framing allows me to explore how experiences and knowledge between species are generated through apparatuses, be they scientific, artistic, queer, evolutionary, ecological, conceptual, sensual or microbiopolitical.

Scientific protocols, despite their aspirations to standardisation, replicability and reliability, rely on consistent laboratory conditions, identical equipment, clear protocols, tacit knowledge and haptic familiarity – meaning that, through repetition, the actions of the practitioner become more consistent and less prone to variation or error. Care of and for another is implicit in the process but lost in translation between phenomenon and data. Failures are frequent and crucial for the process and are also lost in translations to results, conclusions or publication. According to Rocha (2011, p. 330), Foucault describes this system of representationalism as "scientia sexualis," where lived experience is reduced to an informatic body that can be studied, taken apart and comprehended, revealing the "truth" of the thing. However, laboratory conditions are inconsistent, equipment is never identical and breaks down, protocols are rarely clear, and tacit knowledge is difficult to share and takes time to learn. In this sense, scientific experiments are performative iterations that map and manifest "material engagements with the world" (Barad, 2007, p. 49). Conversely, Foucault argues that practices of "ars erotica" value sex as experience, appreciating and preserving actions which can bring about pleasure. They also haunt *scientia sexualis*.

Scientific protocols are also instruction painings, since, as Yoko Ono (1966) describes, "the work becomes a reality only when others realise the work. Instructions can be realised by different people in many ways. This allows infinite transformation of the work that the artist / scientist himself cannot foresee." Artmaking, at least the way I do it, tends towards chance and serendipity. It is more open to performative and affective experiences of bodies, the *ars erotica*, than data generation. This opens diverse spaces for microbial agency and responseability, recognising the value of scientific and artistic practices and interrogating the underlying assumptions and embedded biases of both.

I am interested in the cuts enacted by these apparatuses; how they evoke and generate particular material-semiotics and afford or foreclose material agency. I am interested in the materiality and performativity of microbial ecologies: the matter of bodies; the laboratory equipment necessary for care, nurture, killing and preservation; the imaging devices essential for navigating the spatiotemporal scales between micro and macro; the architectural spaces of laboratory, gallery, hospital and domicile; the art-making materials for care, display, protection and preservation; the paper, books, pens, computers that facilitate knowledge production, consumption and transmission; the texture of surfaces; the caress of smells; the oppressiveness of heat and cold; the flow of liquid and the soft resistance of agar; the durability of plastic; the immateriality of light; and the ability for response. I use scientific protocols and artistic practices to play in microbial worlds, to untangle how humans generate knowledge of microbes and, more interestingly, how microbes use their own knowledge of humans and each other.

Using this queer methodology, my experiments encourage microbial pleasure and responsibility rather than data and solutions. For example, the artwork, *Surface Dynamics of Adhesion* (Figure 4), consists of a series of acrylic boxes in which living candida grows in a pattern adapted from the first drawing of the organism by Charles Philippe Robin in 1853 and reminiscent of patterns popular on the wallpaper of parlours and art galleries in Europe at the time. The candida grows on blood agar, a growth medium that contains my own blood. The work is hung on the gallery wall as a horizontal border approximately one metre from the floor. Although

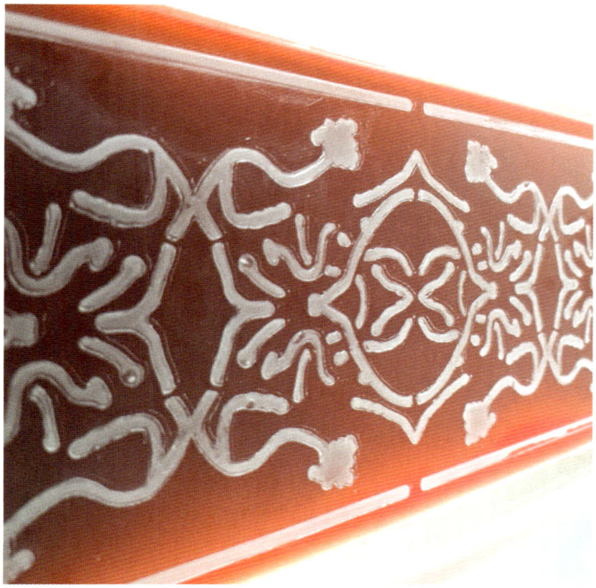

Figure 4: *Surface Dynamics of Adhesion*. Bates, T. (2018). Detail of Candita albicans forming on a surface of agar.

Surface Dynamics of Adhesion is both *scientia sexualis* and *ars erotica*. Emerging from scientific protocols, the work embraces the fecundity of candida and its affinity for surfaces, aggregation and biofilm formation. Optimum growth conditions maximise cell numbers, which are isolated, extracted, concentrated, cleaned and emulsified. The purified cells are applied to artist's blood agar plates and incubated overnight at 30°C, during which time cells proliferate and a living pattern emerges. Engaged in its own jouissance, the candida takes advantage of nutrients and warmth, opportunistically reproducing and replicating, eating and excreting, inhaling and exhaling, indifferent to the human maker and the viewers.

initially constrained by a patterned stencil, in the gallery the candida is free to roam across and penetrate the surface of the agar. Growing on artist's blood, agar enables an interspecies eros between human blood cells, agar (polysaccharides extracted from algae) and candida bodies which proliferate into a flourishing communion. This fecund performativity is consumed by the human viewer and by the candida, which rapidly disrupts the pattern.

Part V: Queer Kinshipping

Through this process, I have become much more interested in how microbes understand and experience their worlds: How and where do microbes live? How are they affected by what we do to their environments, including our bodies? How do they talk to and affect each other? How do they talk to and affect us? How do they experience pleasure? What are the biological, cultural and ethical implications for us and for microbes who think about us as companion species? How do we understand ourselves if we think of ourselves as living in a microbial world rather than them living in ours? Haraway (2016, p. 1) insists that "the task is to make kin in lines of inventive connection as a practice of learning to live and die well with each other in a thick present." I am interested in ways to make microbes kin, even those we don't like.

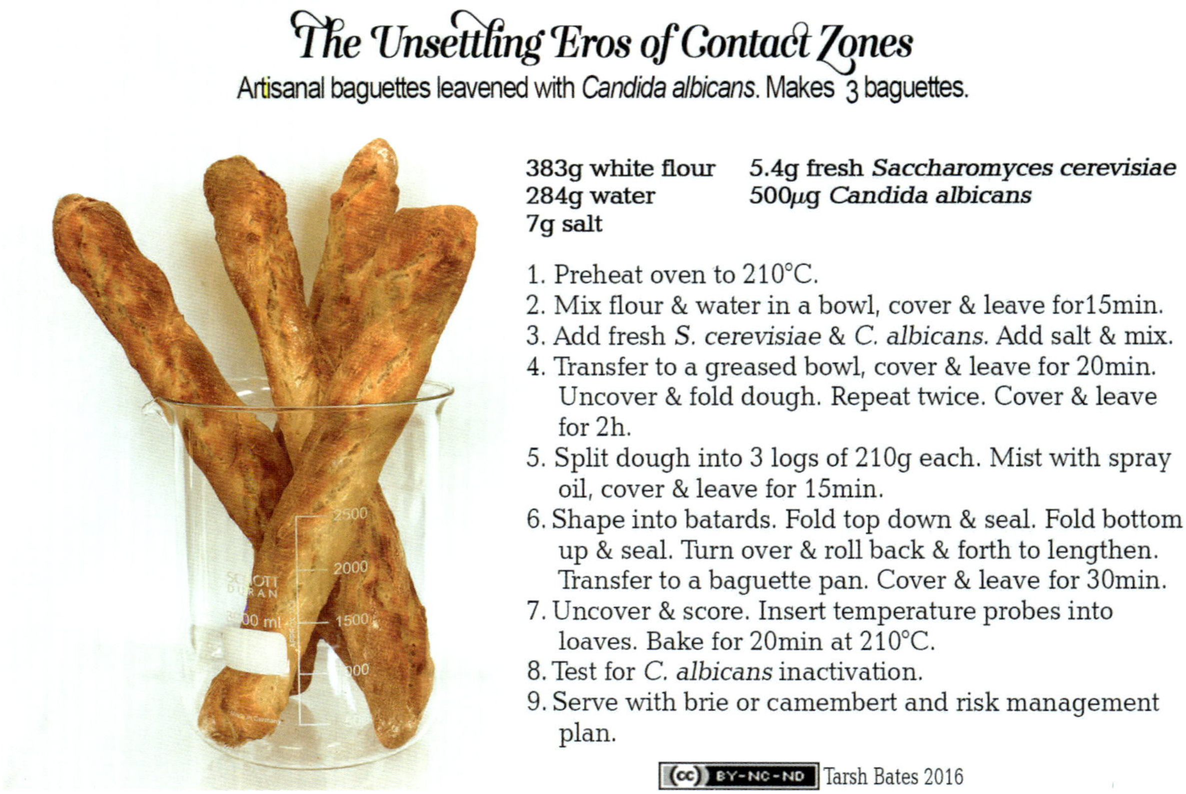

Figure 5: *The Unsettling Eros of Contact Zones*. Bates, T. (2016).
Recipe card, instructions for making artisanal bread leavened with Candida albicans.

Queer kinship is, for the most part, non-biogenetic. Often rejected by our biological families, queers form families of choice based on intimacy and community. These families may include biogenetic kin but are usually uncoupled from genetic relatedness and sexual reproduction and include non-human companions. Queer kinships are more-than-human, generous configurations that embrace other species, reproductive technologies and cultural institutions as companion species (Bates, 2019, p. 33). They are often fraught. However, they also offer opportunities to imagine and live otherwise, re-orienting to the performativities of social behaviour and choice, temporal and spatial contingency, and haptic and nonvisual intimacies that exceed human language and sensation. Such kinships can be powerful tactic for responding to the enormity of climate change and mass extinction and open us to the impersonal intimacies and responsible haptics of queer microbial kinshipping. Making bread leavened with candida which is shared with others is one such tactic to consider who is invited to the table, when, where and how (Figure 5).

Part VI: Scavenging

As I am a generalist and a scavenger, I spend much of my practice struggling with imposter syndrome. Although my queer method helps me pull thrilling and fascinating threads, navigating interdisciplinary practice is challenging. It can be lonely, frustrating and confusing. Learning curves are steep and I am constantly code-switching. I have no home. I identify as genderqueer and my pronouns are she/they, acknowledging that I am always, already, microbial-kind. Afterall, we are all products of the exhalation of cyanobacteria and millennia of evolution. Microbes terraformed the planet during what is arguably the first mass extinction event, the Great Oxygenation. 2.4 billion years later, life continues because of microbial metabolisms and respirations.

I survive because of the generosity and creativity of all my inspiring and inspired queer kind. I am very grateful.

References

- Abram, D., 1996. The Spell of the Sensuous: Perception and Language in a More-than-Human World. Vintage Books, New York.
- Barad, K., 1998. 'Getting real: Technoscientific practices and the materialization of reality', Differences, 10(2), pp. 87–128. https://doi.org/10.1215/10407391-10-2-87.
- Barad, K., 2007. Meeting the Universe Halfway: Quantum Physics and the Entanglement of Matter and Meaning. Duke University Press, Durham & London.
- Barad, K., 2011. 'Nature's Queer Performativity', Qui Parle, 19(2), pp. 121–158. https://doi.org/10.5250/quiparle.19.2.0121.
- Barad, K., 2015. 'Transmaterialities: Trans*/Matter/Realities and queer political imaginings', GLQ: A Journal of Lesbian and Gay Studies, 21(2–3), pp. 387–422. https://doi.org/10.1215/10642684-2843239.
- Bates, T., 2019. 'The Queer Temporality of CandidaHomo Biotechnocultures', Australian Feminist Studies, 34(1). https://doi.org/10.1080/08164649.2019.1605486.
- Dempster, M.B., 1998. A self-organizing systems perspective on planning for sustainability. Master's Thesis. University of Waterloo.
- Foucault, M., 1990. The History of Sexuality: Volume 1, an Introduction. Translated by R. Hurley. Vintage Books, New York.
- Gilbert, S.F. and Tauber, A.I., 2016. 'Rethinking individuality: the dialectics of the holobiont', Biology & Philosophy, 31(6), pp. 839–853. https://doi.org/10.1007/s10539-016-9541-3.
- Hanisch, C., 1969. 'The Personal is Political', in S. Firestone and A. Koedt (eds), Feminist Revolution. Doubleday, New York, pp. 72–82.
- Haraway, D.J., 1992. 'Ecce Homo, Ain't (Ar'n't) I a Woman, and Inappropriate/d Others: The Human in a Posthumanist Landscape', in J. Scott and J. Butler (eds), Feminists Theorize the Political. Routledge, New York, pp. 86–100.
- Haraway, D.J., 1994. 'A Game of Cat's Cradle: Science Studies, Feminist Theory, Cultural Studies', Configurations, 2(1), pp. 59–71. https://doi.org/10.1353/con.1994.0009.
- Haraway, D.J., 2003. The Companion Species Manifesto: Dogs, People, and Significant Otherness. Prickly Paradigm Press.
- Haraway, D.J., 2016. Staying with the Trouble: Making Kin in the Chthulucene. Duke University Press, Durham & London.
- Heidegger, M., 1962. Being and Time. Translated by J. Macquarrie and E. Robinson. Basil Blackwell, Oxford.
- Jaque, A., Otero Verzier, M. and Pietrolusti, L. (eds), 2020. More-than-Human. Het Nieuwe Instituut, Rotterdam.
- Kull, K., 2010. 'Umwelt', in P. Cobley (ed.), The Routledge Companion to Semiotics. Routledge, London, pp. 348–349.
- Margulis, L. and Fester, R. (eds), 1991. Symbiosis as a Source of Evolutionary Innovation. MIT Press, Cambridge, MA.
- Ono, Y., 1966. 'Instruction Pieces. Yoko Ono in 1966 at Indica Gallery, London', Aiu: A Yoko Ono Website. Available at: http://www.a-i-u.net/yokosays.html [Accessed 2 Nov. 2019].
- Ono, Y., 2000. Grapefruit: A Book of Instructions and Drawings. 4th edn. Simon & Schuster, London.
- Paxson, H., 2008. 'Post-Pasteurian Cultures: The Microbiopolitics of Raw-milk Cheese in the United States', Cultural Anthropology, 23(1), pp. 15–47. https://doi.org/10.1111/

- Rocha, L.A., 2011. 'Scientia Sexualis Versus Ars Erotica: Foucault, van Gulik, Needham', Studies in History and Philosophy of Science Part C: Studies in History and Philosophy of Biological and Biomedical Sciences, 42(3), pp. 328-343. Available at: https://doi.org/10.1016/j.shpsc.2011.01.003.
- TCAP Project, [online] Available at: https://tcaproject.net
- Jones, C., [online] Available at: https://catjones.net
- High, K., [online] Available at: https://www.kathyhigh.com
- Hauri-Downing, S., [online] Available at: https://susanhauri-downing.com

Endnotes

1 Holobionts are symbiotic, functional assemblages of eukaryotic hosts and associated microbiomes (Margulis and Fester, 1991; Gilbert and Tauber, 2016).

2 Following environmental scientist Beth Dempster's (1998) characterisation of sympoietic systems as cooperative and amorphous in contrast with self-contained, closed autopoietic systems, Haraway (2016, p. 58) describes sympoiesis as a "making-with."

3 Umwelten refers to the unique perceptual and experiential realities of different species (Kull, 2010).

4 "kinshipping" is a playful portmanteau of "kinship" and the GenZ slang "shipping."

5 "In 1996, ecological philosopher David Abram coined the phrase "the more-than-human world" as a way of referring to earthly nature (introducing it in the subtitle of The Spell of the Sensuous and throughout the text of that book); the term was gradually adopted by other scholars, theorists, and activists, and has become a key phrase within the lingua franca of the broad ecological movement." (Otero Verzier and Pietrolusti, 2020)

6 https://tcaproject.net

7 https://www.kathyhigh.com/

8 https://catjones.net/

9 https://susanhauri-downing.com/

10 In The Companion Species Manifesto, Donna Haraway (2003, p. 11) coins the term "naturecultures," insisting that nature and culture have always been inseparable: that "nature" is both biology and cultural construction and "culture" is both discursive and biological. Naturecultures are co-constitutive, not dialectic; inseparable, mutualistic entanglements of all entailed by each.

FROM ABSENCE TO IMMORTALITY: MAPPING 15 YEARS OF CREATIVE PRACTICE ACROSS ART, SCIENCE AND TECHNOLOGY

Svenja Kratz

This chapter provides a retrospective review of art-science works from 2008 to 2023 exploring the transformative potential of life. Central is the "Absence of Alice" (AOA) project, developed in response to culturing Saos-2 cells, an immortalised bone cancer line derived from an 11-year-old girl in the 1970s. Spanning interrelated exhibitions over five years, AOA examined the liminal nature of cultured cells as fragments of an absent body, probing porous boundaries between life and death, self and other. The project raised ethical concerns surrounding the use of living materials, by referencing the fraught history of the first human cell line, established in 1951. AOA marked a creative pivot, with ideas of biological entanglement and immortality informing later works. From 2013 onward, AOA's legacy evolved into new projects, culminating in Posthuman Genetic Legacies (PHGL), which included the creation of an artist-induced pluripotent stem cell (iPSC) line. This work proposed an alternative form of genetic reproduction, challenging notions of fertility, lineage, and ownership of biological material. The chapter also reflects on the broader use of cell lines in science and art, drawing on contributions from other artists. It concludes by reflecting on the role of speculative art-science research in shaping discourse on biotechnology, reproduction, and posthuman futures.

This chapter explores the intersection of art and science, emphasising the potential of artistic practice, centered around cells as tissue culture, to act as a tool for critical reflection and public dialogue. Moving beyond traditional science communication, this interdisciplinary approach reveals the nuances of scientific lab practices and the sociocultural impact of emerging biotechnologies. As a creative practitioner deeply embedded in this field, I reflect on the past 15 years and how my practice has evolved to illuminate the intricate interconnections between life forms and the broader ethical implications of biotechnological advancements.

Focusing particularly on the *Absence of Alice* (AOA) project and subsequent works, this chapter underscores how art-science practice can activate philosophical posthuman thought. As articulated by Francesca Ferrando, such thought "destabilises the limits and symbolic borders posed by the notion of the human," questioning the binaries between human and nonhuman, natural and artificial, and blurring boundaries between life and death (Ferrando, 2020, p.5). By critically engaging with concepts of biological and social entanglement, immortality, and genetic legacy, these works highlight the ethical and philosophical implications of using living materials in art and science. Through an analysis of selected projects, alongside historical information relevant to the establishment of cell and tissue culture art, this chapter demonstrates the value of speculative, cross-disciplinary research in stimulating debate about alternative forms of reproduction, biotechnological potentials, and the broader ethical, social and legal implications of our evolving relationship with life and technology.

Cell and Tissue Culture Art: Origins and Legacies

Early examples of art and science practices can be traced back to Alexander Fleming's 1928 microbial drawings and Edward Steichen's 1933 genetically augmented delphiniums. However, biological art, or bioart, only emerged as a distinct artistic genre in the late 1980s, with cell and tissue culture as a field of in-depth inquiry gaining prominence in 1996 through the work of Oron Catts and Ionat Zurr as part of the *Tissue Culture and Art Project* (Yetisen et. al., 2015). Their work employed cells and tissue engineering as a medium to critique utopian fantasies of "victimless" technologies and the exploitation of cells as "semi-living" entities (Catts & Zurr, 2013). In 2000, Catts and Zurr founded Symbiotica at the University of Western Australia, the first studio-laboratory providing artists with direct access to biotechnologies. This initiative became a key hub for tissue culture-based projects in Australia, including some of my own.

As a field, cell and tissue culture in both art and science depends on the accessibility of human and animal cells. In most routine studies, these cells take the form as cell lines "immortalised" cultures that when maintained in appropriate conditions can replicate almost indefinitely. This contrasts with healthy cells, which possess an inherent mechanism that limit replication to 50 divisions to prevent genomic instability. This capability allows them to be repeatedly sub-cultured, leading to the production of vast quantities of cells with defined characteristics, thereby enhancing the reproductibility and reliability of experimental outcomes. Consequently, the total biomass of such cell lines can eventually surpass the mass of the original donor tissue. The first immortal human cell line, the HeLa cervical cancer cell line (created in 1951) has a collective biomass of "more than 50 million metric tons," as documented in Rebecca Skloot's *The Immortal Life of Henrietta Lacks* (2010, p. 2). The immense quantity of HeLa cells speaks to their value as a commercial cell stock and corresponding ubiquity in global biolaboratories. Indeed, HeLa cells remain one of the most widely used cell lines and were instrumental in the development of many medical advances including the polio vaccine, cloning technologies and cancer research (Skloot, 2010).

There is an inherent uneasiness when considering the vast scale of HeLa cells, a discomfort further intensified by the history surrounding their creation. Derived from the cancerous cells of Henrietta Lacks, an economically marginalised African American woman, the HeLa cell line was established and shared without her consent, becoming a cornerstone of the billion-dollar biomaterials industry. Although created for scientific advancement and contributing significantly to biomedical research, the disclosure of Lacks' identity brought distress to her family and sparked ongoing debates about donor rights and consent (Skloot, 2010). In recent years, legal actions, including lawsuits by the estate of Henrietta Lacks against Thermo-Fisher Scientific and Ultragenyx Pharmaceutical, have further underscored the need to recognise cells as entities entwined with personal and cultural histories, where consent and donor rights remain a significant issues (Chace, 2024; Philippidis, 2023).

HeLa cells themselves are remarkable entities. Due to their aggressive growth, both in Lacks' body and in vitro, they frequently contaminate and outcompete other cell types and are regarded as "the weeds of cell culture" (Van Valen & Maiorana 1991, p. 72). Some evolutionary biologists have even suggested that HeLa's unique genotype and reliance on lab environments qualify it as a new species, *Helacyton gartleri* (Van Valen & Maiorana, 1991). The narratives surrounding the origin and status of HeLa cells have also inspired numerous artists including Christine Borland, Pierre-Philippe Freymond and Cynthia Verspaget (Senior, 2011). While their works all integrate HeLa cells and aim to highlight the significance and history of the cell line, Cynthia Verspaget's 2004 *Anarchy Cell Line* offers a particularly apt critical response. By creating a new "artistic cell line" by mixing her blood with HeLa cells, she confronts notions of ownership and the roles of both scientists and artists in the manipulation of biological materials. Through accompanying documentary texts, Verspaget also acknowledges the historical exploitation of women and other marginalised bodies in medical research (Senior, 2011). While artistic engagements that directly integrate HeLa cells remain relatively limited, projects involving human cells are inescapably connected to this history.

Entering the Field

My introduction to the field of cell and tissue culture began with a flask of Saos-2 cells. This designation signaled the origins of the cells as Sarcoma Osteogenic (bone cancer). Like HeLa cells, Saos-2 cells are commercially available through various biomedical supply companies, such as the American Type Culture Collection (ATCC). It was through the ATCC that I learned these cells were originally established from a bone cancer lesion of an 11-year-old Caucasian girl in the 1970s. Discovering the origin of these cells profoundly affected me, making it difficult to engage with them without thinking about the young girl and her family. In the absence of her real name and personal history, I chose to call her Alice. This decision served as a reminder that the strange entities I observed under the microscope were connected to other bodies and formed part of a complex network of relations. The commercial availability of the cells also sparked consideration of informed consent and whether the family would approve of their widespread distribution as a biomedical "product". While the use of Alice's cells in cancer research might have been acceptable to her family, the application of these cells in creative practices probably was not considered.

Like HeLa cells, Saos-2 cells are a cell line considered both immortal and genetically stable. However, these terms can be misleading, as cell lines are far from stable and unchanging entities. They are highly responsive to their culture conditions, and prolonged cultivation, or repeated splitting into multiple culture vessels, often leads to changes in both phenotype and genotype. Indeed, over the initial six months, I split the original cell culture 78 times, during which the cells grew increasingly sluggish, elongated, and often developed multiple nuclei, indicating noticeable shifts in their behaviour and morphology (Kratz, 2013). As such, Saos-2 cells occupy a strange liminal territory. On one hand, they remain intimately connected to the donor Alice in terms of genetic and embodied connection. However, as continually evolving cancer cells in vitro, they also exist as individual and independent entities. I often wondered whether the family would find solace in their child's lingering presence, or horror in the amplified legacy of her disease (Kratz, 2013). What would Alice herself think?

It should be acknowledged that biological connections of Saos-2 cells, like all cell types, do not just extend to humans. Indeed, all eukaryotic cells (cells that have a defined nucleus) are considered products of endosymbiosis (where one organism lives inside the other). This is because mitochondria, known as the chemical energy production "powerhouses" of eukaryotic cells, were originally independent organisms that became permanently integrated into the structure of a larger host. They still retain a separate genome in the form of mitochondrial DNA (MtDNA), which is passed along the maternal line. Additionally, all eukaryotes share a fundamental cell structure. Research from the 1980's revealed that the homeobox DNA sequence within genes is crucial in regulating developmental processes, such as body formation, across a wide range of multicellular organisms (Alberts et. al., 2002). Animal and human cells, dependent on cell type and corresponding nutrient requirements, can be cultured together, signaling their shared genetic and ancestral connections. Furthermore, humans share much of their genetic makeup with other species with 8% estimated to be viral in origin (Van Blerkom, 2003).

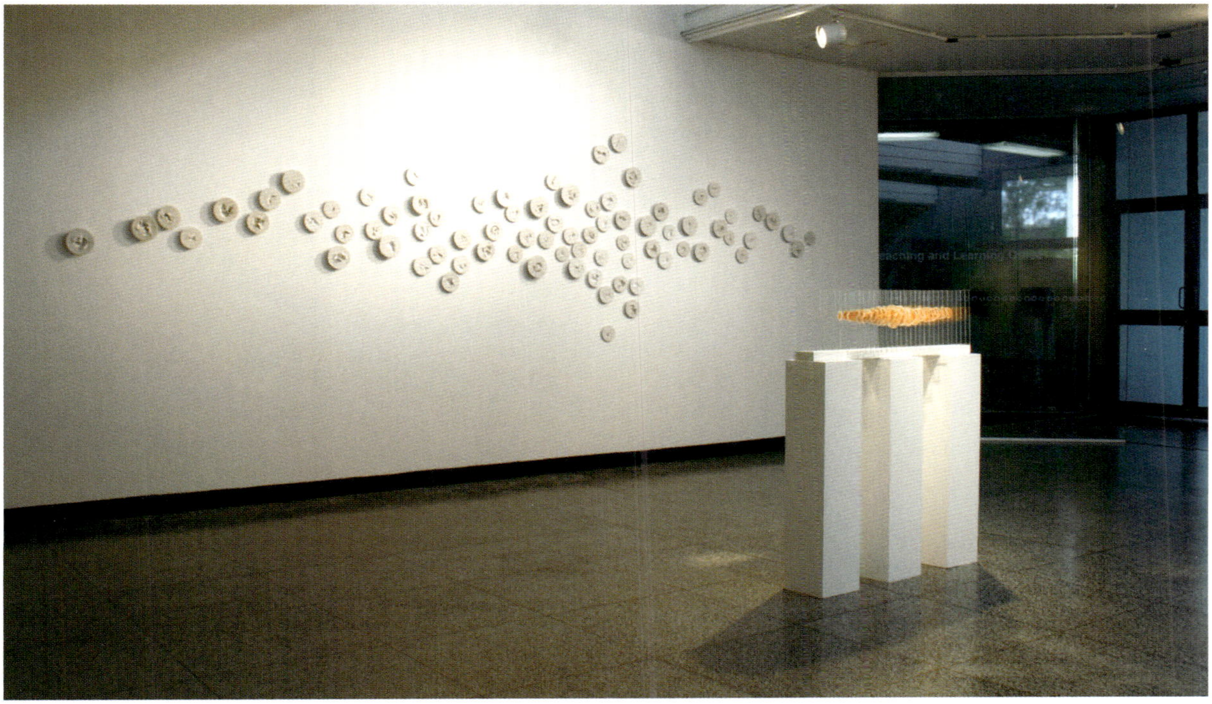

Figure 1: *Impressions of a Single Object.* Kratz, S. (2008). Installation view featuring 78 plaster impressions and *Fragments of a Body in the Process of Becoming Other.* Latex containing Saos-2 cells, acrylic, wood.

The Absence of Alice

These initial observations inspired the creation of an evolving body of work titled: *The Absence of Alice.* This series of interconnected works and exhibitions spanned over five years and positioned Alice's story within an ongoing narrative, with multiple points of connection and divergence. The first exhibition in 2008 at the QUT Visual Art Gallery in Queensland, featured five sculptural and video works that explored the uncanny nature of the Saos-2 cell line as living fragments of an absent body (Kratz, 2013). While the exhibition referenced the origins of the cell line and my lab experiences in its titles and accompanying texts, it primarily focused on themes of continual becoming. This body of work presented the Saos-2 cells not merely as biological specimens, but as entities embodying both memory and transformation. Through works like 78 *Impressions of a Single Object* and *Fragments of a Body in the Process of Becoming Other* (2008), the works also reflected on the limits of scientific and artistic methods, suggesting that all representations of life and biological processes are inherently abstracted and unable to fully capture their complexity (Figure 1).

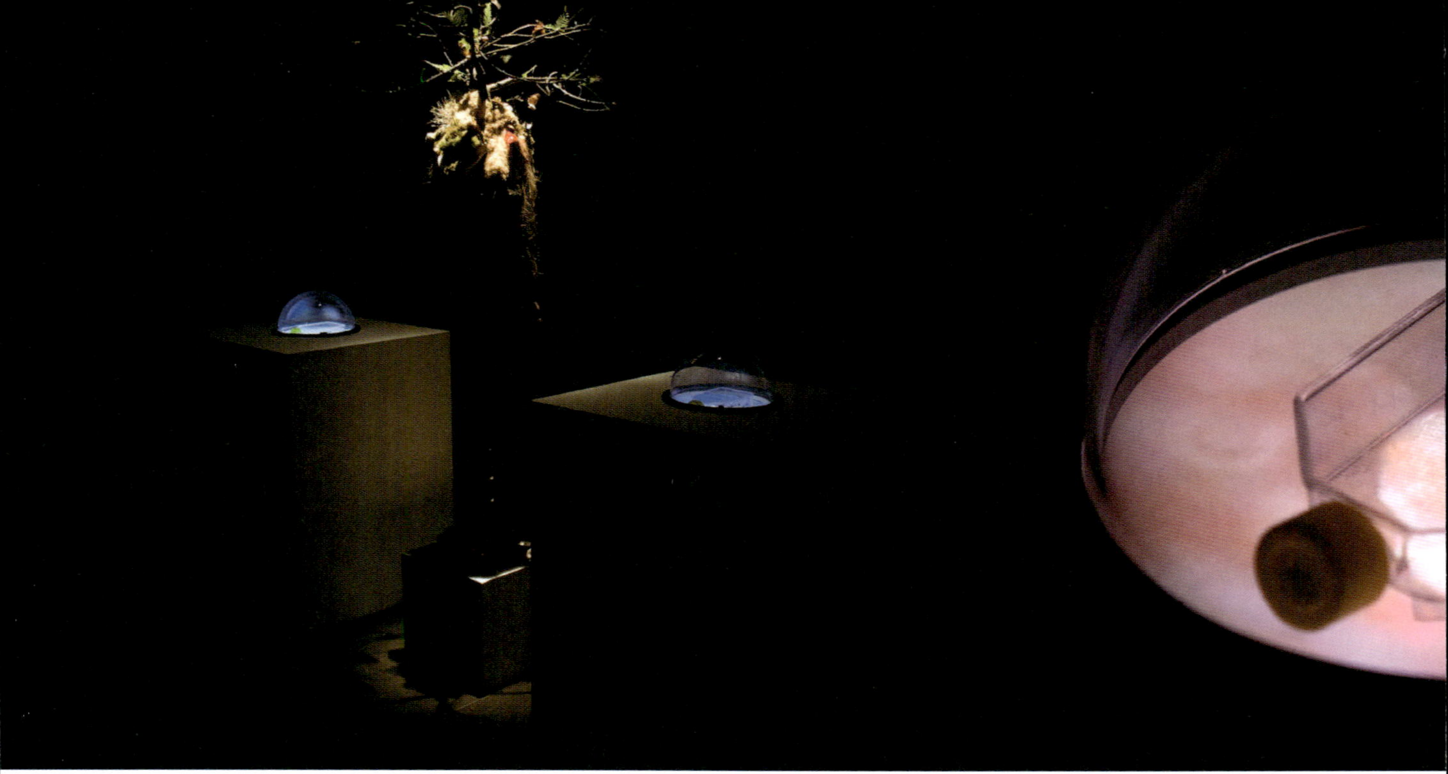

Figure 2: *HEK293T: The Transformation of Johni or Oliver.* Kratz, S. (2010-2012).
Mixed media installation incorporating preserved HEK293T cells in flasks and cryovials, sculpture, and video.

As the development of *The Absence of Alice* continued, other cell lines became interwoven into the expanding narrative. During a residency at SymbioticA in 2000, I was introduced to basic genetic engineering techniques and HEK 293 cells - a cell line established from the tissue of an aborted embryo in 1973. Unlike HeLa and Saos-2 cells, which are naturally immortal due to genetic mutations that make them cancerous, HEK 293 cells were artificially immortalised via the incorporation of sheared adenovirus 5 DNA. HEK 293 cells have given rise to at least 12 derivative cell lines including HEK 293T, a widely used variant (Yuan et al., 2018). The "T" in HEK 293T denotes the expression of the Simian Virus 40 (SV40) large T antigen. This modification makes HEK 293T cells particularly suitable for transfection, allowing for the introduction and expression of additional genetic material, such as DNA or RNA. I used the HEK 293T strain to introduce fluorescent proteins from coral and jellyfish into the cells, resulting in glowing red and green HEK variants. Though routine, what struck me about working with HEK 293T cells was how an organism that never reached full gestation could give rise to unique microorganisms with distinct traits, highlighting the porous nature of taxonomic boundaries. These ideas were reflected in the artwork *HEK293T: The Transformation of Johni or Oliver* (2010-2012) which featured flasks of the fixed cells, video animations alluding to their origin, and timelapse footage of their genetic transformation (Figure 2).

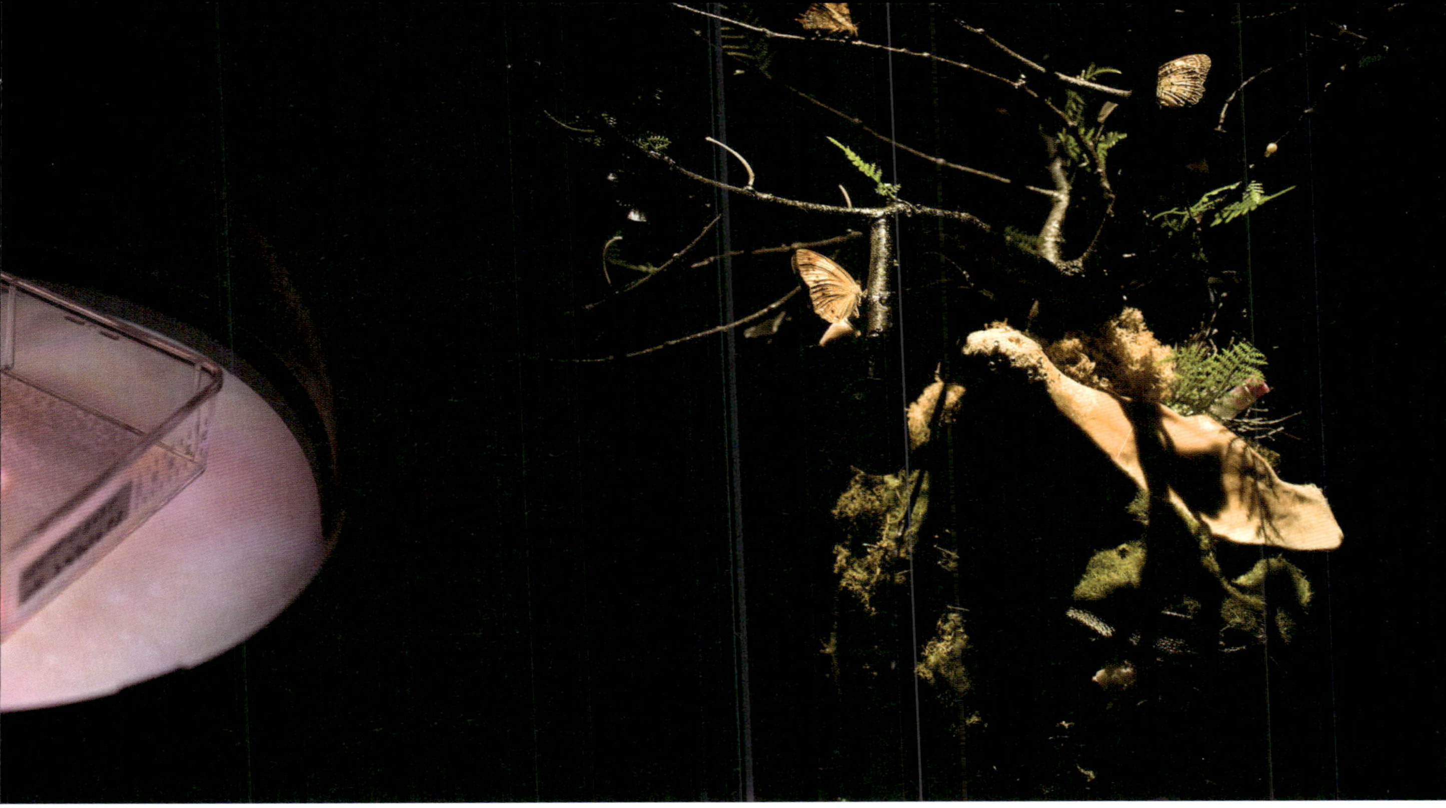

As *The Absence of Alice* series evolved, I began to reflect on the products used in cell culture, particularly fetal bovine serum (FBS), which is derived from the blood of fetal calves as a by-product of the meat industry. The reliance on animal-derived products in cell culture had already been critically examined in earlier works, such as the Tissue Culture and Art Project's *Disembodied Cuisine* and *Victimless Leather* (Catts & Zurr, 2013). These projects questioned the proposition of commercial biotech companies that cell-cultured food and products could be produced from small amounts of tissue without causing harm to animals, given the hidden dependence on animal products such as FBS. This consideration led me to explore the entanglement of consumption and biotechnology by working directly with fetal calves whose blood had been harvested for FBS production.

One of the major projects to emerge from this engagement was *The Immortalisation of Kira and Rama*. Developed during the 2000 SymbioticA residency, the project involved isolating living cells from two deceased fetal calves, Kira and Rama, with the aim of immortalising their cells and presenting these live remnants alongside their preserved bodies. Through multiple exhibition instances, the project explored isolation, cryopreservation, and resurrection, highlighting how creative acts can prompt discourse on the intersections of life, death, and biotechnology. Although time and funding constraints prevented

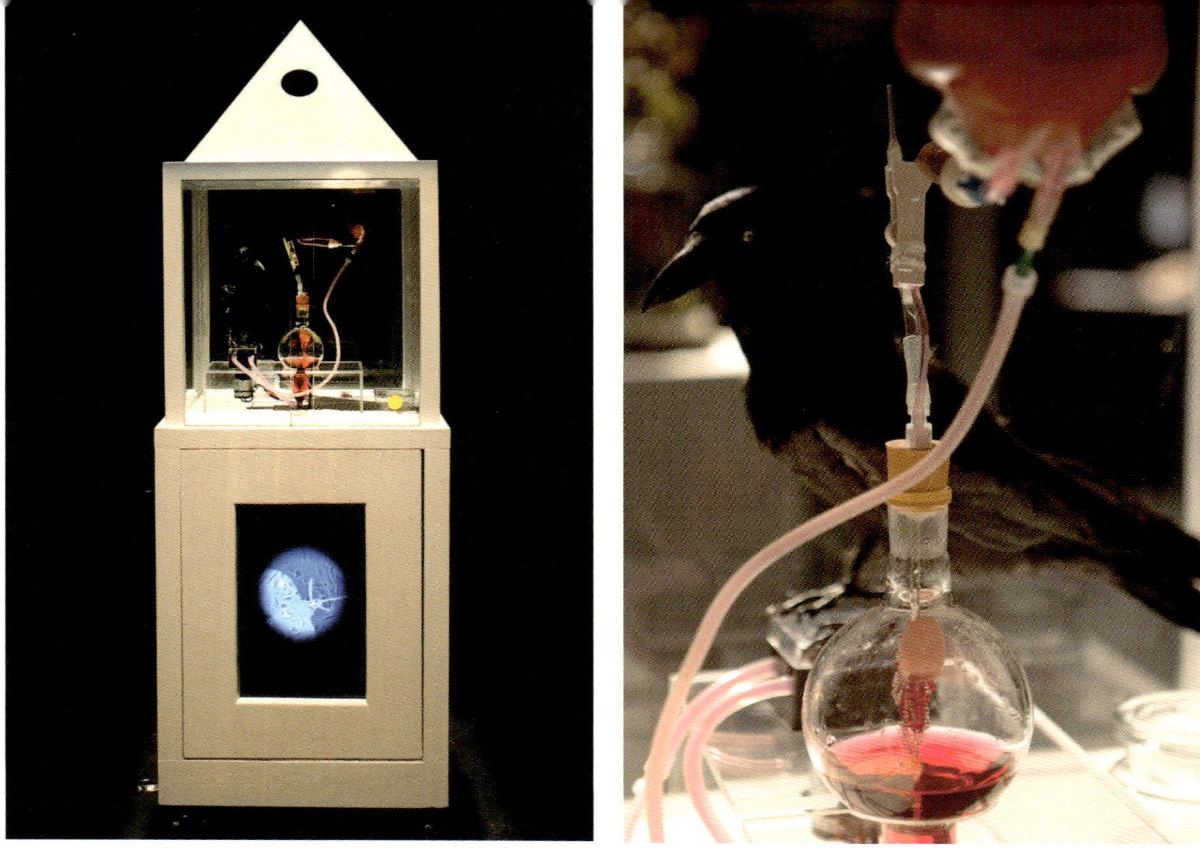

Figure 3a: *Towards the Immortalisation of Kira and Rama: The Temporary Resurrection and Second Death of Kira*. Kratz, S. (2011). Mixed media installation featuring custom bioreactor with a silkworm cocoon seeded with fetal calf cells, accompanied by video and project relics. Photo: Dan Cole.

full immortalisation, the final exhibition in 2011, *Towards the Immortalisation of Kira and Rama: The Temporary Resurrection and Second Death of Kira*, featured Kira's living cells in a custom bioreactor, alongside bodily relics from both calves (hearts, hide, cryovials, and tissue samples). This setup aimed to challenge viewers' perceptions of biotechnology by juxtaposing the sterile presentation of science with the visceral reality of death. Further complicating this tableau, the audience was served pies made from mother cows, a gesture that underscored the often-unseen connections between scientific, industrial, and agricultural systems and the various lives they affect.

Overall, *The Absence of Alice* series operated as a mechanism for revealing and rethinking relations. As Marietta Radomska points out, the series "challenges the normative and human-exceptionalist concept of death" by foregrounding the entangled materialities of the living and non-living, and reframing death not as a definitive endpoint, but as a node within an ongoing ecology of transformation (2020, p.1). In doing so, it also foregrounds the paradoxes of biotechnologically facilitated immortality, where the persistence of cellular life coincides with the absence and fragmentation of the originating subject.

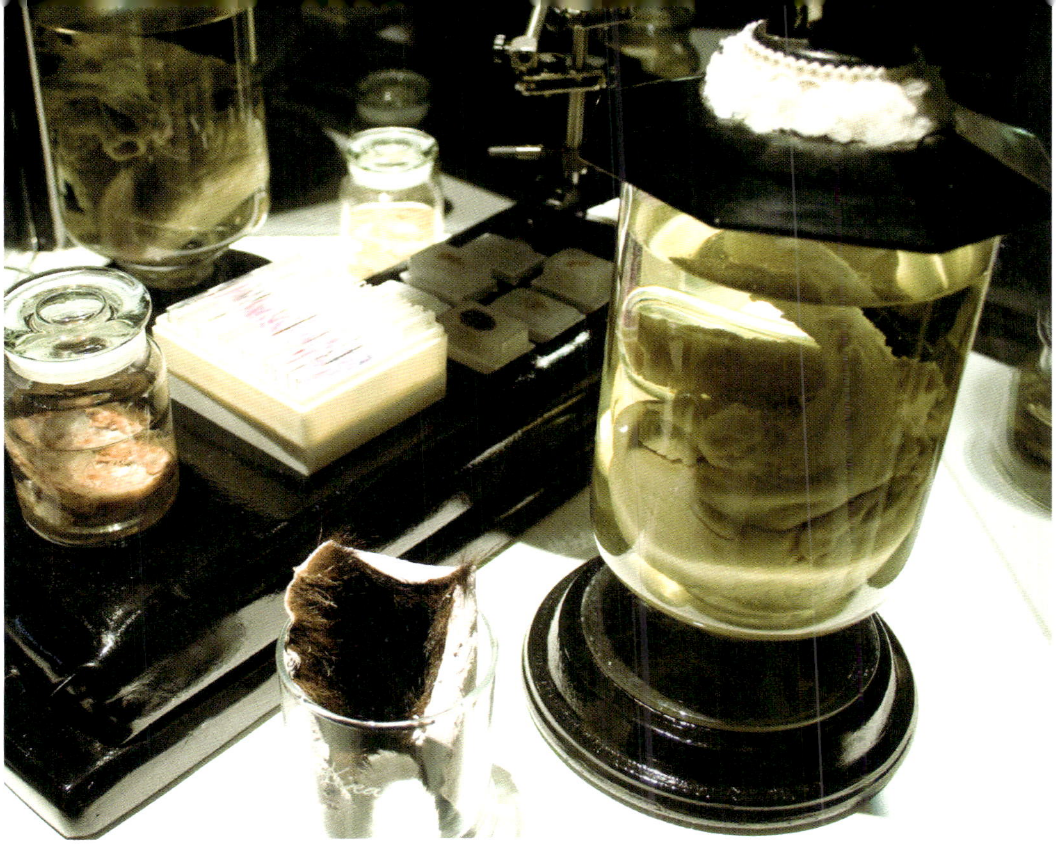

Figure 3b: *Towards the Immortalisation of Kira and Rama: The Temporary Resurrection and Second Death of Kira*. Kratz, S. (2011).

From Absence to Immortality

The Absence of Alice project represented a significant moment within my practice, catalysing an ongoing engagement with the human preoccupation with mortality and the desire for continuity. This thematic trajectory extends into my current project, *Posthuman Genetic Legacies*, which interrogates speculative formulations of immortality through the interlinked frameworks of procreation and genetic inheritance. As a single woman navigating the later stages of reproductive viability, I became interested in how biotechnologies might facilitate the production of alternative genetic progeny. Informed by developments in genetic engineering, gene therapy, and the presence of viral DNA within the human genome, I developed *Self-Portrait #2: Site of Infection* for the 2019 *Pandemic* exhibition at the Plimsoll Gallery, Hobart. In this piece, a wax bust emitting DNA-infused vapor, speculated on using viral infection to disseminate my genetic material, suggesting that DNA fragments could be integrated into host organisms and, by using a retrovirus and targeting germ cells, transmitted to future generations without direct reproduction. By conceptualising viral infection as a conduit for genetic continuity, the work aimed to unsettle normative paradigms of maternity

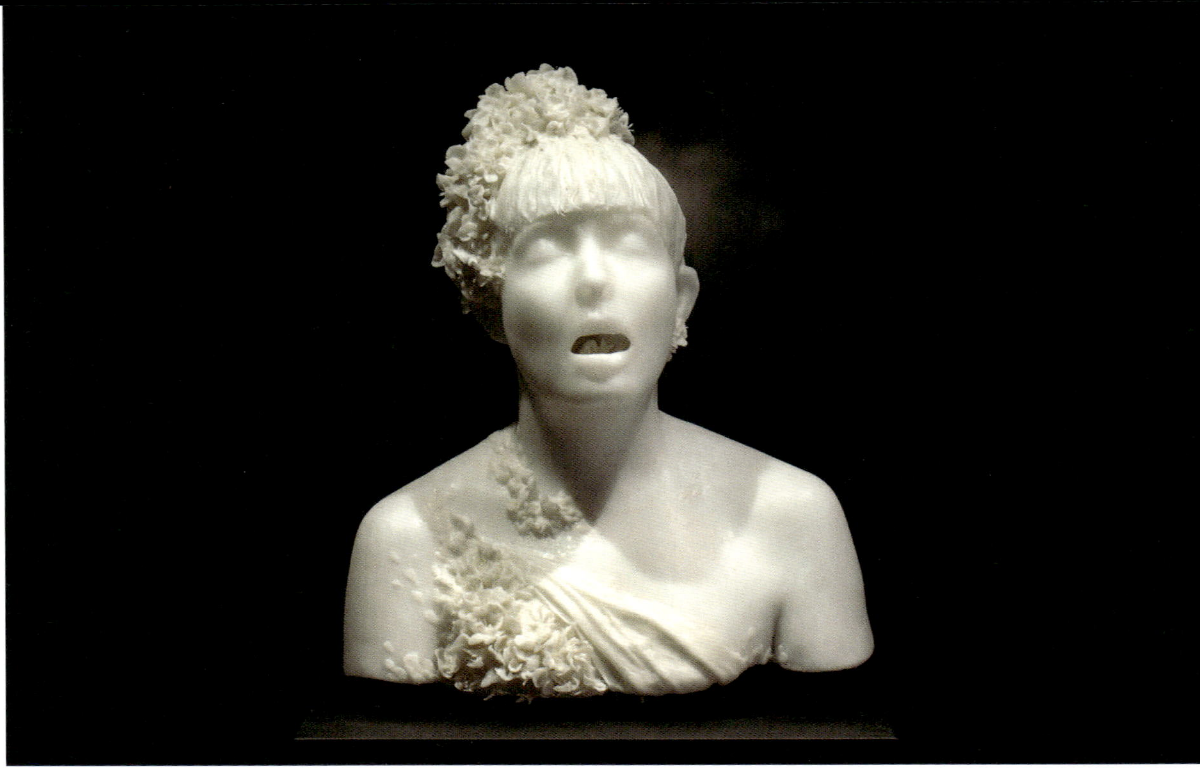

Figure 4: *Self-portrait #2: Site of Infection*. Kratz, S. (2019).
Mixed media sculpture emitting water vapour containing the artist's DNA. Photo: Rémi Chauvin.

and fertility, proposing instead entangled and extended reproductive networks inclusive of the more-than-human (Kratz, 2022) (Figure 4).

Following this work, my practice returned to cell culture, particularly the idea of establishing an immortalised cell line, akin to HeLa, Saos-2 or HEK293 cells, from my own body and making the cells commercially available for scientific and artistic research. While there is an earlier precursor, the Billy Apple® artist cell line, created in 2010 to extend the Apple® brand (Hilton, 2014), my desire was influenced primarily by the experience of uterine pathology. In 2019, I was diagnosed with a large fibroid (benign tumour of the uterus). The experience was deeply unsettling due to a protracted diagnostic and treatment term alongside unexpected grief over the likelihood of remaining childless (See Kratz, 2022). To counter this anguish, I decided to reposition the growth as a "tumour baby" and create a cell line from its tissue.

The 2019 exhibition *Mourning Story: Expectations, Absences, and the Potentials for Self-Persistence* at Rosny Barn in Hobart critiqued cultural constructs of femininity through a series of mixed media works. Using floral motifs, anatomical references, and historical symbolism, the show interrogated idealised femininity and the medicalisation of women's bodies. *After Spring* reinterpreted Botticelli's *Primavera* and *The Birth of Venus*, juxtaposing mythological beauty with visceral anatomical reality. *Time is Topological* included elements like clocks and a bleeding table to address the legacy of hysteria and cultural perceptions of women as reproductive vessels.

The Memento Mori series, along with *Coming to Terms with Being Forgotten*, reflected on the mourning of lost possibilities while also acknowledging humanity's deep connection to a vast genetic and evolutionary history, suggesting that our ultimate role may be to die and re-enter a broader ecological cycle. In contrast, *SVKR-LM: Tumour Baby* explored the creation of a fibroid cell line. As a sculptural work incorporating fixed cells and video animation, it drew on *HEK293T: The Transformation of Johni or Oliver*, hinting at the potential for the fibroid cells to generate a lineage of daughter cell-variants that continued to evolve (Kratz, 2022).

In 2021, I began an Australian Network for Art and Technology (ANAT) Synapse residency, collaborating with Prof. Brad Sutherland, Dr. Jo-Maree Courtney from the University of Tasmania's School of Medicine, and Prof. Jane Nielsen from the Centre for Law and Genetics. The project focused on immortalising and commercialising fibroid cells for both artistic and scientific research. Involvement from legal experts highlighted the aim to use this as a case study to examine ethical, legal, and governance frameworks surrounding the consent, use, intellectual property (IP), and distribution of biomaterials.

This ambition was informed by the history of HeLa cells, alongside the recognition that public understanding of biomaterial laws and precedents remains limited. For example, the "no-property rule" in the UK, US, and Australia states that human bodies and their parts cannot be owned. However, a significant exception arises when "work and skill" are applied to separated body parts, such as cells and tissues (Quigley, 2018). Legal precedents, such as *Moore v. Regents* of the University of California, often grant rights over these materials to researchers or institutions, without requiring donor compensation or input. Exceptions do exist for reproductive materials (egg, sperm, embryos) (Quigley, 2018). However, the development of induced pluripotent stem cell (iPSC) technology, where somatic cells are reprogrammed into gametes, further complicates these legalities.

During the immortalisation process, we discovered that the fibroid cells were unviable, leading us to pivot and reprogram my blood cells into iPSCs as an alternative "blood line." This resulted in two iPSC cell line clones, SK1 and SK2. These iPSCs can be differentiated into almost any other cell type. For instance, we directed SK2 cells into pericytes as stock cells for immediate use in the Sutherland research group's work on perivascular brain health. The next step involved finalising quality control measures and exploring the legal frameworks for potential commercialisation. By establishing an artist cell line and a database that provides insights into key legal precedents, ethical clearances, consent, and regulatory frameworks, this work aims to make information about the use of biomaterials more accessible and transparent. It complemented the feminist art collective subRosa's project *Cell Track: Mapping the Appropriation of Life Materials* (2004-2009), which similarly explored the commercialisation, patenting, and ownership of biological materials (subRosa 2011).

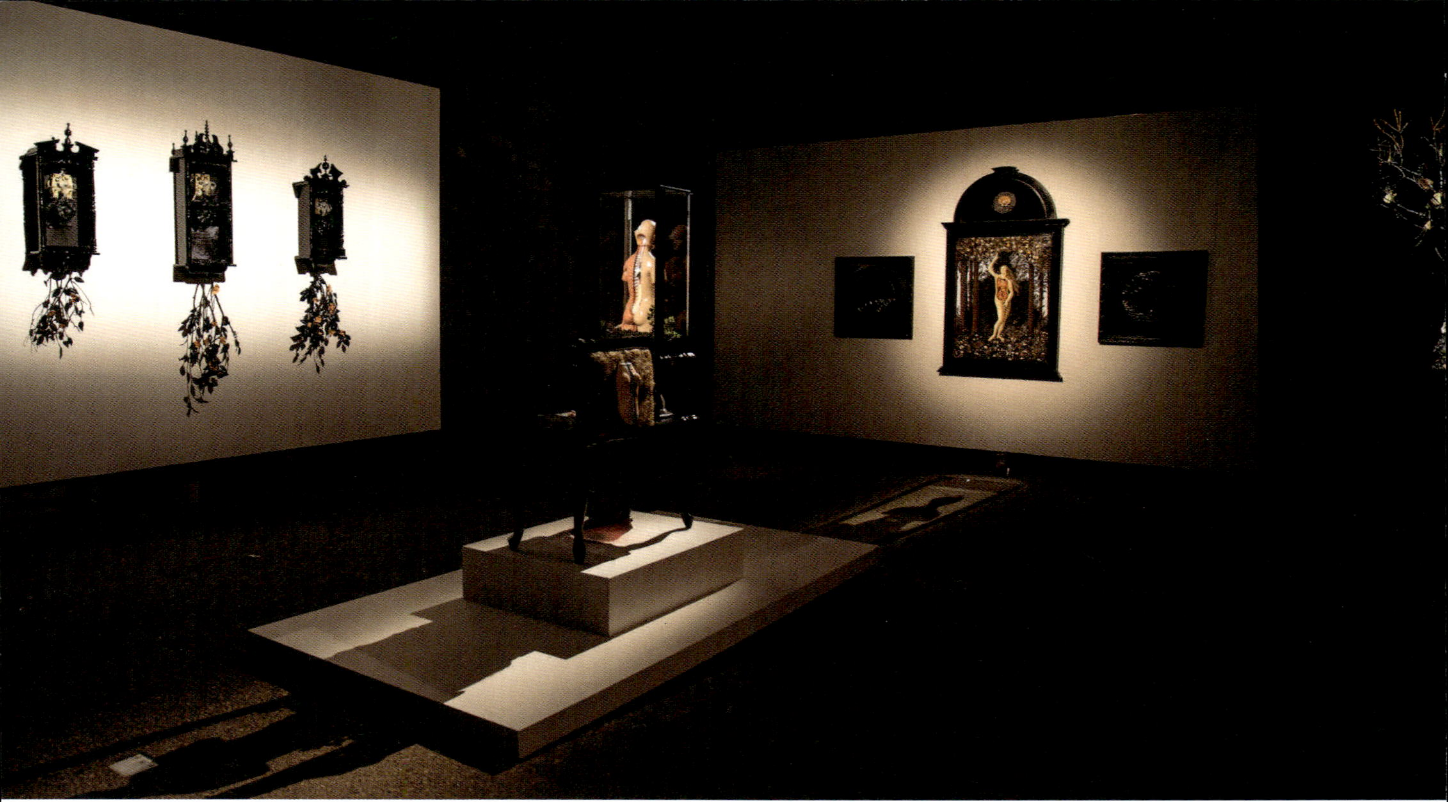

Figure 5: *Mourning Story*. Kratz, S. (2020). Expectations, Absences and the Potentials for Self-Persistence. Installation view.

Conclusion

By using my own cells and including personal information in the cell line data, I aim to deepen the connection between biomaterials, personal values, and family histories. This approach furthers creative research that privileges personal and marginal narratives while addressing privacy, legal, and insurance concerns, especially when publicly shared information may impact family members. As a female artist, the decision to immortalise my cells is a political act, challenging traditional narratives of fertility and highlighting issues of consent with reference to the historical exploitation of marginalised bodies within Western culture. As iPSCs, the resulting cells can be reprogrammed into various cellular lineages, such as their transformation into sperm cells. This potential resonates conceptually with Charlotte Jarvis's *In Posse* (2020), which critically interrogates the gendered hierarchies embedded in reproductive biology by working towards "vitro gametogenesis: the creation of spermatozoa from female stem cells" (Pet, 2024, p. 59). Simultaneously, the cells could be directed toward osteogenic differentiation, becoming bone cells capable of producing a mineralised matrix in vitro. This shift from living tissue to mineral formation enacts a kind of ontological drift, further revealing the material entanglements between the biological and the geological, the animate and the inanimate. Overall, this chapter reflects on the evolution of my artistic practice over the past 15 years, high-

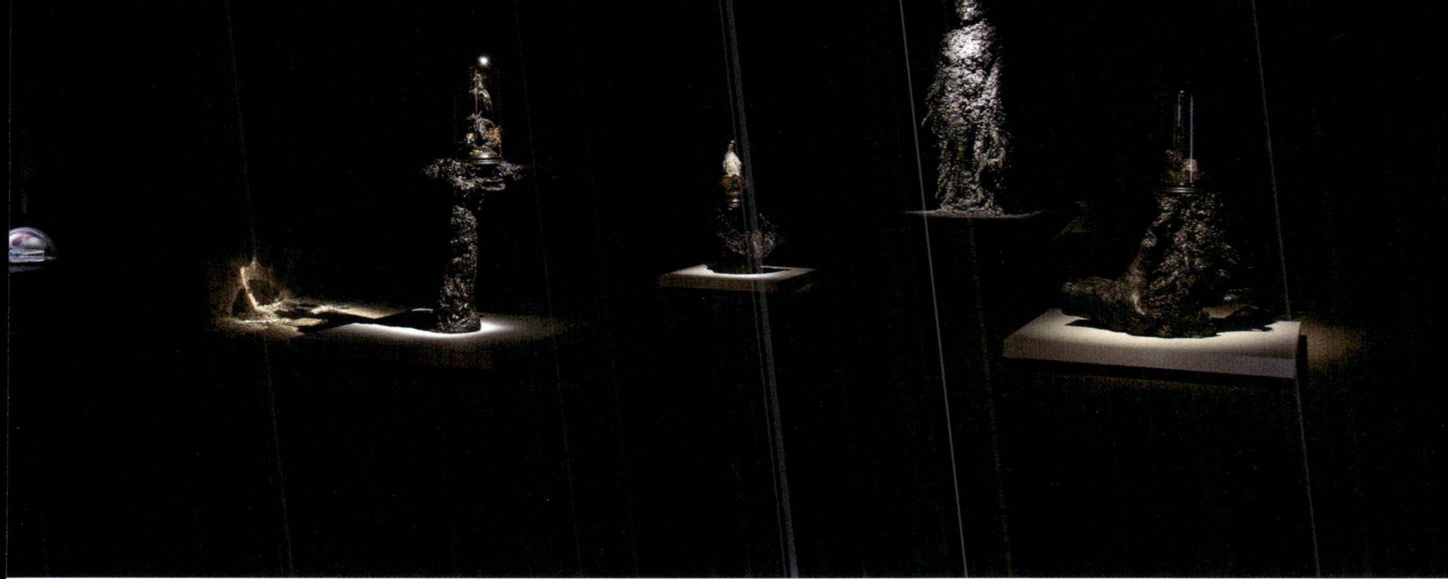

lighting how the integration of biological materials into art opens up transformative possibilities for interdisciplinary dialogue between art and science. Projects like *The Absence of Alice* and the creation of an artist cell line in *Posthuman Genetic Legacies* critically engage with the legal, ethical, and commercial frameworks surrounding biomaterials, while also embedding posthuman perspectives and personal narratives within these broader contexts. Similarly, artists such as Cynthia Verspaget, subRosa and Charlotte Jarvis use biotechnologies to expose how routine lab processes and reproductive technologies are entangled with racialized and gendered power structures and capitalist agendas. Theorists such as Marietta Radomska (2020) further argue that bioart can deterritorialise dominant understandings of death by revealing its relational, processual, and non-anthropocentric dimensions. As, Christine Beaudoin (2021) aptly asserts, bioart generates questions and opens speculative enquiry alternative modes of human existence and ethical relationality. By fostering dialogue across these fields, the work encourages reflection on how biotechnological advancements can reinforce oppressive structure or offer opportunities to reshape societal values, ethical frameworks and scientific practices. Engaging in this discourse is essential not only for advancing knowledge but also for navigating our collective future with greater integrity, respecting the diverse forms of life that these technologies affect.

References

- Alberts, B., Johnson, A., Lewis, J., Raff, M., Roberts, K. and Walter, P., 2015. 'Genetic information in eukaryotes', in Alberts, B. et al. (eds.), Molecular Biology of the Cell. 6th edn. New York: Taylor & Francis.
- Beaudoin, C., 2021. Remaking (Post-) Human Bodies in the Anthropocene. In A. Jarrín & C. Pussetti (Eds.), Remaking the human: Cosmetic technologies of body repair, reshaping, and replacement (pp. 165-185). New York: Berghahn Books.
- Catts, O. and Zurr, I., 2013. 'Disembodied livestock: The promise of a semi-living Utopia', Parallax, 19(1), pp. 101-113.
- Chace, A., 2024. 'Medical taking of human biological material v. traditional "Art Looting": Henrietta Lacks and the complex ethical and legal liability questions raised by her unfortunate case', Touro Law Review, 39(2), pp. 1-19.
- Ferrando, F., 2020. Philosophical posthumanism. London: Bloomsbury Publishing.
- Hilton, C., 2014. 'The immortalisation of Billy Apple®', Leonardo, 47(2), pp. 109-113.
- Kratz, S.J., 2013. 'Artscience in practice: Exploring the critical and creative potentials of transdisciplinary art and science practice using a methodological and conceptual framework of creative becoming', PhD thesis, Queensland University of Technology.
- Kratz, S.J., 2022. 'Posthuman Genetic Legacies: Rethinking (Im)mortality and the Limits of Reproduction Through Hybrid Bioart Practice', View. Theories and Practices of Visual Culture, 32, pp. 1 - 41.
- Pet, L., 2024. 'The excess of meaning: Developing an ethical attitude toward biological life through engaging with bioart'. [Doctoral dissertation, Leiden University]. Available at: https://hdl.handle.net/1887/3717696.
- Philippidis, A., 2023. 'Ultragenyx Gene Therapies spark lawsuit from Lacks family', Human Gene Therapy, 34(17-18), pp. 759-762.
- Senior, A., 2011. 'Haunted by Henrietta: The archive, immortality and the biological arts', Contemporary Theatre Review, 21(4), pp. 511-529.
- Skloot, R., 2010. The immortal life of Henrietta Lacks. New York: Crown Publishers.
- subRosa, 2011. 'Bodies Unlimited: A decade of subRosa's art', n.paradoxa: International Feminist Art Journal, 28, pp. 16-25.
- Radomska, M., 2020. 'Deterritorialising death: Queerfeminist biophilosophy and ecologies of the non/living in contemporary art', Australian Feminist Studies, 35(104), pp. 116-137.
- Van Blerkom, L.M., 2003. 'Role of viruses in human evolution', American Journal of Physical Anthropology, 122, pp. 14-46.
- Van Valen, L.M. and Maiorana, V.C., 1991. 'HeLa, a new microbial species', Evolutionary Theory, 10, pp. 71-74.
- Yuan, J., Xu, W.W., Jiang, S., Yu, H. and Poon, H.F., 2018. 'The Scattered Twelve Tribes of HEK293', Biomedical Pharmacology Journal, 11(2), pp. 621-623.
- Yetisen, A.K., Davis, J., Coskun, A.F., Church, G.M. and Yun, S.H., 2015. 'Bioart', Trends in Biotechnology, 33(12), pp. 724-734.

FROM BOTANY TO ART AND HOW TO CREATE YOUR OWN ART AND SCIENCE HEURISTICS

Christa Sommerer

My artistic journey spans over three decades, beginning with studies in biology – focusing on botany and anthropology – at the University of Vienna. Early on, I experienced a tension between scientific objectivity and artistic interpretation, especially during a botanical illustration class where my professor critiqued my drawings as "too artistic." Later, I realized that scientific and artistic perspectives can benefit from "cross-pollination." Throughout my art studies in sculpture, botanical motifs persisted, culminating in the creation of Phyllologia: a speculative botanical art system based on Linnaeus' classification of leaf shapes. This system underpins many of my projects, from drawings to sculptures to videos. In 1992, I started to collaborate with Laurent Mignonneau and to merge botany, electronics, art and media science in installations like Interactive Plant Growing, where visitors can touch real plants to grow virtual ones. Here, I reflect on the challenges of interdisciplinary practice, the role of women in media arts, and my evolving position within the Austrian art/science landscape. I discuss my contributions to these fields and how my work has been shaped by these intersections. Artistic research can engage biology, technology and ecology to foster new dialogues and creative possibilities.

It all started with a trip to two Viennese museums back in the mid-1970s. Together with my parents, we visited the Natural History Museum in the morning and the Art History Museum in the afternoon. These two museums, located along the Ringstrasse in Vienna, are like twins facing each other. They were built around 1868 to house the imperial collections of the then Austrian Emperor. I vividly remember the morning we walked through the exhibits at the Natural History Museum, with its collections of fossils, minerals, stuffed animals, insects, and herbaria. The sheer quantity and inventiveness of nature completely blew my mind. I knew right away that this is what interested me, especially since I had already begun my own small herbarium at home, where I tried to collect as many different plants as I could from the meadow near my parents' home.

When we visited the Art History Museum in the afternoon, I was equally enthusiastic. The works of Bruegel, Arcimboldo, Rembrandt, Vermeer, the Egyptian collections, plant, still-life images... there was so much to see and learn. I felt that this was also something I wanted to do in the future, in one way or another. In high school, my favorite subjects were biology, drawing, and English. After graduating, I began studying biology with a special focus on botany and anthropology. My most interesting courses were systematic botany, electron microscopy, botanical excursions, and all subjects related to the classification of plants. We also had plant morphology courses where we drew plants as accurately and scientifically as possible.

During my studies, I also started creating biology-inspired drawings (Figure 2). Living in Vienna, I visited many museums and modern art exhibitions. I visited several abstract art exhibitions featuring works by Sonia Delaunay, Wassily Kandinsky, and other artists from the early 20th century. I also discovered the Dadaist art movement, and I was impressed by Kurt Schwitters (Schwitters, 1961) and his free, unconventional approach to art, using found objects, trash, and collage techniques.

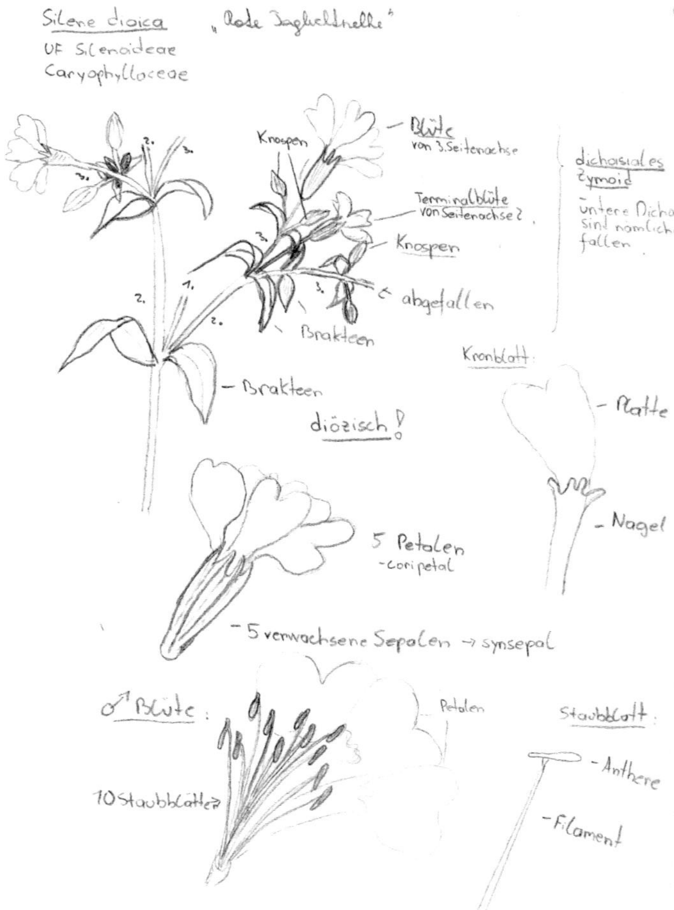

Figure 1: *Scientific botanical drawing of Silene Dioica.* Sommerer, C. (1983).

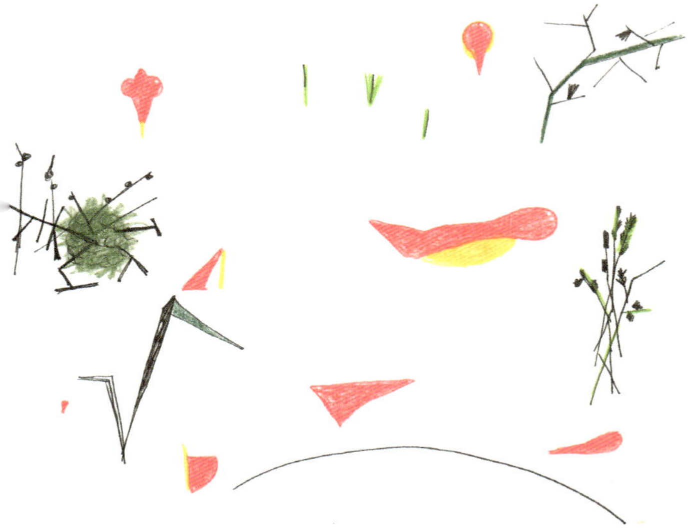

Figure 2: *Artistic drawing of abstract plants.* Sommerer, C. (1984).

I soon began to create my own experiments, building small sculptures with found objects, leftover wood, fabrics, plastic animals, cork… basically anything that looked interesting to me. Soon, my little apartment was filled with projects, sculptures, reliefs, drawings, paintings, and even costumes. I also wrote theatre pieces and film scripts, where randomness and chance played important roles. An artist friend of mine suggested that I try the entrance examination at the Academy of Fine Arts in Vienna, just as a trial. Since I had nothing to lose and I was quite happy with my botany studies anyway, I decided to document all my projects and attend the entrance examination at the sculpture department of the Academy. To my own big surprise, Professor Gironcoli, a famous Austrian sculptor, agreed that I could become his student, but under one condition: he urged me to stop studying biology. His argument was that one could either be an artist or a scientist, but never both.

What an error from today's perspective! But back then, I had to make a choice. Reluctantly, I decided to give up my botany studies and become an art student. My parents were shocked and opposed my decision, especially since I had already completed most of the coursework in botany and anthropology. However, I considered it a privilege to be accepted to the art university, especially since the overall acceptance rate was quite low. Thus began my new life as an art student. I created reliefs, sculptures, and installations, and took as many art courses as possible to learn something new. My favorite classes were art history, the excursions, and the photography class. Yet, in the background, the regret of not continuing my biology studies lingered. It wasn't surprising when botanical motifs crept back into my art practice. Carl von Linnaeus (1806), the renowned botanist who created the plant classification system, became an inspiration for me. I examined his leaf classifications and used them as a foundation for artistic exploration. One example was a set of 35 reliefs I created as cutouts in wood, each measuring approximately 60 x 45 x 10 cm. I arranged them in a 5x7 grid to form a large wall installation (Figure 3), which was showcased at the Secession in Vienna as part of the exhibition Junge Szene 1991 (Amanshauser, 1991).

I also created several light boxes in which I integrated abstracted leaf shapes into existing images from the book *Wissenschaft und Menschheit* (Urania Verlag, 1967). These images, which depicted various scientists at work, searching for new knowledge, inspired me. I collaged my own leaf shapes into their investigations, creating the impression that the leaves were the focus of their work. Some of these light boxes were exhibited in Austria, which

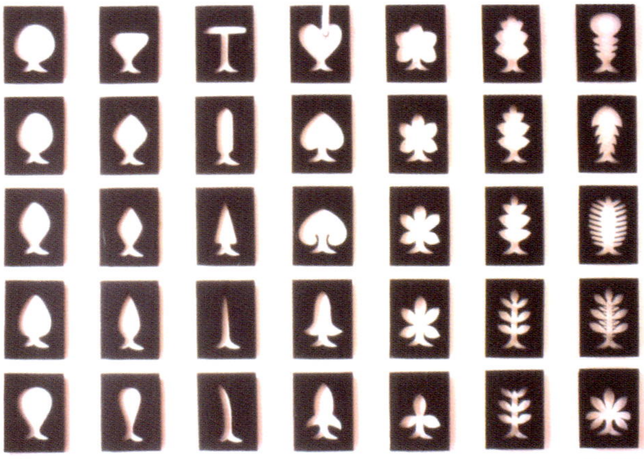

Figure 3: *Phyllologia.* Sommerer, C. (1991).
Installation with 35 wooden reliefs. Secession, Vienna.
Photo: Alexandra Eizinger.

included the Neue Galerie Graz in 1992 (Skreiner, 1992).

In addition to the light boxes, I self-published a book called *Ikonophylla*, featuring many of my leaf shapes in different contexts: with astronauts, in Antarctica, and in labs with scientific instruments. The entire artistic investigation of leaf shapes needed a scientific name, so I called the series *Phyllologia*, which loosely translates in to "science of the leaves". By creating my personal art/science heuristics, I wanted to merge botany and art - something my art school professor deemed impossible. But I was convinced it could be done and set out to create my own heuristics, where science and art would intersect, regardless of "scientific truth" or the prevailing artistic conventions of the time. Looking for other artists with scientific elements in their work, I found several inspirations. The work of Tassilo Blittersdorff, who used electrochemical processes and galvanization to create automatically growing images with fractal features, resonated with me. Another artist who influenced me was Johanna Kandl, who incorporated organic elements into her paintings and drawings, interpreting nature through her artistic lens. The artist duo Lois and Franziska Weinberger also impressed me, using plants found in trash dumps and other "non-places" to show that no plant is inherently "bad" and that it is humans who fail to appreciate them. I felt their work was an important ecological statement, highlighting the intersection of art and environmental consciousness.

Another Austrian female artist who also studied sculpture and was interested in art and science combinations was Gertrude Moser-Wagner. But overall, there were very few artists who tried to combine art and science as this was not deemed artistic enough. I even remember that my professor told me that artists should not think too much. He said that real art does not come from the brain but needs to "come from the belly." With my scientific background I felt that this could not be really correct - that there must be a way to combine these two cultures, as C.P. Snow has described them.

For my final diploma in 1990 (Sommerer, 1990) at the Academy of Fine Arts in Vienna, I created an installation of 35 small wooden sculptures (each 40 x 30 x 30 cm), all based on Linnaeus' leaf classification system. These sculptures were presented alongside four large metal tents. After completing my diploma and obtaining a Master of Art, I decided these sculptures should return to nature. I placed them in the damp cellar of my studio in Vienna to decompose. After 15 years, I revisited the cellar and discovered they had almost completely rotted, with only a few fragments remaining. Today, this would be called bio art! After graduation, I entered a difficult period. As my parents had predicted, living from art proved nearly impossible. I sought representation from galleries, but it proved an uphill battle. At the time, most galleries promoted male artists, who were also more prominently featured in exhibitions around Vienna. Even in my sculpture department, there were very few women, and most of the male students demonstrated exceptional craftsmanship skills. With my botanical themes and conceptual approach to art, I often felt like an outsider. In one particularly upsetting experience, my professor, Bruno Gironcoli, a respected artist and teacher, advised me to marry after graduation, as he didn't see a future for me in making a living from my art. I was deeply offended – having given up my cherished botany studies for art, I found his advice insulting. But it also motivated me to prove him wrong!

However, I was fortunate to have several exhibitions in various museums and art spaces in Austria. At one of my exhibitions featuring a video work combining plant leaves and images of scientists, I met gallerist Georg Kargl. He suggested I show my work to Peter Weibel, one of Austria's most famous media artists at the time and a professor at the University of Applied Arts in Vienna. I had already admired Weibel's conceptual and avant-garde video works (Schuler, 1996). In 1991, after recovering from a stroke, Weibel was editing books and organizing exhibitions. I visited him in a sanatorium near Vienna, bringing my portfolio. I showed him my book, videos, and the *Phyllologia* and *Ikonophylla* series, explaining my ideas for combining art and biology. Peter was immediately enthusiastic and mentioned that other artists had done similar work. He recommended a list of books and invited me to become a post-graduate student at his newly established Institute of New Media in Frankfurt. This institute, part of the renowned Städelschule, was one of the first places where art students could work with high-end graphic computers. Peter suggested that the computer would be the ideal medium for bringing my ideas of growing plants to life.

After meeting Peter and receiving his encouragement, I eagerly followed up on his recommendation. I found a book by Louis Bec (1991), president of the fictional *Scientifique de Recherche Paranaturaliste*, that explored epistemology based on Artificial Life and Technozoosemiotics. Bec's designs of zoomorphic types and forms of communication between artificial and natural species deeply impressed me. I saw a connection between my *Phyllologia* series and Bec's *Zoosystematic* approach, as both used scientific principles and nomenclature to create personal art/science heuristics. Excited by the prospect of studying in Frankfurt, I applied for a DAAD (Deutscher Akademischer Austauschdienst) scholarship, which supported me for nearly two years.

At the Institute of New Media in 1991, I was introduced to computers and programming. We also had courses in sound and video art. The postgraduate group was small and international, and the atmosphere was vibrant and creative. The institute had only three Silicon Graphics computers, so we had to sign up for shifts. During my turn, I applied what I learned in the 3D animation program Wavefront to create 3D leaf models as an extension of

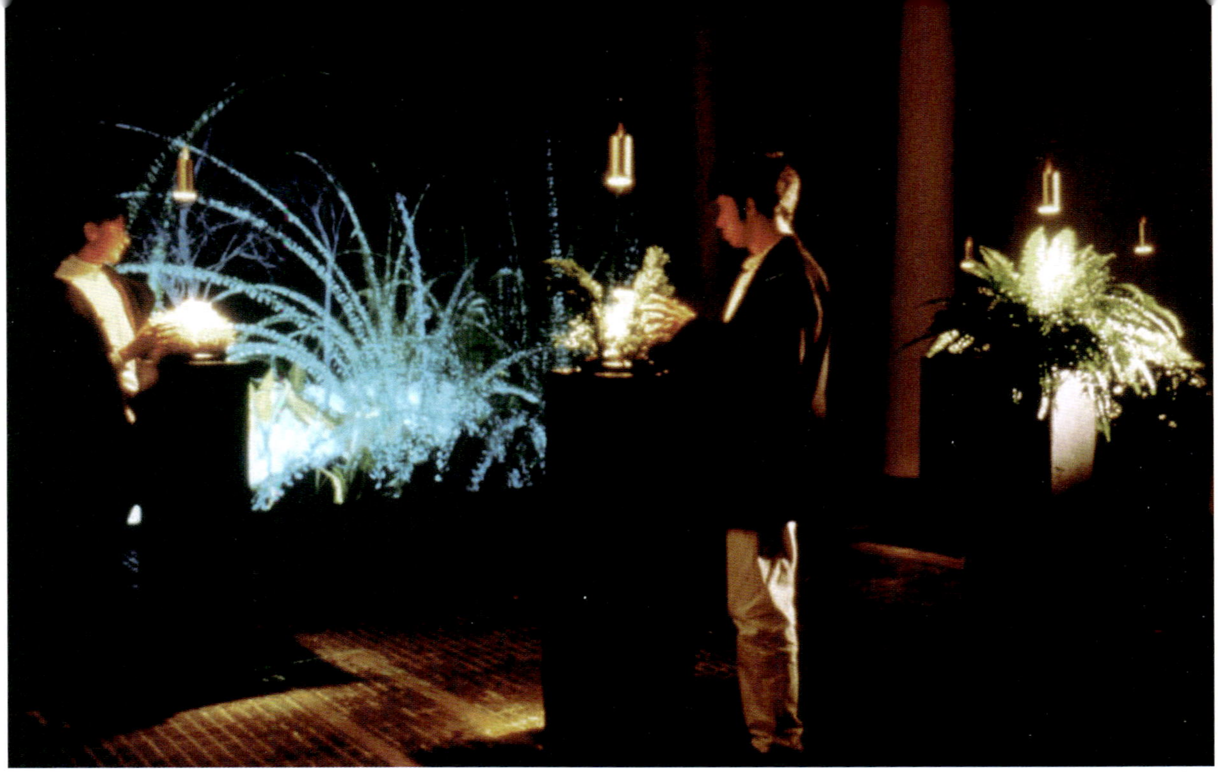

Figure 4: *Interactive Plant Growing.* © Sommerer, C. and Mignonneau, L. (1992). Photo: Sepp Berlinger.

my *Phyllologia* series. I was thrilled that my 3D leaves could move, and I made an animation where the leaf shapes swayed in the wind.

Among my fellow post-graduates were Ulrike Gabriel, Christian Möller, Johannes Deutsch, Constanze Ruhm, Akke Wagenaar, Alba d'Urbano, Michael Saup, and Anna Saup. The atmosphere was competitive but very inspiring. Peter Weibel was often present, and his hard work late into the night motivated me. He also invited international guests such as Matt Mulligan, Dara Birnbaum, and Steina and Woody Vasulka (Vasulka & Vasulka, 1996). I vividly recall Steina and Woody's lecture, where they showed their video works on laser disks and Steina's performance of controlling videos with her violin. Since then, Steina and Woody have remained role models for me as powerful individual artists, as a creative couple, and as organisers of electronic art events.

During my shifts, a young French artist named Laurent Mignonneau approached my desk and asked to watch me model the 3D leaves. He hadn't yet secured his own computer shift, so I agreed, but with little time to spare. After two weeks, Laurent suggested a faster way to create the leaves. He knew how to program and proposed that we write a computer software from scratch to grow the leaves in real-time. Together, along with my botanical knowledge, we shaped the growth algorithm to generate plants like moss, ivy, trees, ferns, and even a virus. We experimented with connecting real plants to an interface. Laurent

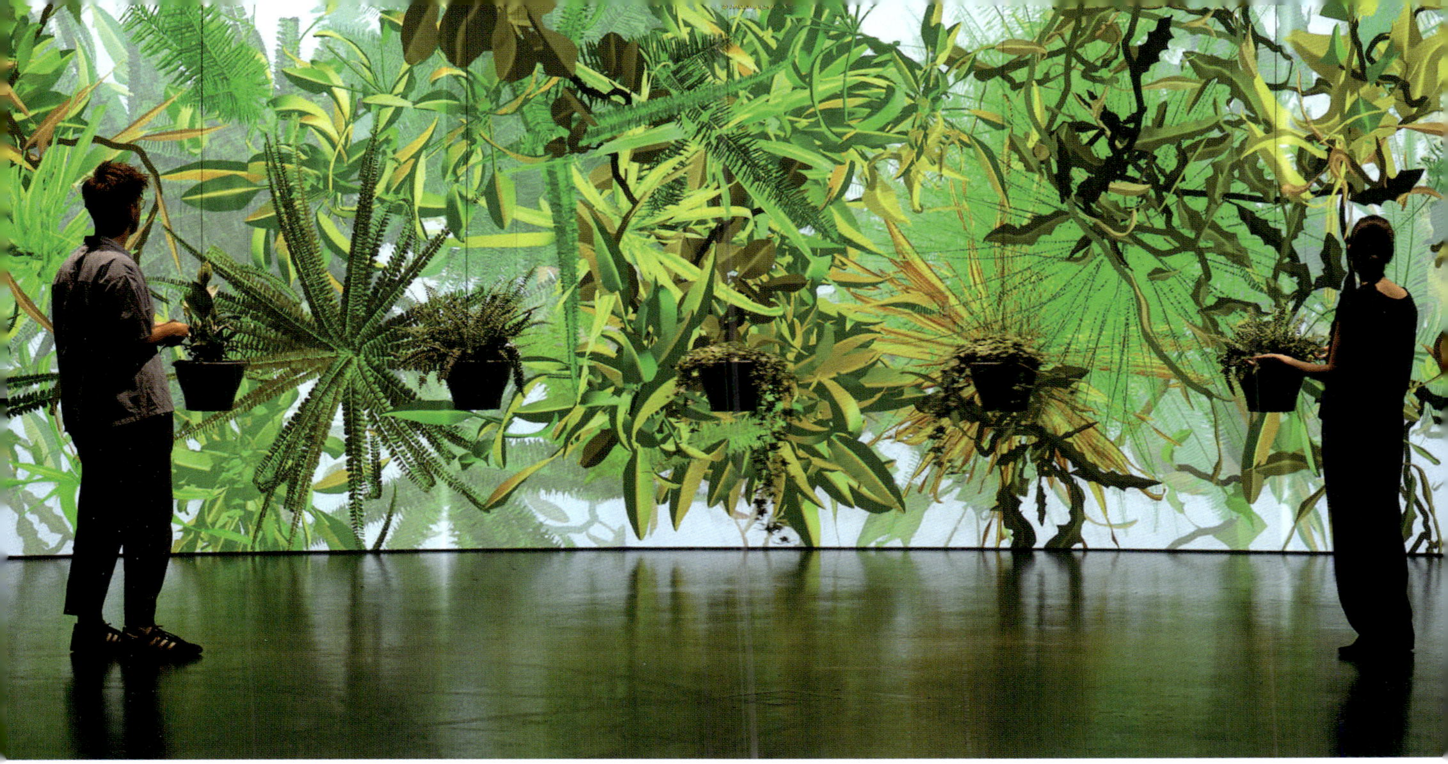

Figure 5: *Eau de Jardin* at *The Artwork as a Living System*. Sommerer, C. and Mignonneau, L. (2024). Interactive installation at ZKM Karlsruhe. Photo: Tobias Wootton.

built to capture the voltage differences between a plant and a person approaching it. It worked! The real plants could control the growth parameters of the virtual plants. We then looked for real plants that were similar to our computer-generated plants and found a real fern, moss, ivy, small tree and a cactus. With my exhibition date fixed for autumn 1992 in Vienna, we worked throughout the summer to create a new interactive installation, which we called *Interactive Plant Growing* (Figure 4). Drawing from my background in sculpture and installation, we designed a scenography to invite visitors to interact with the real plants. We staged five real plants on black pedestals, lit with dim lights, in front of a large projection screen. This created a mysterious atmosphere, encouraging visitors to touch the plants. The project debuted in Vienna at the Sal de Balle during the exhibition *Zeitschnitt - Differenzen, Affinitäten, Brüche* in 1992 (Michalka, 1992). It received positive feedback, with the interaction working smoothly as visitors touched the real plants and the virtual garden grew in response. Soon, *Interactive Plant Growing* became a popular sensation and within just a few months after its first presentation, the project was presented at the Mediale in Germany, the Otso Gallery in Finland, the Machine Culture exhibition in Siggraph93 in Anaheim, at the Ars Electronica Festival in Linz (Sommerer & Mignonneau, 1993), at Imagina in Monaco and subsequently in more than 50 exhibitions worldwide. Hailed a masterpiece of media art (Zielinski,2023, pp. 345-350), *Interactive Plant Growing* is now part of the ZKM Collection in Karlsruhe.

Since 1991, Laurent Mignonneau and I have worked as an artistic duo, creating approximately 50 interactive exhibits and presenting our artworks in around 380 international exhibitions over the past 33 years. Our collaboration has been instrumental in realising concepts and ideas, as well as in the continuous research on new interfaces, algorithms, and forms of human-machine interactions. Reflecting on the genesis of *Interactive Plant Growing*, I recognise a clear progression: it evolved from my initial studies of leaves in the *Phyllologia* series, which combined botanical motifs with an artistic vocabulary. The introduction of computer technology enabled us to cultivate these leaves in real time and design a plant-human interaction through sensor technologies. This fusion of science, art, and technology completed the circle. Beginning with drawing, painting, sculpture, video, animation, and computer art, interactive art was the next logical step. By involving the public in the art creation process through interaction, as well as utilising generative art, growth, evolution, diversification, and mutation, we achieved a more complex level of art creation. We refer to this creation as *The Artwork as a Living System* (Ohlenschläger, K., Weibel, P., & Weidinger, A., 2023). This has been also the title of our large retrospective exhibition where we presented 14 interactive artworks that combine artistic principle with scientific topics (Figure 5).

The media art scene in the early 1990s was relatively small, vibrant, and international. Main gathering places for this community included the Ars Electronica Festival in Austria, Siggraph in the US, Imagina in Monaco, and many other smaller international festivals. The media art scene had its own circles, and artworks of this type were scarcely present at major art museums or galleries. However, there was always a significant number of female artists in digital art, such as Lynn Hershman, Jill Scott, Monika Fleischmann, Rebecca Allen, Victoria Vesna, Catherine Ikam, Orlan, Ulrike Gabriel, Alba d'Durbano, Agnes Hegedüs and many others.

In Austria during the 1990s, several female media artists were prominent figures. Valie Export was already well-known, especially for her collaborations with Peter Weibel in the 1980s. Ruth Schnell's work was also highly regarded in the media art community. The artist Margot Pilz combined many forms of media including computers, creating early interactive works such as the Delphi Oracle in 1991. An artist duo that began collaborating in the 1980s was Station Rose (Elisa Rose and Garry Danner), who created audiovisual performances, light boxes, and media artifacts with their unique aesthetics. Another media art duo in Austria was Sylvia Eckerman and Mathias Fuchs, who created large public media installations. From the mid-1990s onwards Margarete Jahrmann often collaborated with Max Moswitzer to create complex media art installations.

So media art duos have often been an inspiration for me, considering such influential couples as Peter Weibel & Valie Export, Steina and Woody Vasulka, Monika Fleischmann and Wolfgang Strauss, Station Rose, Karen Lancel and Hermen Maat, and more recently Varvara & Mar. Knowing how challenging and time-consuming it is to create media art, working as a duo is optimal: one can easily exchange ideas, rely on each other's skills, and, if needed, receive a motivational boost to keep going.

However, I should also honestly mention that, overall, my path was not straight and easy: I gave up an almost completed science study to become an artist, only to realise that, as a female artist, I would have no professional future in Vienna in the late 1980s. Neither my art professor, nor the gallerists, nor my mostly male colleagues believed in me. In addition, my ideas of combining art and science were also deemed too strange and not artistic enough. One must also consider that in the late 1980s, there were no female professors at the art academies (except in the textile and fashion departments), and we had no role models to look up to. So much has changed now! In Austrian art academies today, nearly half of the faculty staff is female, and it is beyond question that female artists take their place in important exhibitions and in art history.

What I have learned over the years is that the only person one can rely on is oneself and one's own intuition. One must cultivate one's own inner drive and creativity. This has helped me to develop a resistance against others who wanted to discourage me, because my art, in their opinion, was "too this" or "too that" or "not enough of this and that." As a female artist I felt judged more severely and the lack of female role models at the art academies or in the art market was also discouraging.

It was only later, when I became part of the very international and open-minded media art community in the 1990s, that I discovered a new spirit. In fact, it became irrelevant if one was male or female or diverse. It was the work that counted and in general, a great openness towards new ideas and new combinations of various disciplines. The work of Jill Scott is a great example of how artistic ideas are combined with scientific principles to create engaging new interactive experiences. Nowadays, we can find many great examples of artists/scientists or scientists/artists. For example, the female biologist turned artist Špela Petrič combines biomedia and performativity to enact relations between organisms, often using plants or fungi. Even in biology, a new attitude towards other disciplines is emerging as scholars begin to investigate the arts and humanities to understand the intricate connections between plants and humans (John C. Ryan et al., 2017).

Returning to one's own intrinsic motivation, I would therefore recommend any young artist to trust their intuition and surround themselves with colleagues who believe in them and help bring out the best in themselves. As we can see, art and science can indeed be combined, and creating one's own art/science heuristics has now become common practice (S+T+ARTS) and now it is even part of quite a few university curricula.

References

- Allen, R., n.d. Rebecca Allen. Retrieved September 2024, from https://www.rebeccaallen.com/about
- Skreiner, W., 1992. Christa Sommerer: Phyllologia. In: Junge Szene Wien ´91, Vienna, pp. 44-45. Wiener Secession.
- Amanshauser, H., 1992. Christa Sommerer: Phyllologia, 1991/1992. In: Transformationen - 13 Positionen österreichischer Skulptur einer neuen Generation, Neue Galerie am Landesmuseum Joanneum, Graz, pp. 30-32.
- Bec, L., 1991. 'Vorläufiger Versuch über die Upokrinomenologie oder: Eine verheerende zoosystemische Expedition durch ein Glossar.' In: Rötzer, F. (ed.), Digitaler Schein Ästhetik der elektronischen Medien, Frankfurt am Main: Edition Suhrkamp, pp. 379-416.

- Blittersdorff, T., n.d. Tassilo Blittersdorff. Retrieved September 2024, from https://de.wikipedia.org/wiki/Tassilo_Blittersdorff Eggerman, S. & Fuchs, M., n.d. Sylvia Eckerman and Mathias Fuchs. Retrieved September 2024, from https://digitalartarchive.at/database/work/1988/
- Export, V., n.d. Valie Export. Retrieved September 2024, from https://www.valieexport.at/
- Fleischmann, M. & Strauss, W., n.d. Monika Fleischmann and Wolfgang Strauss. Retrieved September 2024, from https://www.fleischmann-strauss.de/
- Hegedüs, A., n.d. Agnes Hegedüs. Retrieved April 2025, from https://zkm.de/en/person/agnes-hegedus
- Hershman, L., n.d. Lynn Hershman. Retrieved September 2024, from https://www.lynnhershman.com/about/
- Ikam, C., n.d. Catherine Ikam. Retrieved September 2024, from https://www.ubikam.org/bio-c190m
- Kandl, J., n.d. Johanna Kandl. Retrieved September 2024, from https://www.hjkandl.at/de/
- Lancel, K. & Maat, H., n.d. Karen Lancel and Hermen Maat. Retrieved September 2024, from https://www.lancelmaat.nl/about/about/
- Linnaeus, C. von, 1806. A General System of Nature: Through the Three Grand Kingdoms of Animals, Vegetables, and Minerals, Systematically Divided Into Their Several Classes, Orders, Genera, Species, and Varieties ... Vol. 1. London: Lackington, Allen, and Company.
- Michalka, M., 1992. 'Christa Sommerer & Laurent Mignonneau, Ästhetik und Wissenschaft, Interactive Plant Growing 1992.' In: Drechsler, W., Spiegl, A., Steiner, B., Wurzer, I. (eds.), Differenz, Affinitäten und Brüche, Zeitschnitt´92 - Aktuelle Kunst aus Österreich, Vienna: Bundesministerium für Unterricht und Kunst, pp. 192-195.
- Ohlenschläger, K., Weibel, P. & Weidinger, A. (eds.), 2023. Christa Sommerer & Laurent Mignonneau, The Artwork as a Living System 1992-2022. The MIT Press Leonardo Book Series.
- Orlan, n.d. Orlan. Retrieved September 2024, from https://www.orlan.eu/
- Petrič, S., n.d. Špela Petrič. Retrieved April 2025, from https://www.spelapetric.org/about
- Pilz, M., n.d. Margot Pilz. Retrieved April 2025, from http://www.margotpilz.at/Allen
- Ryan, J.C., Vieira, P. & Gagliano, M. (eds.), 2021. The Mind of Plants: Narratives of Vegetal Intelligence. Santa Fe, NM: Synergetic Press.
- Schmalenbach, W. (ed.), 1967. Kurt Schwitters. Munich: Prestel Verlag.
- Schuler, R. (ed.), 1996. Peter Weibel - Bildwelten 1982-1996. Munich: Triton Verlag.
- Scott, J., n.d. Jill Scott. Retrieved September 2024, from https://www.jillscott.org/
- Schnell, R., n.d. Ruth Schnell. Retrieved September 2024, from https://ruthschnell.org/en/
- Snow, C.P., 1959. The Two Cultures. London: Cambridge University Press.
- Sommerer, C., 1990. Phyllologie, 1990, Diplom für Bildhauerei, Meisterschule Gironcoli. In: Akademie der Bildenden Künste, Diplomarbeiten 1990, Vienna, p. 42.
- Sommerer, C. & Mignonneau, L., 1993. 'Interactive Plant Growing.' In: Gerbel, K. & Weibel, P. (eds), Ars Electronica '93 - Genetic Art Artificial Life, Vienna: PVS Verleger, pp. 408-414.
- S+T+ARTS, n.d. S+T+ARTS is an initiative of the European Commission to foster alliances of technology and artistic practice. Retrieved September 2024, from https://archive.aec.at/startsprize/
- Station Rose, n.d. Station Rose. Retrieved September 2024, from https://www.stationrose.com/
- Vasulka, S. & Vasulka, W., 1996. Machine Media. San Francisco: San Francisco Museum of Modern Art.
- Weibel, P., 1992. Die Eigenwelt der Apparatewelt - Pioneers of Electronic Art, Vasulka, W. & S. (curators), Ars Electronica.
- Weibel, P. & Export, V., n.d. Peter Weibel & Valie Export. Retrieved September 2024, from https://www.peter-weibel.at/portfolio_page/aus-der-mappe-der-hundigkeit-1968/
- Weinberger, L. & F., n.d. Lois and Franziska Weinberger. Retrieved September 2024, from https://www.loisweinberger.net/
- Vesna, V., n.d. Victoria Vesna. Retrieved September 2024, from https://victoriavesna.com/
- Varvara & Mar, n.d. Varvara & Mar. Retrieved September 2024, from https://var-mar.info/
- Zielinski, S., 2023. 'Positioning a Masterpiece of Media Art. Christa Sommerer's and Laurent Mignonneau's Installation Interactive Plant Growing.' In: Ohlenschläger, K., Weibel, P. & Weidinger, A. (eds.), Christa Sommerer & Laurent Mignonneau, The Artwork as a Living System 1992-2022, The MIT Press Leonardo Book Series, pp. 344-353.

EXHIBITIONS

FEMEL_FISSIONS: WOMEN ARTISTS INSPIRED BY WOMEN SCIENTISTS

Curated by Rachael Parsons, Lubi Thomas and Trish Adams

This unique exhibition premiered at the QUT Creative Industries Precinct, Australia in 2016. The main aim of Femel_Fissions was to show that both the artist's studio and the scientist's laboratory are sites for unrestricted inquiry and experimentation. Femel_Fissions traced the historical influence of women on scientific discovery and research through newly commissioned works by leading Australian and international artists. As curators, we explored the scientific fields of neurology, biology, cytogenetics, psychology, primatology and anatomy. The gallery pages of this book are divided into three sections. In the section titled Curators' Contributions, the background to the project by Rachael Parsons, Lubi Thomas and Trish Adams is featured. In Science Contributions, the three curators present a written survey of the scientists that were chosen by the artists. The scientists featured are Lucia Gialeazzi Calvani, Allison Jolly, Esther Lederberg, Rita Levi-Montalcini, Lynn Margulis, Barbara McClintoch and Margaret Floy Washburn. While other scientists are discussed in the book, these were the main influences behind the artistic works in Femel_Fissions. In the next section called Artists' Contributions and Their Comments, each artist reflects on how these scientists influenced their ideas and presents the resulting works. The international artists featured here are: Trish Adams, Tarsh Bates, Gina Czarnecki, Svenja Kratz, Rachel Mayeri, Helen Pynor and Jill Scott.

Femel_Fissions is a major exhibition featuring significant Australian and International female artists who work in the field of art/science. *Femel_Fissions* traces and highlights the critical influence of women from the past on scientific developments and theory. Seven selected contemporary female art/science practitioners were commissioned to create new artworks in response to the groundbreaking research of female scientists, thereby mediating their historic discoveries through art. Each newly developed work was based on the pioneering research of a female scientist from various fields of practice such as neurobiology, cytogenetics, and primatology.

Curators' Contributions

The first *Femel_Fissions* curatorial meeting took place at Merlo Café, QUT Gardens Point, in mid-2014, although at the time we did not recognise it as such! Back then, the exhibition was still a nebulous concept rotating around our mutual enthusiasm for art/science practice, where the collaborative intersects with and converges into hybrid forms. In 2014, this growing field of contemporary art included a range of pioneers, as well as a profusion of emergent artists, researchers and writers: an innovative, transdisciplinary community generating exciting work through knowledge, ideas, skills and techniques from both art and science. Since the foundation of the Arts Catalyst in London in 1993 and Art & Science Collaborations, like ASCI in New York in 1998, the enthusiasm for art/science has expanded dramatically. The ongoing vitality of programs like SymbioticA Research Laboratory at the University of Western Australia, founded in 2000, Artists-in-Labs at the Zurich University of the Arts (ZHdK) in Switzerland (founded in 2003) and the establishment of institutions such as Singapore's Art Science Museum, (opened in 2011), along with dedicated publications like *Artlink's 2014 Bio Art* edition, show the impact of art/science on contemporary culture.

At the same time as engaging with this growing practice space, however, we became increasingly aware of the problematic and continued underrepresentation of women in both the arts and sciences. Over the past fifteen years, there has been a broadening recognition of the gap between male and female representation within science, technology, engineering and mathematics (STEM) fields, and in art that engages with science and technology. The Athena Swan Charter (SAGE), initiated in the UK in 2005 and subsequently introduced in Australia, provided clear goal-based incentives for organisations to move towards gender equality by including more women scientists. However, one only needs to read *The CoUNTess* report (2016), or engage with the *Art+Feminism* Wikipedia project (started in 2014), or read the many newspaper articles reflecting on the challenges facing women working in STEM or the arts, to find that the contemporary landscape - physical and digital, career and cultural - continues to reflect a gender gulf.

As curators and practitioners within the digital new media/media arts landscape, we became increasingly concerned about this gulf. Our initial conversations regarding the representation deficit of women began back in 2009, when *Mellifera* was shown at The Block. Part of The Block's ongoing program of exhibitions and project presentations drawn from creative practice positioned at the nexus of art, science, technology and engineering, *Mellifera* was one of the few co-female-led projects at that time, and for us, it was a tipping point in recognising that the divide was already establishing itself within the Australian QUT Creative Industries Precinct (CIP) program. Even though the CIP program was run by women with a conscious policy of including female practitioners in all exhibitions, work by women was still underrepresented. *Mellifera* explored aspects of gender through its use of the Internet software platform, *Second Life*, the inclusion of a resident gender-neutral 'bot', and the corporeal ambiguity introduced by avatars. But the issue of unequal gender representation continued to vex us over the years until a café meeting in 2014, when the idea of *Femel_Fissions: Women, Art & Science* was conceived.

Clearly, we were not alone in this thinking. By 2016, we had seen several high-profile women-only shows, including one at the renowned blue chip gallery Saatchi, London, and Hauser Wirth & Schimmel's inaugural Los Angeles show. Maybe this culmination may have been built upon the traction of reports and articles addressing the representation gap, including the previously mentioned *CoUNTess report* (2016), *ARTnews Women in the Art World* issue (June 2015), and *The White Review* (2013). As expressed in a New York Times article, *Female Artists Are (Finally) Getting Their Turn*, the representation challenge is a multifaceted one that requires engagement across the whole art landscape, including public, private and commercial galleries, festivals and fairs. In 2014, *Femel_Fissions* came to fruition as part of a broader project focusing on female artists in the CIP's 2016 program.

It is important, however, to note that while engaging with this vital critical discourse, we also witnessed the work of women who, despite these challenges, produced the most innovative and cutting-edge research and practice. Women, within the arts and sciences - both past and present - have been succeeding, leading and innovating. Yet, as projects such as *ART + Feminism* reveal, the contribution of women to art and science is not widely known. It was this realisation and the desire to make visible the historic achievements of women, as well as supporting contemporary work, that formed the conceptual basis for *Femel_Fissions*.

Femel_Fissions traced and highlighted the critical influence of female scientists from the past on scientific developments and theory through the work of contemporary female art/science practitioners. The premise of the commissioning program was to create new artworks in response to the groundbreaking work from selected female scientists in various fields, including neurobiology, cytogenetics, and primatology. The exhibition presented works by seven contemporary female artists, each of whom taking as their starting point the pioneering research of one female scientist. Through these creative, transdisciplinary intersections, *Femel_Fissions* illuminated the ongoing contributions and innovations of women in multiple fields of practice and explored a return to more fluid boundaries between art and science.

Science Contributions

As curators, we chose female scientists and then asked the artists to voice their identifications with these researchers. These scientists included Lucia Gialeazzi Calvani, Allison Jolly, Esther Lederberg, Rita Levi-Montalcini, Lynn Margulis, Barbara McClintock, and Margaret Floy Washburn. Though other scientists are mentioned in the book, these are the key figures who inspired the artistic works featured in *Femel_Fissions*.

Lucia Galeazzi Galvani was an Italian scientist. She was the daughter of anatomist Domenico Gusmano Galeazzi and Paola Mini, and granddaughter of painter Domenico Galeazzi. In 1762, she married the doctor Luigi Galvani, a professor at the University in Bologna (1775). Alison Jolly was a primatologist, known for her studies of lemur biology. She wrote several books for both popular and scientific audiences and conducted extensive fieldwork on Lemurs in Madagascar. Esther Miriam Zimmer Lederberg was an American microbiologist and a pioneer of bacterial genetics. She discovered the bacterial virus lambda phage and the bacterial fertility factor F. Rita Levi-Montalcini OMRI OMCA was an Italian neurobiologist. She was awarded the 1986 Nobel Prize in Physiology or Medicine, jointly with colleague Stanley Cohen, for the discovery of nerve growth factor. From 2001 until her death, she also served in the Italian Senate as a "Senator for Life". Lynn Margulis was an American evolutionary biologist and the primary modern proponent for the significance of symbiosis in evolution. Barbara McClintock was an American scientist and cytogeneticist who was awarded the 1983 Nobel Prize in Physiology or Medicine. McClintock received her PhD in botany from Cornell University in 1927. Margaret Floy Washburn, a leading American psychologist in the early 20th century, was best known for her experimental work in animal behaviour and motor theory development.

Artists' Contributions

Gina Czarnecki

United Kingdom
I Too. 2016

Margaret Floy Washburn has inspired me through her pioneering cross disciplinary research between psychology, philosophy, ethics and cognition. *I Too* is composed of imaging and visualisation technologies and explores the relationship (and assumed equation) between seeing and knowing, between data, information and knowledge. Woven into the tapestry of scientific images are iris scans, portraits of the artist's mother, "slipping away" with Alzheimer's, and photos of her daughter's selfies from Snapchat - one paired with each message. The image becomes the dominant and necessary part of communication, making up for that which cannot be expressed in words. *I Too* is fundamentally about the spaces between that which can be currently measured. The eye has long been thought to reveal something of the person, even the soul. Current research has shown that various medical conditions can be diagnosed through the examination of the eye. Analysis of the iris reveals biometric information unique to each person, and we rely primarily on our vision for our understanding of our situation and the wider world - we equate observation

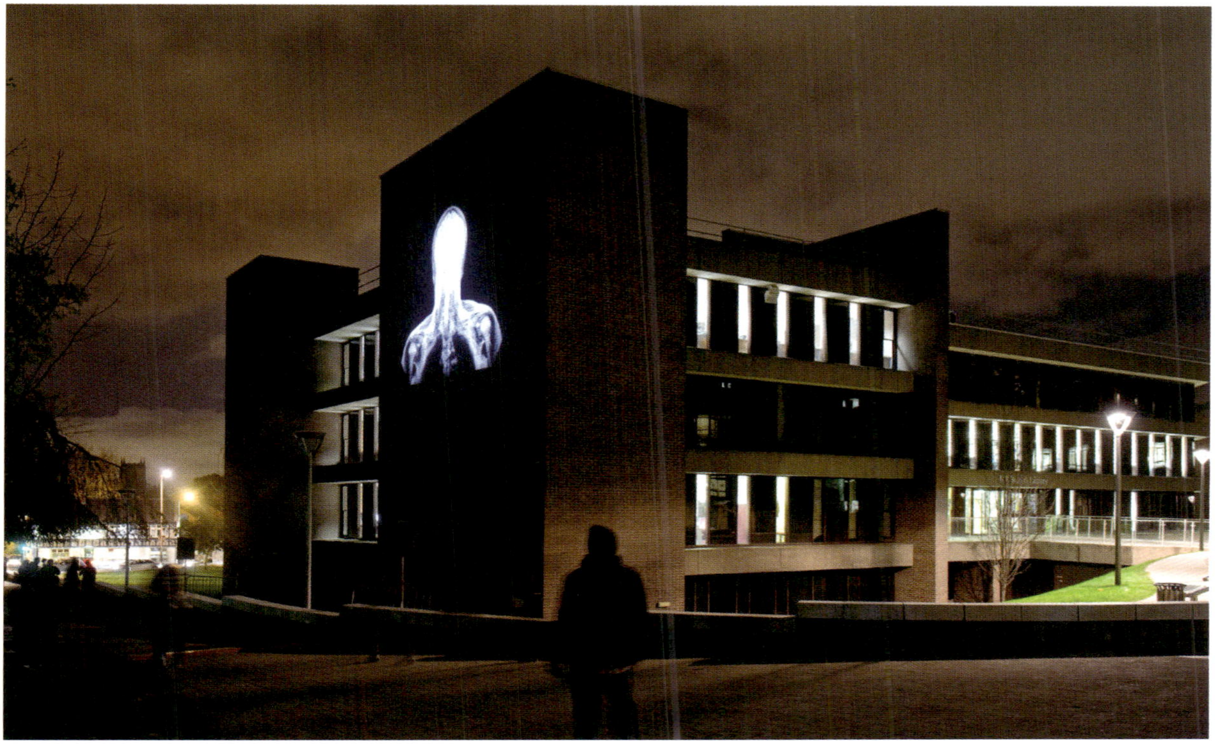

Figure 1 and 2: *I Too.* Czarnecki, G. (2016). Twin screen video installation with stereo sound loop.

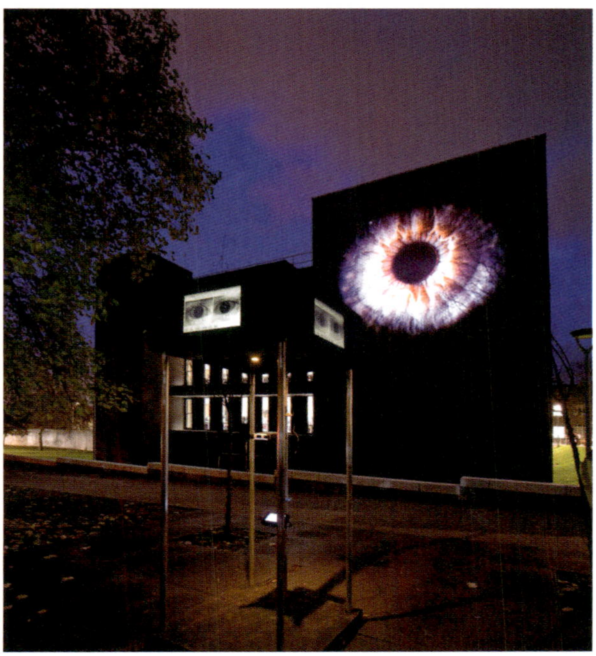

with knowledge and truth. *I Too* connects these themes of vision, cognition, surveillance and belief. It combines images of biomedical research, extreme close-ups of human irises by Suren Manvelyan, footage I have filmed and, through an Iris scanning booth, unique biometric portraits of the viewers themselves. Data analysis of iris scans from the public determined the sequences of sound and image.

https://www.ginaczarnecki.com/artworks

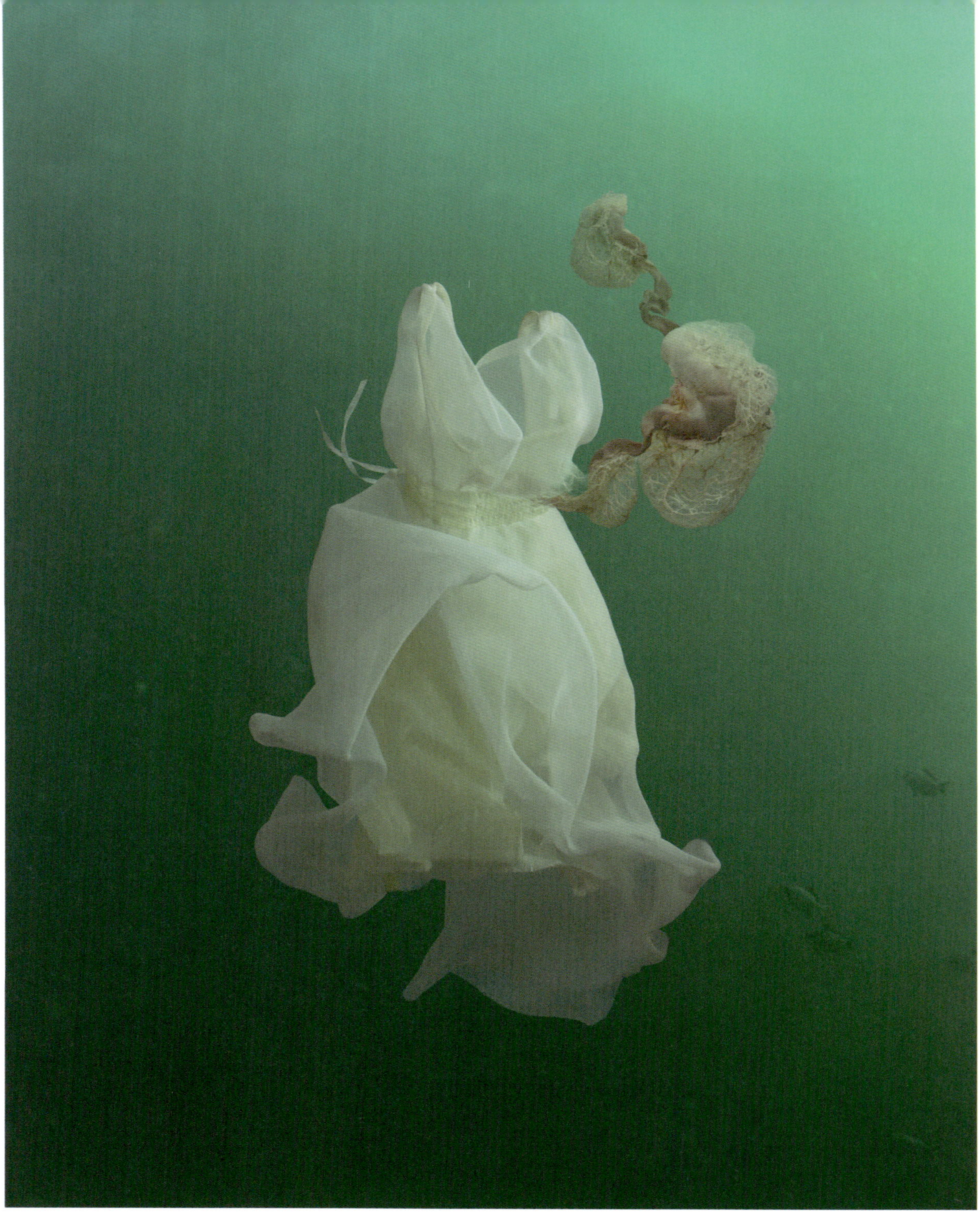

Figure 3: *Liquid Ground 1*. Pynor, H. (2011). C-type photographic print face-mounted on glass.
Image courtesy of the artist and Dominik Mersch Gallery, Sydney.

Helen Pynor

Australia

Animal Electricity: Moments and *Slit series*. 2016

Lucia Galeazzi Galvani is unusual among the scientists whose work is celebrated in *Femel_ Fissions*. Lucia Galeazzi Galvani was an 18th-century Italian scientist, based in Bologna. She worked alongside her more famous husband, Luigi Galvani, in his electrophysiological research and his surgical and obstetrics practice. She also edited his medical texts. The contributions of women were less rigorously recorded or acknowledged when Lucia was working - space and absence surround her intellectual contribution. Within this absence, I imagine and riff on some of the dominant motifs of the Galvani's shared practice.

In the most famous experiment credited to Luigi Galvani, he found that the muscles of dead frogs' legs twitch when struck by an electric spark. From this, he hypothesised that animal tissues possess intrinsic electricity - "animal electricity" - that is fundamental to nerve conduction and muscle contraction. Even though the explanation was incorrect, the insight represents the birth of the contemporary study of electrophysiology and is a founding moment in the development of neurology.

Animal Electricity: *Moments* is an imagined dialogue across centuries between three women - scientist, writer and feminist scholar - who invoke "animal electricity" in their work. Lucia Galeazzi Galvani opens the dialogue with her absent words, represented in a simple, bound black book filled with blank pages alongside a single blank page extracted from the book. The book proportions and number of pages mimic Luigi Galvani's famous publication: *De Viribus Electricitatis in Motu Musculari* (Commentary on the Effect of Electricity on Muscular Motion).

Mary Shelley picks up the thread in her classic 19th-century science fiction novel *Frankenstein*, powerfully influenced by several scientific concepts of the time: Galvani's revivifying of dead tissue seems to have had the most obvious impact on *Frankenstein*. In 1791, he experimented on "animal electricity" that was substantially produced from the brain and conducted to muscles and other organs through the nerves (Jansson, S. 1999, Introduction to Frankenstein, Wordsworth Classics: Ware, Hertfordshire, p.ix).

In 2004, feminist scholar Elizabeth Wilson invoked an uncanny 19th-century experiment on the electrophysiology of decapitated frogs to challenge the brain centrism of contemporary neurology and to support the notion of "distributed" consciousness and the "thoughtfulness" of the peripheral nervous system.

The *Slit Series* references the Galvani's surgical and obstetrics practice and the opening of bodies- human and animal - for medical treatment and scientific learning. The sexual undertones of the title and some of the imagery foregrounds the penetrative nature of surgery and dissection amidst its apparent clinical neutrality. *Animal Electricity: Moments* and *Slit series* invoke a period aesthetic and a quasi-analogue approach in homage to the era in which Lucia Galeazzi Galvani was working.

http://www.helenpynor.com

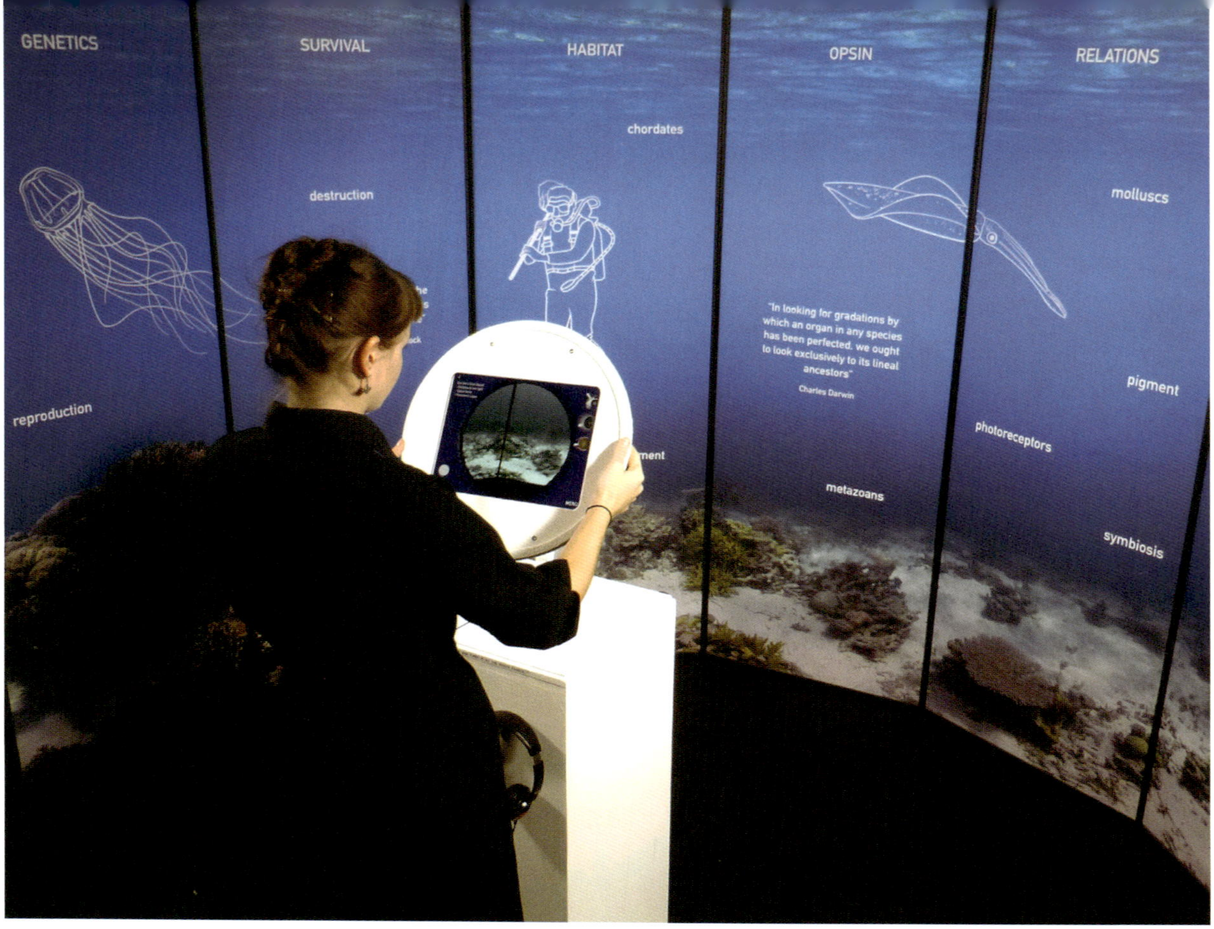

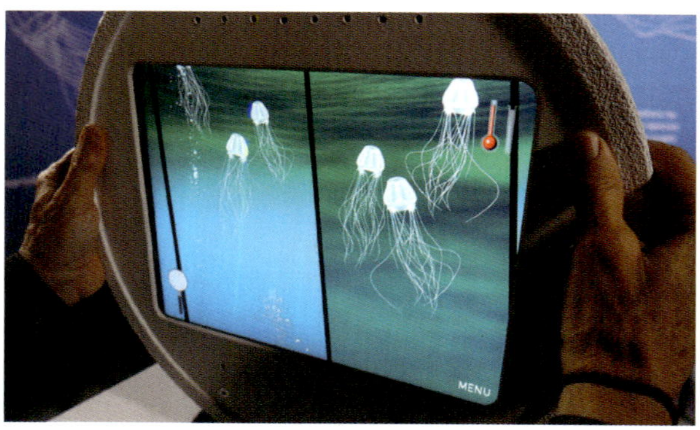

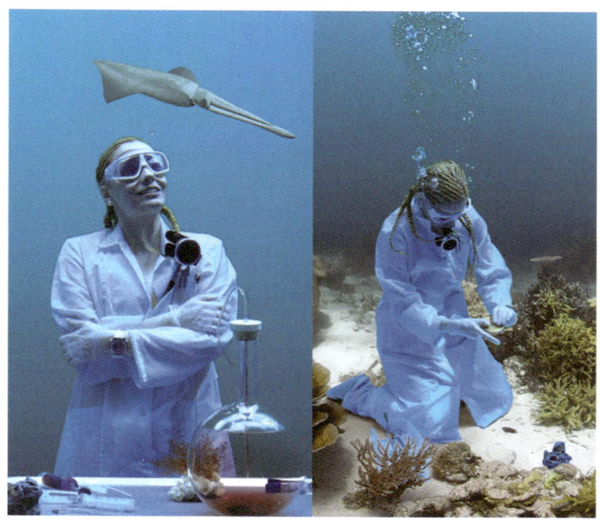

Figure 4 above: *Jellyeyes.* Scott J. (2016).
Photo-wall, iPad inside interface with software for augmented reality.

Figure 5 below: *Jellyeyes.* Scott J. (2016).
Metaphor: When viewers warm the water, blue green algae and jellyfish multiply.

Figure 6: *Jellyeyes.* Scott J. (2016).
The daughter of Margulis, a marine biologist conducts experiments in the coral reef.

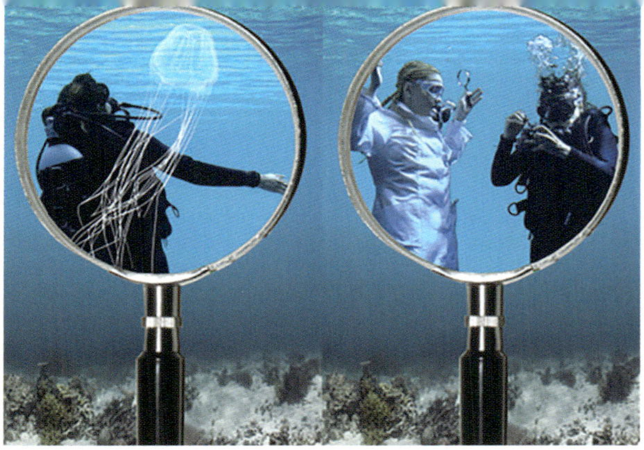

Figure 7a: *Jellyeyes.* Scott J. (2016). Fiction: The careless tourist (performed by the artist) and the scientist (Daniela Rodler) meet to discuss climate change and human behaviour.

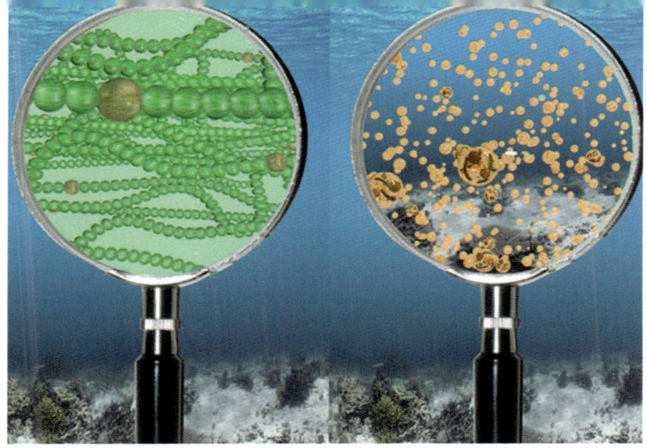

Figure 7b: *Jellyeyes.* Scott J. (2016). Fact: Biodiversity disruption: the increase in toxic blue-green algae and the exodus of good algae from the coral.

Jill Scott

Australia | Switzerland

Jellyeyes. 2016

Lynn Margulis was the primary modern proponent for the significance of symbiosis in biological evolution. In Jellyeyes, I was particularly inspired by her statement that "Bacteria are the agents of change." I found her concept of endosymbiosis especially fascinating, especially after my own experiences as a diver in the Great Barrier Reef. Endosymbiosis is the phenomenon that eukaryotic cells were once invaded by protobacteria and cyanobacteria, which eventually evolved to become essential powerhouse components of any cell: the chloroplasts and mitochondria. In the Barrier Reef climate change is affecting many symbiotic relationships. While the colourful zooxanthellae alga provides their hosts with energy in the form of fixed carbon compounds, the coral provides the zooxanthellae with protection and access to nutrients for survival. In the first part of Jellyeyes, called *Co-evolution*, viewers can discover how our own interventions may affect these symbiont interdependencies. In the second part of Jellyeyes, called *Structural Evolution*, I was inspired by Margulis' idea about the evolution of the cilia in the photoreceptors of the retina. She posited that the formation of these phototransductive cilia might also be attributed to the infiltration of spiral (spirochete) bacteria. Although this concept has since been hotly debated, the similarity between the photoreceptors and jelly like cells from the character's eyes that I have chosen to portray - the jellyfish, the squid and the human - is very revealing. What will happen to this evolution in warmer waters? In the third part of Jellyeyes, called *Comparative Evolution*, the inspiration came from the writings of Margulis in her book *What Is Life?* Here, the viewer can choose to "see through" the eyes of two other species, the squid and the jellyfish, to view serious changes in reef life. My aims were to use augmented reality to create an immersive and empathetic experience and to raise human awareness about the fragility of these evolutionary developments. Here, viewers can reflect about the preconditions for a sustainable level of biodiversity but also question their own role to keep it healthy.

Funding ProHelvetia_ The Swiss Arts Council
https://www.jillscott.org

Scientific advisors: Neuroscientist: Stephan Neuhauss, Aquatic Scientists: Christopher Robinson, Lisa-Ann Gershwin

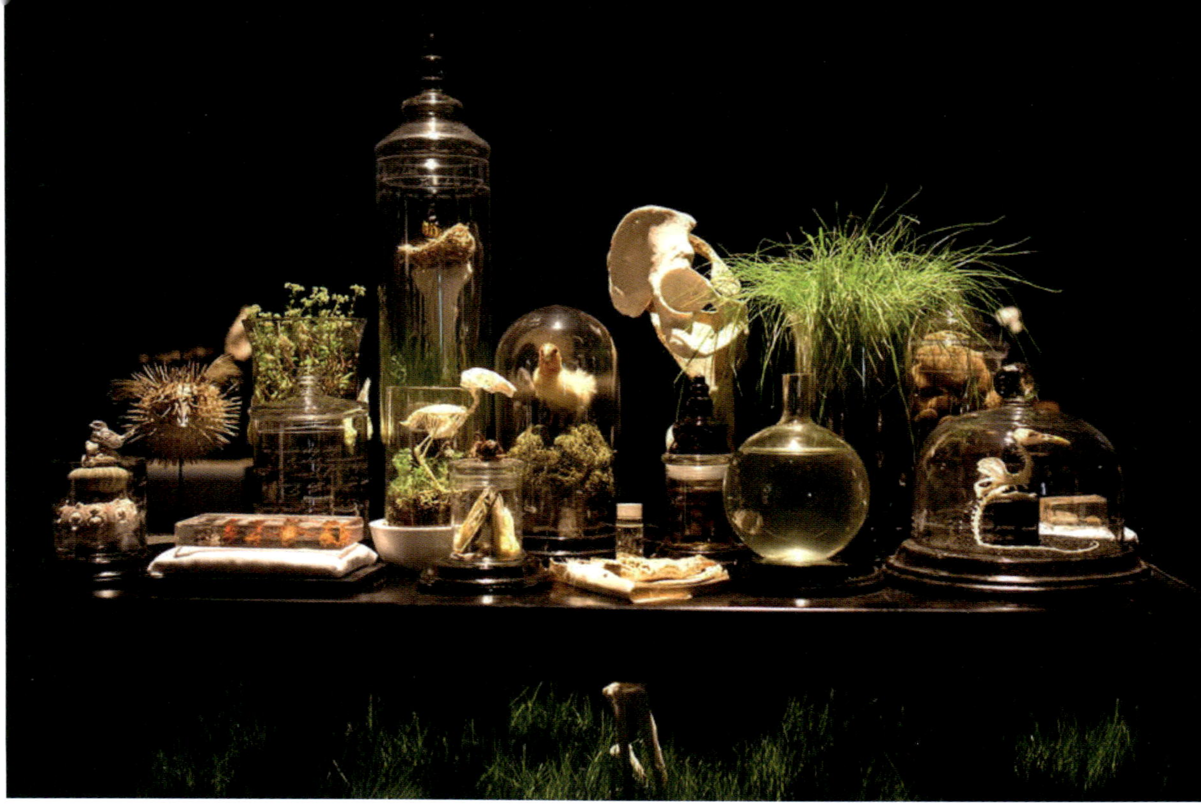

Figure 8a: *Foundations and Ripples*. Kratz, S. (2016).
Clay, varnish, enamel, wire, wood, Perspex, LED lights, glass, beads, plastic and metal.

Svenja Kratz

South Africa | Germany | Australia
Foundations and Ripples, 2016

Foundations and Ripples responds to the pioneering work of Lynn Margulis and Esther Lederberg and reflects on how their research has contributed to scientific thought and formed part of the foundations for contemporary research projects, including my own engagements across art and science. Lynn Margulis was an evolutionary theorist and one of the first scientists to advocate for the theory of Serial Endosymbiosis, arguing that bacterial symbiosis and mutually beneficial microbial relationships were an important part of evolution. She also highlighted the significant role of the microbial world in all aspects of life. Microbiologist Esther Lederberg made major contributions to the field of bacterial genetics, including the discovery of the lambda bacteriophage and numerous insights into how bacteria mutate.

The two white-coloured LED light panels refer to Margulis and Lederberg and include visual components that relate to their work and scientific contributions across evolution and bacterial genetics. The third, purple, light panel links to an Art- Science residency I completed at Leiden University in 2013. As part of this residency, I worked with PhD candidate and female scientist Srividya Ganapathy to induce mutations into archaerhodopsin-3-AR3 - a protein that creates energy from light, with the

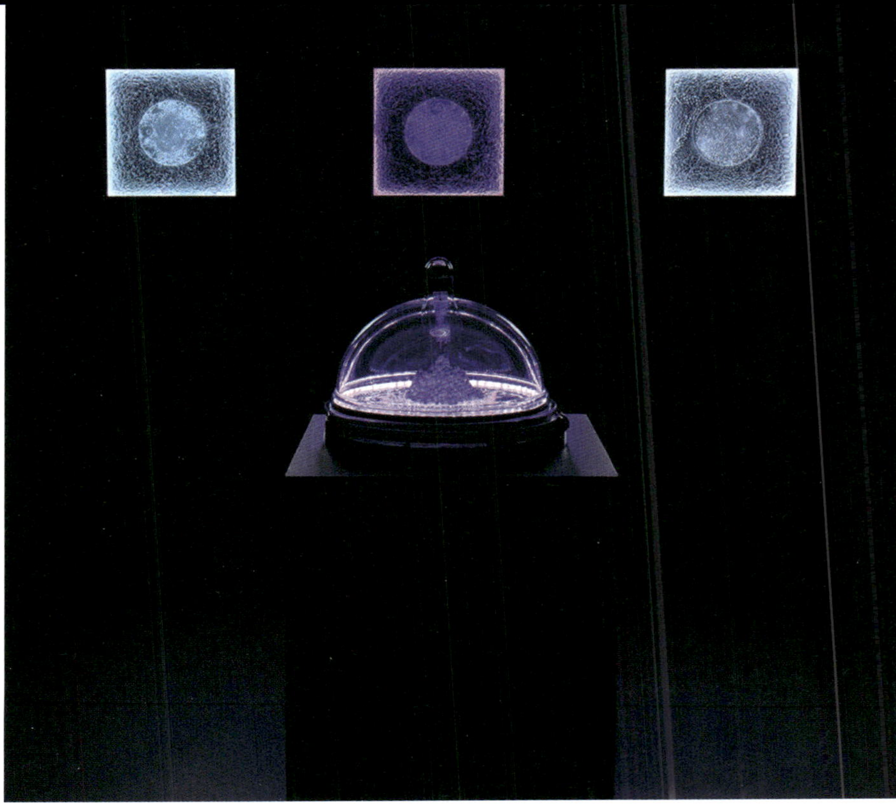

Credits: Thanks to Robert Zwijnenberg and David Louwrier, Art and Genomics Centre; Huub de Groot, Wim de Grip, Srividya Ganapathy, Siebren Frohlich, and Andrean Razomovski from Gorleus Laboratories at Leiden University.
The Art-Science residency: QLD Premier's 2012 New Media Scholarship from QAG/GOMA. Sound by Carly Dickenson (Anise) and metal.

Figure 8b: *Foundations and Ripples*. Kratz, S. (2016). Perspex, purple LED lights, glass, beads, plastic and metal.

aim to shift the absorbance spectrum to use more of the available light spectrum to generate energy. The diorama includes a light bulb obtained from the laboratory in Leiden in which the research was carried out and incorporates the original mutant protein ARS-FS (Figure 8a and 8b).

The colour purple is significant, as the archaerhodopsin molecule is purple and is most efficient at absorbing green light. The bacterial shapes incorporated into the various components reference the origin of the protein from the archaebacteria *Halorubrum sodomense*, as well as the E. coli bacteria used to manufacture the protein. The work of Lynn Margulis was instrumental in understanding the complex interrelationships of microorganisms and their components. Her work was also a great source of wonder and inspiration as I started my own journey into science. Esther Lederberg's work with plasmids, antibacterial resistance and replica plating were instrumental in the understanding of bacterial genetics and genetic engineering. In many ways, their work contributed to the understanding of evolution and genetics, and helped to lay the part of the foundations for this project. The recurring ripples integrated into each component of the installation reflect on the ripple effects of their research that continue to impact on scientific understandings, even today.

https://www.svenjakratz.com/projects

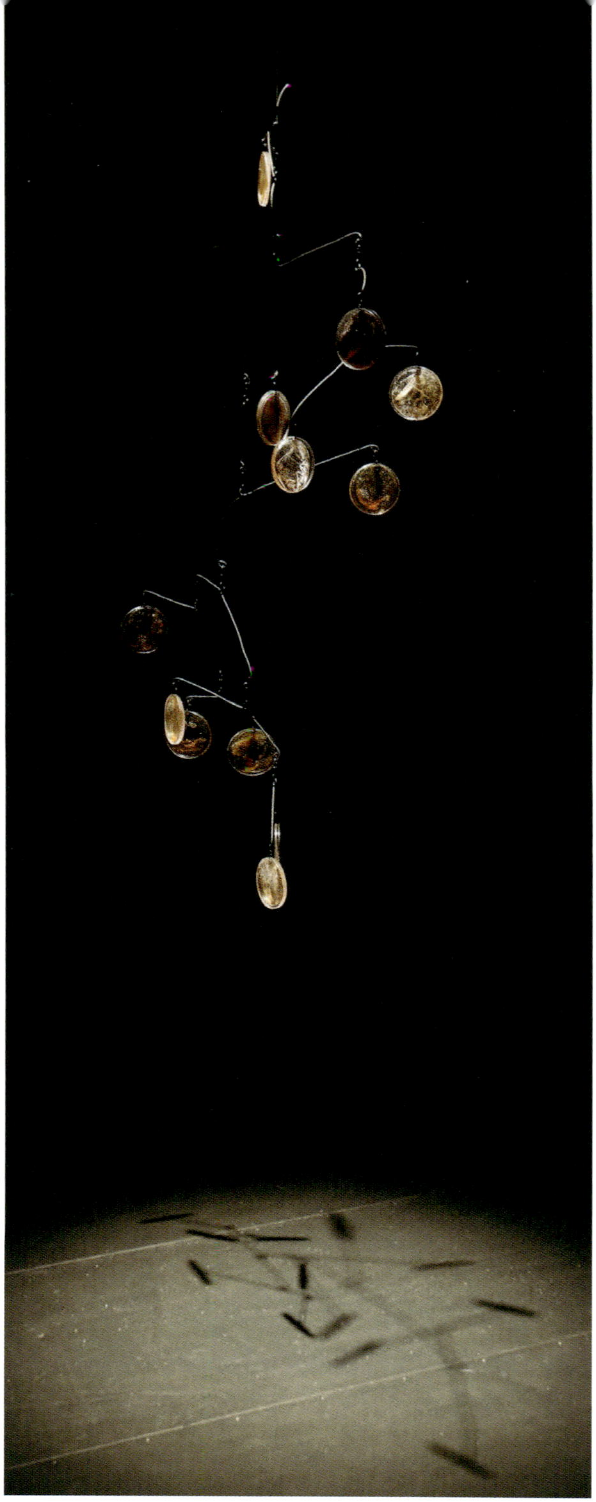

Figure 9: *The Tangled Field: After McClintock.* Bates, T. (2016). Candida albicans, agar, resin.

Tarsh Bates

Australia

The Tangled Field: After McClintock. 2016

The Tangled Field: After McClintock responds to geneticist and Nobel Prize winner Barbara McClintock's 1931: the discovery of genetic regulation ("controlling elements") as an evolutionary mechanism. She traced the evolution of maize through its various chromosomal and phylogenetic characteristics and proved that genes "jump" around chromosomes and are "controlled" to produce particular characteristics. *The Tangled Field* traces the evolution of phenotypic changes in *Candida albicans*. *Candida albicans* is one of the hundredsof species that live in the ecosystems of the human body. They dwell in multispecies communities within our bodies, on our dark, moist, warm folds, consuming sugars and other nutrients. We have co-evolved; human bodies are the ecological niche of *C. albicans*. Within a host body, *C. albicans* are omnisexual and polymorphic, able to switch between asexual and sexual reproductive strategies and several morphological states: distinct cell types involved in different modes of pathogenicity and virulence. *The Tangled Field* brings evolution into a time scale perceptible to human viewers and reminds us that our bodies are dynamic more-than-human ecologies.

https://www.tarshbates.com

Trish Adams

Australia | Great Britain

Obverse. 2016

My chosen scientist is Rita Levi-Montalcini, whose Nobel Prize winning scientific discovery of the nerve growth factor has underpinned much subsequent neurological research. For me, the circumstances surrounding the early stages of her research are also fascinating. At the commencement of World War II, she was dismissed from university by Mussolini, along with other Jewish nationals. To continue her investigations, she set up the silver-staining microscopy process in her bedroom, created makeshift tools from sewing needles, and experimented on chickens' eggs.

Whilst her primary focus was on the nerve growth factor, Montalcini clearly understood that cell death was an essential and integral part of the nerve growth factor physiological cycle. It was literally the obverse or "other side of the coin"- in the nerve growth factor process.

The artwork *Obverse* is composed of a video showing time-lapse micrograph imagery of fibroblast cells from my forearm cultured in vitro and chemically "instructed" to die - to undergo apoptosis, also known as "induced cell death." When a viewer/participant interacts with *Obverse,* their own forearm provides a living canvas upon which the video images are projected, almost as if the skin had been peeled back to reveal the cellular biology beneath the body's surface, where cell death is a fundamental part of the life process.

https://trishadams.tv/obverse/

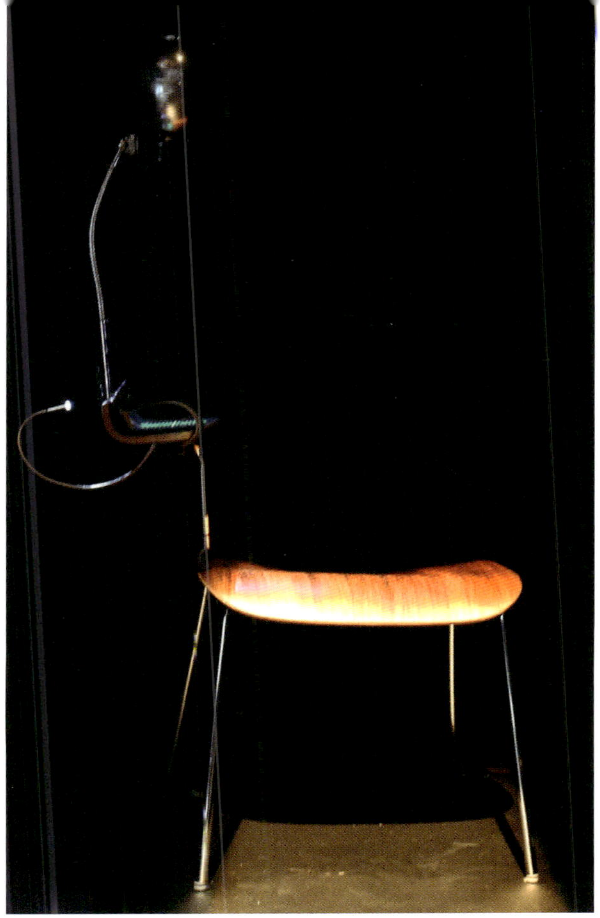

Figure 10: *Obverse*. Adams, T. (2016).
Chrome, metal, wood, leather, pico projector, speaker, Raspberry Pi, switch and wiring.

Viewer Instructions:

Enter the artwork space and sit in the chair.

Place your right arm on the arm rest, inner arm facing upward.

Slot your hand through the grip at the end, palm facing upwards, with your thumb touching the switch button.

The green grid design will be projected onto your inner arm.

Press the switch and watch the video as it replaces the green grid.

The video can be repeated by pressing the switch again.

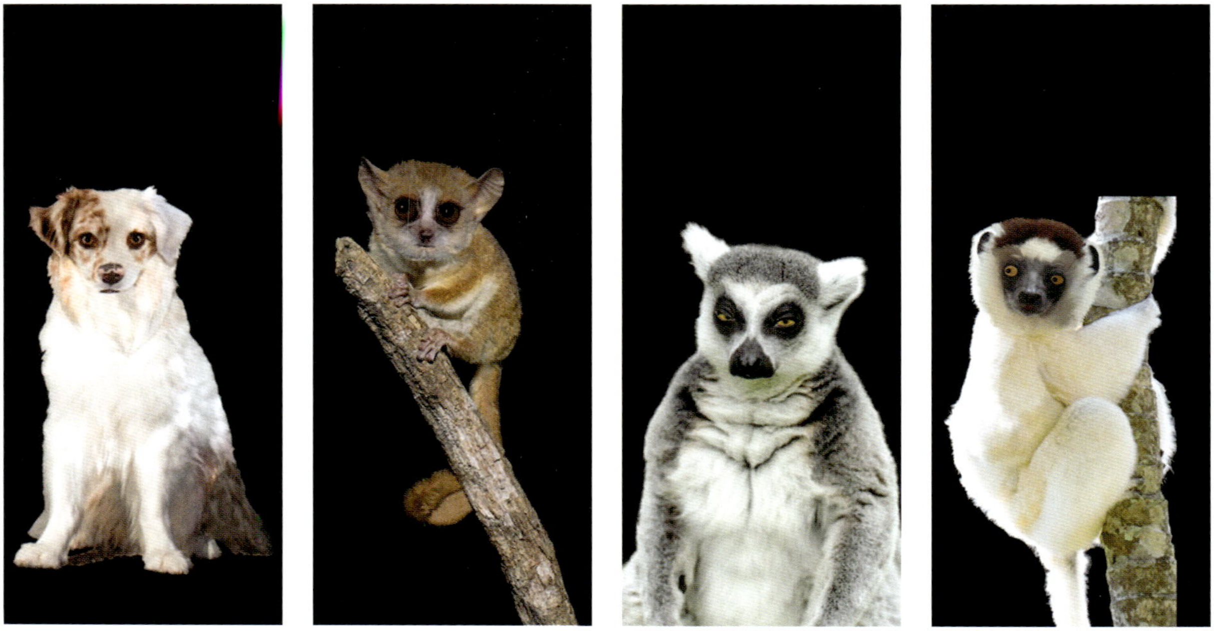

Figure 11: *The Jollies*. Mayeri, R. (2016). A four channel video installation with talking animals. Donna Haraway as Australian shepherd dog with primatologists Hanta Rasamimana as mouse lemur, Patricia Wright as ring-tailed lemur, and Alison Richard as sifaka.

Rachel Mayeri

USA

The Jollies. 2016

The primatologist Alison Jolly (1937-2014) was known for her pioneering theory on the evolution of social intelligence, developed through her study of ring-tailed lemurs. Her scientific and conservation work drew worldwide attention to the unique ecosystem of Madagascar. In this biographical artwork, the artist presents interviews with Jolly's network of colleagues, friends, and family. Many voices articulate the significance of her scientific discoveries as well as her career: group living over tool making as a driver for evolution, her description of a female dominant primate society, the role of play in learning, as well as her place in the first generation of women in the field of primatology and her development of community-based conservation. Monkeys, lemurs, and other nonhuman characters animate the conversation, producing reflection about humans as part of the primate order, social network, and ecosystem.

https://www.rachelmayeri.com/blog/2017/05/23/the-jollies/
Watch the film at: https://vimeo.com/175264125

See also this essay on the making of the project: Mayeri, R. (2019). *The Jollies*: A Biographical Artwork about Primatologist Alison Jolly. A/b: Auto/Biography Studies, 34(3), 461-465. https://doi.org/10.1080/08989575.2019.1664177

Essay by Jennifer Lynn Peterson forthcoming on the Los Angeles Filmforum series she curated called Experimentations 1, Feminist Film Experiments with Science.

Conclusion of the exhibition

The works in this exhibition were created using a range of techniques that explore the return to more fluid boundaries between art and science. They address the historic and ongoing lack of adequate acknowledgement or representation of women practitioners in both art and scientific fields. Aiming to highlight the work of women who have been overshadowed within social structures and written history, *Femel_Fissions* was a landmark exhibition that sought to address this imbalance by celebrating women, their works, ideas, and impact.

Femel_Fissions was presented at Queensland University of Technology Creative Industries Precinct's premier new media exhibition space, *The Block*, in July/August 2016. The exhibition coincided with Australia's National Science Week.

Credits

The exibition *Femel-Fissions* was funded by
Creative Industries, QUT Australia
Scientific Collaborator - Dr. Victor Nurcombe,
School of Biomedical Science, The University of Queensland
Erik North - OBVERSE "Chair" Construction
Ross Eldridge - Software Development
Roundhouse - Soundtrack
Andrea Rassell - Video Post-production
OBVERSE design supported by CiArt, RMIT University;
Director, Dr. Jonathan Duckworth

Reference

– Jansson, S. (1999) Introduction to the Wordsworth Classics edition of Frankenstein. Wordsworth Editions.

FEMINIST CLIMATE CHANGE: BEYOND THE BINARY AND ACROSS GENERA

Victoria Vesna

This essay reflects on the 2017 exhibition Feminist Climate Change: Beyond the Binary, co-curated for Ars Electronica, as a lens through which to explore the entangled crises of gender, ecology, and technology. Anchored in personal narrative and historical analysis, it centres the story of Iranian designer Maryam Razi, whose trajectory - from transnational creative collaborator to climate-displaced artist - mirrors the escalating precarity faced by women worldwide. Set against the backdrop of the #MeToo movement, Greta Thunberg's rise, and Ars Electronica's own internal reckoning with gender bias, the essay situates the exhibition as both a critical intervention and a generative archive of feminist, intersectional climate justice. Drawing on ecofeminist scholarship and the work of some of the participating artists, it calls for a reimagining of institutional and ecological systems rooted in care, interdependence, and radical transformation. With the selected works, we aim to converge the issues in feminism with environmentalism. By framing the exhibition in this way, it was our hope to reinvigorate the eco-feminism that emerged in the 70s and was ignored for much too long. In this particular context, at the Ars Electronica festival in Linz, we address the local and transnational issues of feminism in media arts and the global issue of climate change – thus the very obvious title.

Introduction: Reimagining Feminist Climate Futures

The Feminist Climate Change: Beyond the Binary exhibition, which I co-curated with Xin Xin for Ars Electronica in 2017, emphasised that feminism is not exclusively about women; rather, it advocated for the dismantling of all systems of inequality, inviting participation from all genders, including men, non-binary, and gender-diverse individuals. The exhibition underscored that feminism is about challenging and transforming power structures that have traditionally marginalised not only women but also other underrepresented communities and the environment.

At the time, this perspective felt urgent but also full of potential. There was a sense that emerging generations of artists, scientists, and activists could still intervene in the course of climate destruction and systemic inequality. The conversations fostered through the exhibition - between disciplines, across borders, and among identities - reflected a kind of feminist futurism grounded in care, interconnection, and resistance.

Maryam Razi and the Art Sci Collective

It was during this moment that Maryam Razi, a young Iranian designer, walked into the center and became deeply engaged with this project. Maryam embodied the very spirit of transnational feminist energy that the *Beyond the Binary* exhibition aimed to cultivate. She moved between Tehran and Los Angeles, contributing innovative work and insights that wove together cultural memory, technology, and ecological thinking. In 2017, Tehran's creative community was thriving despite underlying tensions. Maryam represented the powerful and poetic vision of what a feminist future could look like - global, experimental, and inclusive.

But that vision has become increasingly difficult to hold onto. In the years since, Maryam - like many Iranian women - has found herself unable to return home. The intensification of state surveillance, the repression of free expression, and the targeting of women who dare to speak, create, or move freely has made it unsafe. Meanwhile, in the United States, the reversal of reproductive rights with the 2022 Supreme Court ruling, marked a devastating regression. Young women today are coming of age with fewer protections than the generations before them. The illusion that democratic nations are inherently progressive on women's rights has been shattered.

An Exhibition Rooted in Urgency and Solidarity

The Feminist Climate Change exhibition showcased a vibrant constellation of artists and scientists whose works interrogated climate change, gender, and power through a feminist, anti-binary lens. The lineup was made up mostly of UCLA's *Art Sci Collective*: featuring Pinar Yoldas, Silvia Rigon, Mary Maggic Tsang, Xin Xin, Noa P. Kaplan, Sanglim Han, Sarah Brady and Jen Agosta; *The Design Media Arts* alumni with additional invited artists: Erika Blumenfeld, Nancy Baker Cahill, Inhye Lee, Fabiola

Menchelli, Bahareh Khoshooee, Angelina Oleksy-Wawrzyniak, Nandita Kumar, Eunice Luk, Yaloo and the collective *voidLab*. Young feminist-aligned scientists including Christina Agapakis, Olivia Osborne and Rita Blaik also contributed.

The exhibition was intergenerational, celebrating students, recent graduates, emerging artists, scientists, and educators alike. It was also a deeply personal moment for me: my younger daughter, Aleksa Mara, joined us during the installation. Seeing her engage hands-on with the labour of building this space for imagination and resistance made tangible the intergenerational urgency of feminist climate action. Her participation echoed the exhibition's core message - that change is collaborative, that it crosses generational and gendered lines, and that the future depends on how we nurture these connections now.

Cultural Flashpoints: #MeToo, Greta and Institutional Critique

The exhibition unfolded in 2017 - a year of seismic shifts around gender and power. As we installed *Feminist Climate Change* in Linz, the *#MeToo* movement erupted globally, revealing the pervasive scale of gender-based violence. At the same time, Greta Thunberg began her solitary climate strike in Sweden, a quiet act that soon sparked a global youth movement. Both were led by young women. Both exposed the violence of systems - whether against bodies or the planet - and insisted on radical change.

These movements echoed the core ethos of the exhibition: that dismantling systems of domination requires confronting both the exploitation of bodies and the extraction of Earth's resources. The timing was not incidental. Feminist Climate Change, as articulated through the artists' works, was a lived, urgent response to these intersecting crises.

Responding to Critique: Ars Electronicas' Evolution

The tensions addressed in the exhibition were not only directed outward. Ars Electronica itself was facing growing criticism for its lack of gender equity - particularly in its prestigious Golden Nica awards, which had historically favored male recipients. The *Kiss My Ars* campaign, initiated by artist Heather Dewey-Hagborg, brought this disparity to public attention. At the same time, Christa Sommerer, in charge of the campus exhibitions extended an invitation for me to curate the annual Campus exhibition, a platform typically reserved for showcasing the technological innovation of international academic institutions. Christa Sommerer is the director of *Interface Cultures* at the University of Linz. I agreed - on the condition that we could confront these institutional issues openly. From this exchange emerged *Feminist Climate Change: Beyond the Binary*, a project that reflected the festival's willingness to engage with critique and begin addressing its own structural biases.

As an extension of the exhibition, we co-organised a symposium with Ars Electronica titled with the same name, held on September 9, 2017, at the *OÖ Kulturquartier* in Linz. The panel brought together artists, theorists, scientists, and curators to explore intersections of feminism, ecology, and technology. It opened with *From C to X: Networked Feminisms*, a session featuring Virginia Barratt, Alla Mitrofanova, and Annie Goh, moderated by Diana McCarty. This session traced the lineage from cyberfeminism to xenofeminism. This was followed by *Emerging Voices*, with participants including A.M. Darke, Kate Hollenbach, Mary Maggic, Silvia Rigon, Echo Theohar, and Christina Yglesias, moderated by Xin Xin of *voidLab*. Another panel, *Feminism and the Sciences / Environmentalism*, featured Rita Blaik, Olivia Osborne, Byron Rich, and Silvia Rigon, moderated by James Gimzewski. The final discussion, *Practices and Initiatives*, brought together an international cohort including Diana Arellano, David Familian, Ine Gevers, Satinder P. Gill, Waltraud Grausgruber, Beatrix Hausner, Haytham Nawar, Genoveva Rückert-Sommerauer, Elisabeth Schimana, Rosa von Suess and Eveline Wandl-Vogt, and was moderated by me. The discussions were vibrant, unapologetic, and transformative. At the same time, Ars Electronica began building an archive of women artists working with technology - *Women in Media Arts* - a meaningful step toward institutional repair. This process affirmed that feminist critique, when met with humility, can lead to real structural change.

Feminist Ecologies: Highlighted Works and Practices

Artists such as Pinar Yoldas, Mary Maggic, Xin Xin, Scott Hessels, and John Brumley - all part of the *Art Sci Collective* - contributed works that exemplified the exhibition's interdisciplinary and activist ethos. Yoldas envisioned speculative ecosystems shaped by microplastic contamination. Maggic's estrogen hacking workshops revealed how hormonal regulation, surveillance, and environmental toxicity are entangled. Xin Xin blurred digital design with feminist accountability. Hessels translated environmental data into poetic media, while Brumley's open-source tools promoted access and transparency. Their works created a network of resistance and reimagination. They offered not just critique, but proposals for how art, science, and feminism could work together to forge livable futures.

Cycles of Suppression and Resistance: A Historical Perspective

The feminist climate movement is not new. Its roots stretch back to the ecofeminist theories of Vandana Shiva, Carolyn Merchant, Maria Mies, and Silvia Federici. Merchant's *The Death of Nature* traced how science reshaped Earth into a passive machine. Federici's *Caliban and the Witch* revealed how witch hunts disciplined women's bodies to serve capitalist accumulation. Shiva famously wrote, "What we do to nature, we do to ourselves."The work in *Feminist Climate Change: Beyond the Binary* is part of a this longer arc - one that stretches across decades, geographies, and generations. The roots of ecofeminism, emerging in the 1970s through thinkers like Vandana Shiva, Carolyn Merchant, and Maria Mies, made explicit the links between the domination of women and the domination of nature. They argued that the logic of patriarchy, capitalism, and colonialism depended on a binary worldview - one that separated reason from emotion, human from nature, masculine from feminine - and that this false dualism justified violence against both bodies and ecosystems.

Merchant's *The Death of Nature* traced how the Scientific Revolution replaced a living, organic view of the world with a mechanical one, relegating the Earth to a passive resource to be controlled. Silvia Federici, in *Caliban and the Witch*, showed how the witch hunts of early modern Europe were part of a larger campaign to discipline women's bodies in the service of capital accumulation - a campaign that, arguably, never ended. These histories remind us that the current rollback of rights and the environmental collapse we are witnessing today are not aberrations - they are the continuation of a long, cyclical pattern of suppression and resistance. These scholars help us see today's crises - from Roe v. Wade's reversal to climate catastrophe - as part of a long, recurring pattern of domination. But just as these patterns persist, so too do resistance and renewal.

Loss and Legacy: Maryam's Story and the Fires of 2025

Maryam's story, too, is part of this lineage. Her journey - from an active participant in the *Art Sci* community to a displaced artist navigating the tightening restrictions of the Iranian regime - reflects both the vulnerability and the resilience of young women today. But her struggle did not end with exile. In early 2025, Maryam lost everything in the catastrophic wildfires that swept through Pacific Palisades in Los Angeles and swept through her neighborhood, erasing her home, her studio and her archives. What she escaped politically, she could not escape ecologically.

Her loss is not isolated. It is emblematic of the entangled crises of our time: the climate emergency no longer looms as a distant threat - it arrives suddenly, on wind and flame, and takes without warning. And it arrives most violently for those already precariously positioned. Maryam's life has been shaped by the convergence of geopolitical borders and planetary boundaries, both of which have become increasingly unforgiving. And yet, she continues to create, to speak, to resist.

Her voice, like those of the artists in *Feminist Climate Change: Beyond the Binary*, reminds us that the fight for gender equity and ecological survival is not abstract. It is ongoing, recursive, and deeply embodied. These losses are personal. This work is urgent.

FEMINIST CLIMATE CHANGE BEYOND THE BINARY

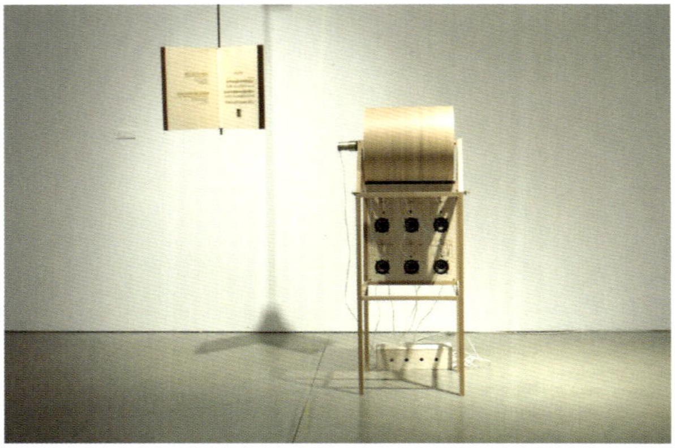

Figure 1: *Vexation.* Hui, P. (2017). Musical instrument.

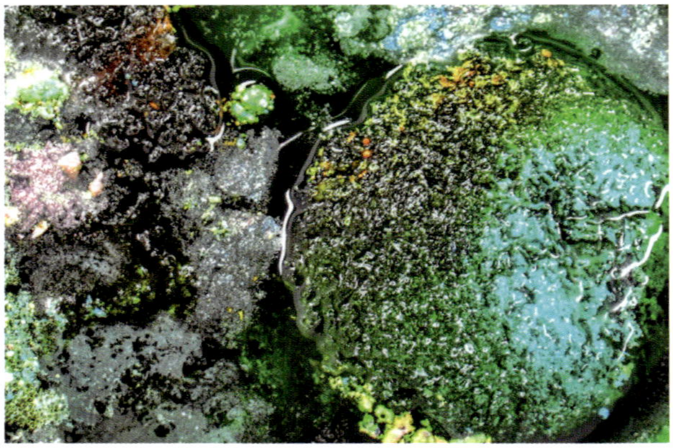

Figure 2: *Meltings of the Heart Change Glacial Landscapes.* Osborne, O. (2017). Chemicals, coloured dyes, paint.

Some artists in the exhibition:

Vexation by Phoebe Hui (HK)

Vexation is a musical instrument built especially to play Erik Satie's composition *Vexation.* Satie apparently instructed that the same music should be played 840 times. Inspired by Samuel Biderman's octave spinet, *Vexation* builds upon traditional drawing pencils and woodwork together with modern electronics. I made a moving wooden cylinder on which I drew marks using pencils with different-sized leads. These pencil marks function as a score. The contact between the sound circuit and the pencil marks produces audible music. The cylinder can also be seen as a sculptural piece. Its cylindrical shape evokes my understanding of vexation - an endless circulation. In *Vexation,* I tried to collapse score and performance: The drawing in itself is the physical material that generates the tone. I am interested in transforming existing artworks, presenting them using new forms of notation or mechanical instruments, in order to raise the question: When does something become a different work of art?

http://www.earthlinginger.com

Meltings of the Heart Change Glacial Landscapes by Olivia Osborne (UK)

The ice domes represent both the environment in the form of glaciers and their defenselessness against climate change. In addition, they also represent the vulnerability of "frozen" human hearts, susceptible to melting. The salt symbolises the action of a xenobiotic tainting the environment. In the heart, it represents a powerful, evocative emotion that penetrates the organ, both through a chemical reaction. When this occurs, it leaves a tainted colour that is forever encapsulated within the environment and the heart, "trapped." The water that surges in and out represents the people who enter and leave our lives, both in the environment and in our hearts. Only a few powerful individuals or chemicals have the capacity to make an impression - or "love" - in this landscape. Their touch upon the impressionable, delicate emotions and susceptible landscapes remains there permanently, hybridising one another, interconnecting. These actions are represented by hydrophobic coloured dyes and paint.

https://oliviaosborne5.wixsite.com/oliviaosborneart/art-work

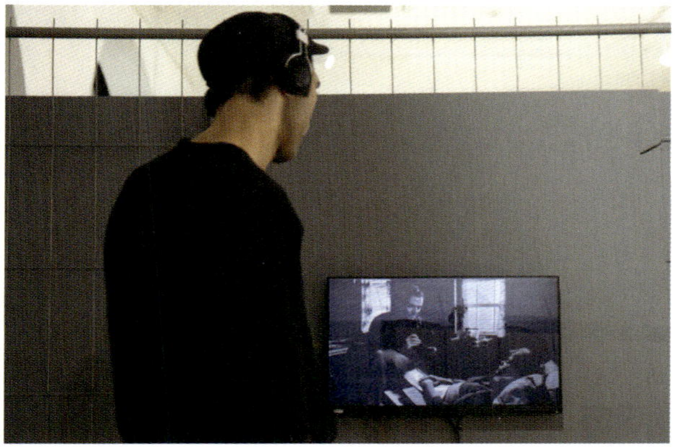

Figure 3: *Cyborg Portrait.* Kaplan, N. (2017). Video.

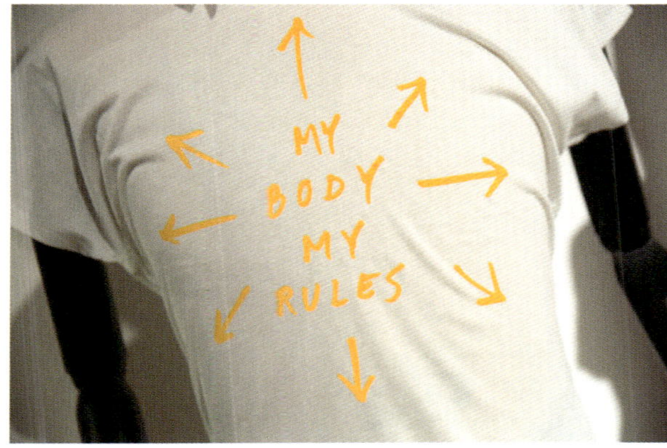

Figure 5: *Believe Campaign.* Tomorrow Girls' Troop. (2017). Performance.

Cyborg Portrait by Noa Kaplan (US)

Why do the female cyborgs defy the pattern? Using the four mysterious characters from the US television series Westworld as a starting point, I began an obsessive process of de-interlacing their narratives - by capturing and recutting each character's story arc so that I could watch each uninterrupted.

https://www.noapkaplan.com

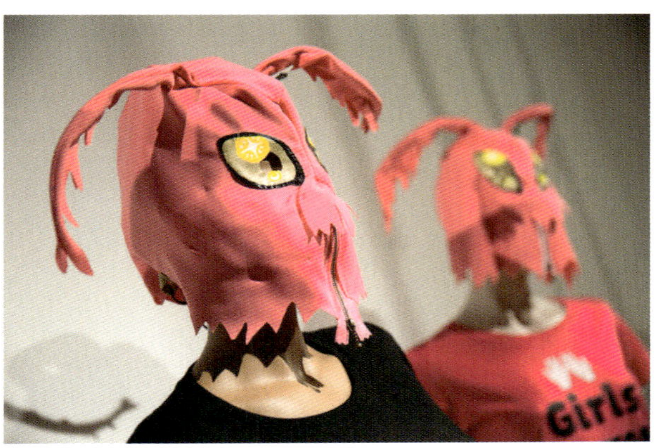

Figure 4: *Believe Campaign.* Tomorrow Girls' Troop. (2017). Performance.

Troop (JP/KR)

The Believe Campaign was launched to raise awareness of sexual violence in Japan and to demand modernisation of the penal law, which has not been modified since its establishment in 1907. The *Tomorrow Girls' Troop* contributed the design elements, targeting women in their 20s, and staged the art performance *Believe March* to demonstrate the public's demand for the amendments. Participants wore feather-shaped masks to maintain anonymity, with messages of support. The march was filmed and premiered in 2017 in Tokyo as part of a group show on socially engaged art (Figure 4 and 5).

https://tomorrowgirlstroop.com

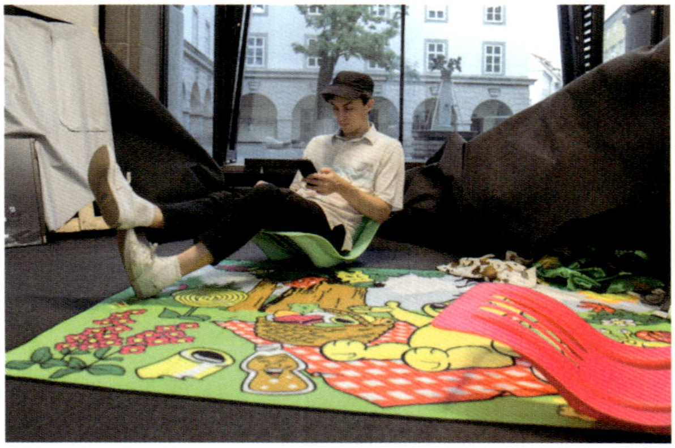

Figure 6: *Compliant Gait*. Brumley, J. (2017). Installation with social media.

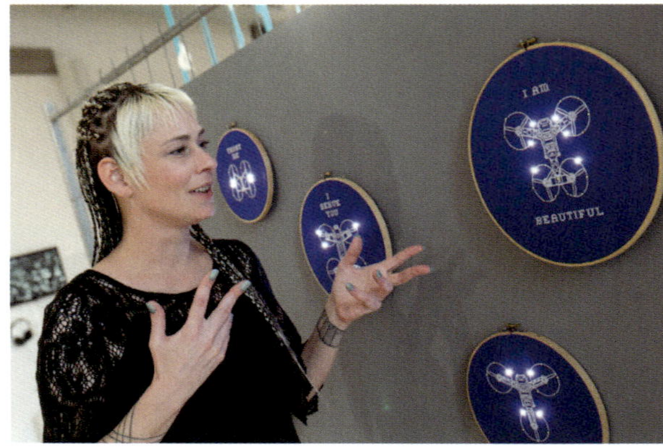

Figure 7: *Drones Sweet Drones*. Niemetz, A. (2017). Embroidered blueprints using Arduino-powered lights.

Compliant Gait by Sharmi Basu (US) and John Brumley (US)

Digital bodies are constructed through the various gestures, data and objects we release into virtual space. Our own digital labours maintain such beings, and it is only through constant engagement with social media that the elusive memories of our own selves momentarily breach into the feeds of our followers and friends. As such, the corporate filters imposed by the apps that support and display our patchwork bodies partially imbue our digital selves with branding via watermarks, limited distribution, and licensing. In *Compliant Gait*, an invisible creature is given temporary form through the labour of an audience. After connecting to a local wireless network, audience members can use their mobile phones to instantiate digital objects within the hull of the creature. One by one, these objects fill the hollow shape of the creature's body, revealing its form as it moves with a compliant gait across a barren landscape.

https://www.sharmi.info/recent-upcoming

Drones Sweet Drones by Anne Niemetz (NZ)

Home Sweet Home was an expression that was popular with troops on both sides of the American civil war, and through the glorification of drones, the installation aims to open up discussion about the uses of drone technology. As embroidered blueprints using Arduino-powered lights, the aesthetic of the drones combines techniques associated with the past and the future, art and science, the amateur and the professional, and the feminine and the masculine. The blueprint text prompts us to further consider the potential of drones, as well as the gendered logics under which they operate. *Drones Sweet Drones* is purposely conspicuous rather than stealthy. Turning surveillance on its head, it wants us to study the fly on the wall that is becoming a greater part of our lives.

https://adime.de/

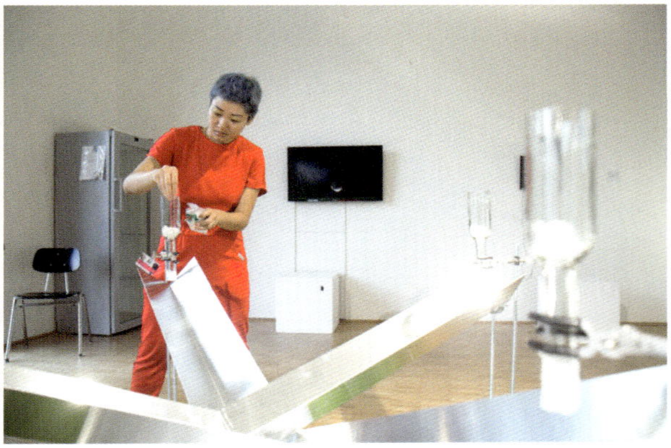

Figure 8: *Molecular Queering.* Tsang, M.M. and Rich, B. (2017).

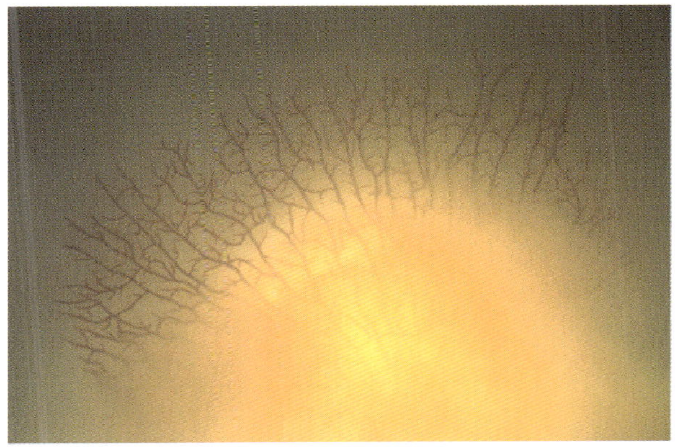

Figure 9: *TyndallLandscapes.* Blaik, R. (2017).

Molecular Queering by Mary Maggic Tsang (US), Byron Rich (CA)

Bodies queer in many ways, most actively through the molecular colonisation of our planet. Thanks to petrochemical, agricultural and pharmaceutical industries (markers of our anthropogenic time), these queering molecules are hormonally active and bio-politically pervasive as a state of toxicity. Our bodies and bodies of non-human species are all undergoing a collective mutagenesis - our kin are both the intersex frogs as well as the gender-bending chemicals in their bloodstream. So what does it mean to identify with our chemically induced world? To create discourse that turns toxic shame into toxic embrace? Am I not only inheriting the genomes of my parents but also the plastic molecules my mother is exposed to as I incubate in her womb? It is with this queering power of xeno-biochemicals that the *Molecular Queering* workshop performs a urine hormone extraction and analysis, a DIY/DIWO recipe for gender-hacking. Bring your own urine!

https://maggic.ooo/About
https://byronrich.com

TyndallLandscapes by Rita Blaik (US)

TyndallLandscapes is the creation of artificial skyscape sculptures utilising nanoparticles as the primary means of scattering light. These sunsets invite the viewers to contemplate as one might contemplate an actual sunset. They are also presented with the concentration of the nanoparticles used to create the "sunset" and show the analogous, parts-per-million concentrations of highly polluted cities where particulate concentrations are so high as to cause serious health complications. The emergence of nanoparticles as a technology so promising for technological and societal advance, also comes with negative effects on our health and the environment. These are difficult to study due to the size-specific effects and traits of nanomaterials.

https://ritablaik.com

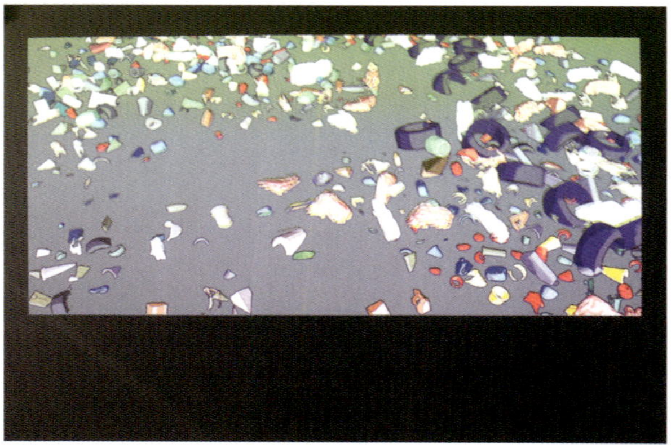

Figure 10: *Panta Rei (Everything Flows).* Rigon, S. (2017). Video.

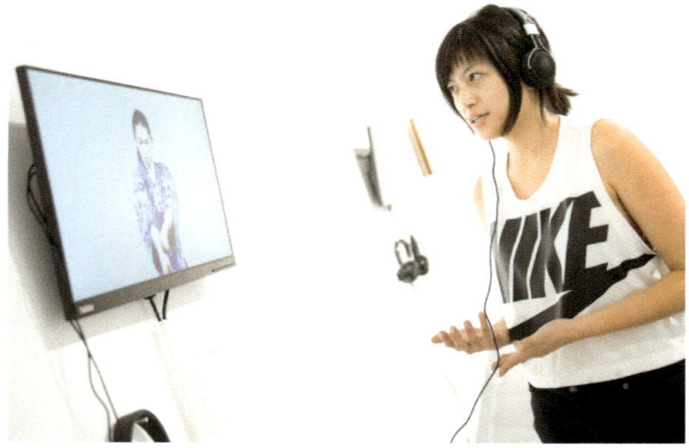

Figure 11: *Prologue.* Xin, X. (2017). Video.

Panta Rei (Everything Flows) by Silvia Rigon (IT)

Inspired by real media news events, *Panta Rei* is a socio-political commentary on the desensitising effects of the media, but also a metaphor of the passage we are facing epochally, with water at the center of the struggle for sustainability and survival, and the choices we make - or fail to make.

http://www.silviarigon.com/#/pantarei/

Prologue by Xin Xin (US/TW)

Prologue questions whether the decentralisation of surveillance software tools, created by governments, corporations and institutions to manipulate our relationship with politics, can undermine the individual's sense of responsibility toward themselves and others. It also questions whether sovereignty can possibly be achieved without centralised protocols.

https://www.newschool.edu/parsons/faculty/xin-xin/

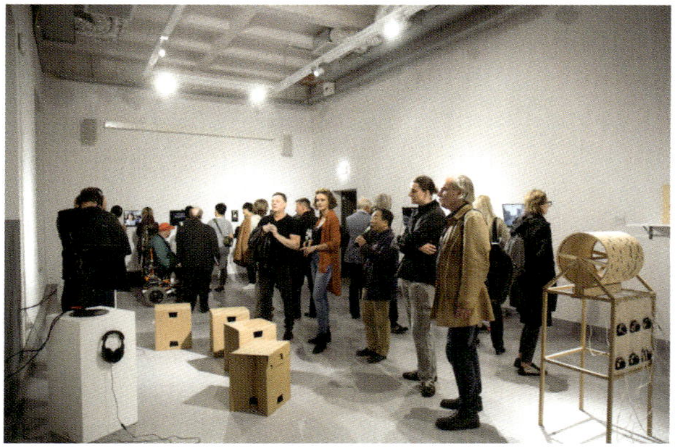

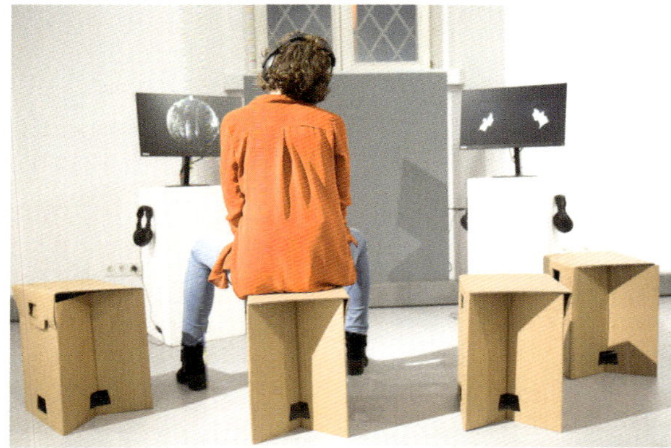

Figure 12 and 13: Images fron the exhibition, *Feminist Climate Change: Beyond the Binary.* (2017). Ars Electronica, Austria.

Other Artists in the show included:

Extreme Environments Arts-Based Field Research by Scott Hessels (US)
Dirt by Christina Agapakis (US), Ellie Harmon (US)
Cyborg Portrait by Noa Kaplan (US)
Xerodrome by Christopher O'Leary (US)
Fog Light by Doug Smarch (CA)
Light Echoes by Aaron Koblin (US)
The Antmaster by Ben Tricklebank (US), Gil Kuno (US/JP)
Oh Dear Me (Documentation) by Knifeandfork (US)
Follower by Lauren McCarthy (US)
In Passing by A.M. Darke (US)
Shapeshifting VoidLab by Nora Khan (US), Sarah Brady (US), Sanglim Han (KR), Jen Agosta (US)
Shadow Glass by *VoidLab* by Jen Agosta (US), Sanglim Han (KR), Xin Xin (US/TW)

All Photos: Tom Mesic.

Conclusion of the exhibition:

Feminist Climate Change as Living Archive

What *Feminist Climate Change: Beyond the Binary* offered in 2017– and what it continues to offer today – is a vision of solidarity that crosses binaries and borders. It reminds us that care is strength, that the feminine is a force of resistance, and that the future is neither gender-neutral nor politically inevitable.

As we face worsening climate and political conditions, we must return to the lessons of this exhibition – not as nostalgia, but as blueprints. The stories we tell, the networks we build, and the art we make are tools of survival. This is not just history. It is a living archive.

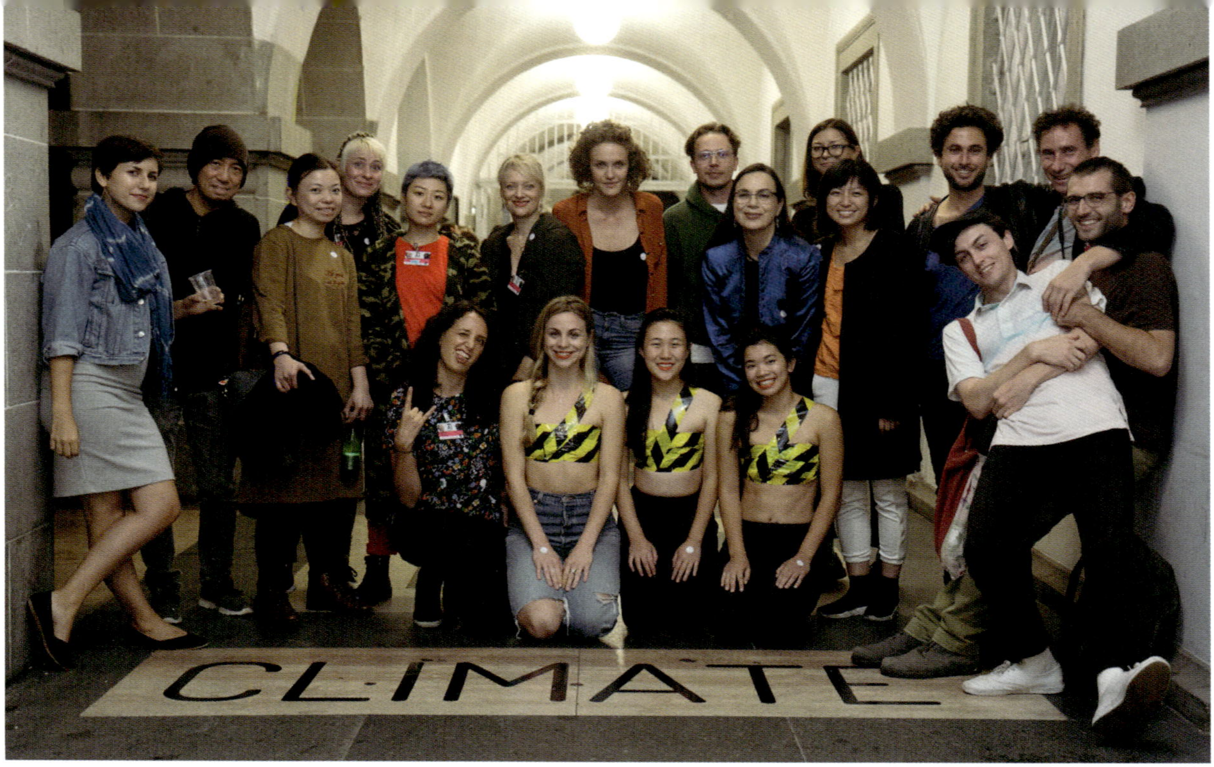

Figure 14: Artists in the exhibition.
Feminist Climate Change: Beyond the Binary (2017). Ars Electronica, Austria.
Photo: Tom Mesic.

References

- Ars Electronica. 2017. Feminist Climate Change: Beyond the Binary. Festival Archive. Available at: https://webarchive.ars.electronica.art/festival/2017/ai//en/index.html%3Fp=1491.html. [Accessed 22 May 2025].
- Ars Electronica. 2017. Feminist Climate Change: Beyond the Binary Panel. Festival Archive. Available at: https://webarchive.ars.electronica.art/festival/2017/ai//en/index.html%3Fp=3015.html. (Accessed 22 May 2025).
- Dewey-Hagborg, Heather. 2016. Kiss My Ars: On the Lack of Gender Diversity in Ars Electronica's Awards. Available at: [insert URL]. Accessed 22 May 2025.
- Federici, Silvia. 2004. Caliban and the Witch: Women, the Body and Primitive Accumulation. Autonomedia.
- Haraway, Donna J. 2016. Staying with the Trouble: Making Kin in the Chthulucene. Duke University Press.
- Merchant, Carolyn. 1980. The Death of Nature: Women, Ecology, and the Scientific Revolution. HarperOne.
- Shiva, Vandana. 1988. Staying Alive: Women, Ecology and Development. Zed Books.
- Thunberg, Greta. 2019. No One Is Too Small to Make a Difference. Penguin Books.
- Women in the Media Arts -Achive at Ars Electronica.
- https://ars.electronica.art/archive/en/women-in-media-arts/

CONVERSATIONS

BORDERLANDS IN THE SPACE OF ART-SCIENCE PRACTICE

Helen Pynor and Bigna Lenggenhager

In a conversation format, we suggest that art and science share aspects of the experiential process of creativity, including experiences of uncertainty and risk, and a reliance on presentiments, intuition, serendipity and synchronicity. Art and science sometimes share the same objects of study - for example, living entities. However, they use and produce different methodologies, outputs and criteria to assess the 'truth' or success of their work, and modes of criticality. Whilst they may borrow from each other, this borrowing is not "symmetrical". This conversation explores these issues from our perspectives - as an artist first trained and practising in science, and a scientist whose research extends beyond traditional scientific scopes - considering how our interdisciplinary backgrounds, practices and gender influence, facilitate, deepen and channel our artistic, scientific and art-science work. We contextualise our experience within a broader frame of artistic and scientific practice, recognising the centrality of intuition, serendipity and other 'chaotic' forces as engines powering the 'logical' progression of science. Our work challenges and exposes the unworkability of certain binaries in Western conceptions of selfhood, including life - death, self - other, male - female, embodied - disembodied, objectivity - subjectivity and human - nonhuman. Through our art and science practice, we trouble the convenience and certitude of these binaries, highlighting the uncertainty of hazy boundaries and complex transitional states.

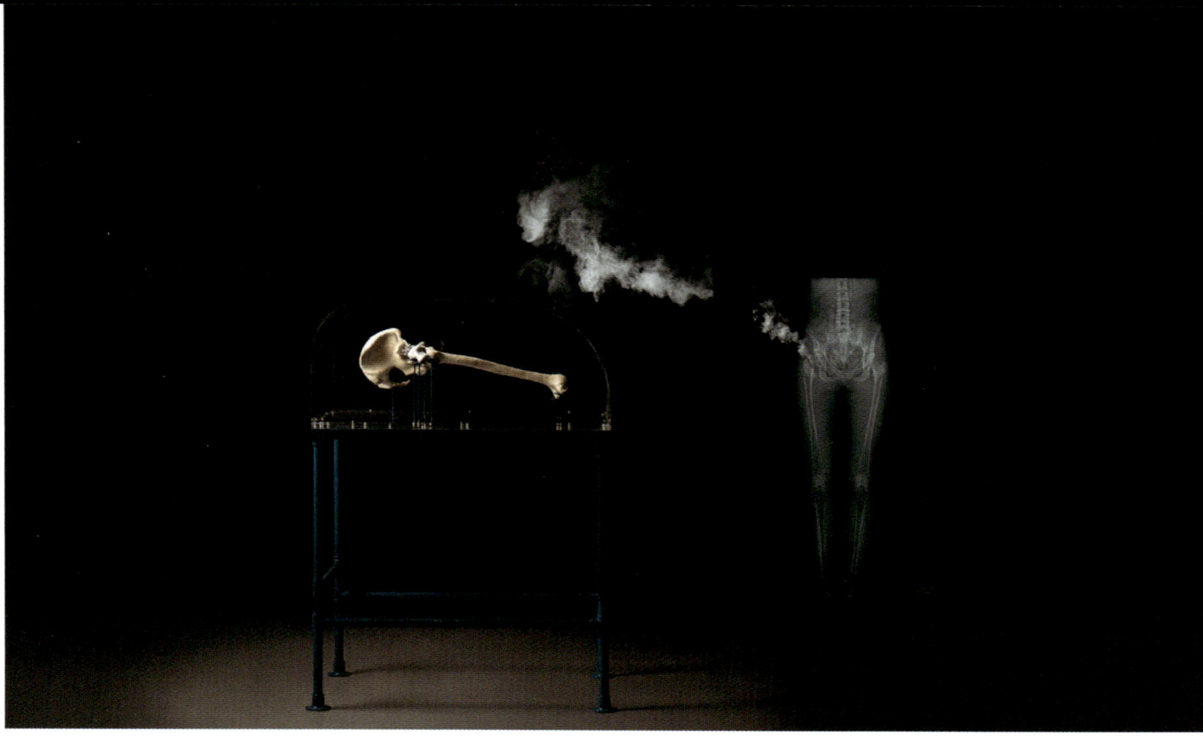

Figure 1: *Habitation*. Pynor, H. (2021). Unglazed bone china (made from the artist's bone removed during surgery, supplemented by animal bone), unglazed earthenware, felt, coral, metal, acrylic, archival pigment prints (drawn from the artist's own archive of CT and X-Ray scans), lightboxes. Dimensions variable. Photo: Helen Pynor.

UNCERTAINTY, INTUITION AND SERENDIPITY IN SCIENTIFIC AND ARTISTIC PRACTICE

Bigna Uncertainty is both fascinating and powerful. Though humans are naturally inclined to avoid it, seeing it as threatening, destabilising, and draining, it underpins exploration, learning, innovation, and change. In my psychotherapy training, we explored the value of "not knowing yet" as vital for both therapist and patient. While many traditional approaches seek to resolve uncertainty quickly, system-based approaches highlight how uncertainty and stochastic processes can benefit therapy. Recognising the role of uncertainty is crucial in art, science, and psychotherapy. I believe that enduring this state of uncertainty - and allowing time for doubt - plays a key role in fostering exploration, discovery and progress.

Helen It's interesting to think about uncertainty in the context of our personal lives and how deeply uncomfortable it is to live with it. I'm thinking about a work I made a few years ago, *Habitation* (2021) that was in part my response to dealing with rapid change and the uncertainties that accompanied it (Figure 1). In the work, I made a bone china object from bone that was surgically removed from my body during hip replacement surgery (and other images and objects). In a book chapter I wrote more recently, I explored the process of working with the bone as a vehicle to facilitate an exploration and integration of the radical bodily transformation I was experiencing – the visceral forcefulness of the surgery and the long, incremental rehabilitation process afterward (Pynor, 2024). I was interested in how artmaking can function as a form of "ritual making," supporting people to cope with uncertainty and change. I dipped briefly into the anthropological literature around "rites of passage" as "technologies" that create structures of support and safety through significant life uncertainty and transformation, mitigating the risks and anxieties that accompany such change (Stenner and Zittoun, 2020). Although it may not be framed in such terms, I think artmaking frequently assumes a kind of 'ritual making' that supports such processes.

Bigna Yes, I believe these aspects are more transparent in artistic work than in science. However, recent years have seen a shift in how scientific practice is understood, with growing recognition that it involves trials, errors, and unpredictability. Traditionally, only final, polished, often positive results were published, contributing to the replication crisis, (Open Science Collaboration, 2015) – especially in psychology, where many findings have failed to replicate. This has prompted efforts to improve research practices. One example is "pre-registration," which I and many others now use. By outlining a study's framework and hypotheses in advance, pre-registration increases transparency, showing which hypotheses remain unconfirmed and which ideas go unexplored. Furthermore, it highlights the exploratory nature of research by revealing that some of the most interesting findings often emerge unexpectedly, rather than from pre-planned predictions. Pre-registration helps expose the full scientific process, including its trial-and-error phases, and stochastic elements. Still, I believe science could go further in acknowledging this complexity. One reason some experiments fail to replicate under different conditions – such as in a new lab or at another time – may be an overestimation of our ability to control all experimental variables. There is likely much "noise" and randomness influencing results in ways we don't fully grasp. Embracing this complexity could help us better navigate the uncertainties of scientific discovery.

Helen I have not heard of the term "replication crisis" but I feel like it gets to the heart of how much uncertainty there is in science. This is like the "unconscious" of science – science needs to find stable truths to progress and build knowledge, but it doesn't fully acknowledge how much uncertainty is inherent in the process. I am not just referring to unexplored areas of research; I also mean the areas that have already been "worked out," yet still contain vast areas of uncertainty. These types of uncertainties don't result from a lack of rigour or from sloppiness, but rather because, particularly in the life sciences, life has so much elasticity, complexity and compensatory capacity that it's very difficult to pin down everything in the way science demands. Uncertainty is often viewed as a flaw, but perhaps it simply reflects the fact that the things we're studying are way too complex to be as objective as we strive to be, with the tools we currently have.

I'm now working on a project with a number of early career scientists from four science labs across Europe, studying the epigenetic control of

DNA replication at the earliest stages of life, from the single-celled zygote to the 4-cell stage (Replifate, 2025). The molecular processes taking place during DNA replication are happening at flickering speeds, with a dynamism and complexity beyond human perception and almost beyond human imagination. What is striking is the large degree of stochasticity in the process. Whilst the broader process of DNA replication happens in a predictable fashion, at a detailed molecular level there are significant variations in how the process proceeds, layers of unpredictability, and molecular compensatory mechanisms to address more extreme deviations. This complexity and stochasticity present profound challenges when attempting to describe these processes at a detailed level in traditional mechanistic terms.

We're both interested in the role of intuition and serendipity in both scientific and artistic practices, that highlight the creative and often unpredictable nature of these practices. The Nobel Prize-winning biologist François Jacob distinguishes between "day science" and "night science," where the former represents organised, public knowledge, and the latter refers to the messy, intuition-driven process of idea formation. Jacob describes his experiences of wandering blindly, doubting everything, experiencing "vague presentiments" and "hazy sensations" accompanied by night sweats and anxieties, emphasising the role of instinct and intuition over logic (Jacob, 1995, pp. 296-7). His description mirrors my own experience during the early stages of creating artworks, where an initial clear vision often gives way to uncertainty and anxiety when I realise the idea needs 'more'. When I open up to experimentation, unexpected insights emerge during the making process through the embodied, experiential encounter between my ideas, my body, other people I'm in dialogue with, and the materials and processes I'm using to make the work. This process is part intentional experimentation, part uncontrolled collisions of human, non-human and inanimate forces, in which serendipity and stochasticity play a huge part. Through this process I can eventually find an outcome far more complex and coherent than the original idea. Perhaps both artists and scientists share comparable creative struggle during their work's emergence.

Bigna I absolutely love your description of this process, and I find the concept of "day science" and "night science" very compelling. While the "dark" aspects of night science might feel less familiar to me, the "messy" and intuitive elements resonate strongly. We could also conceptualise it as the more female side of science. This part of the process - the hunches, the trial-and-error, and the seemingly chaotic moments that might lead to breakthroughs - is something I relate to in my own work. As I've mentioned before, I think it's crucial to talk more openly about this side of science. I think we're slowly moving towards scientists acknowledging these more ambiguous areas of practice, perhaps more in my field than some other fields. My hope would also be that with women being increasingly influential in science this insight might naturally grow.

THE SUBJECTIVE NATURE OF SCIENTIFIC AND ARTISTIC RESEARCH AND PRACTICE

Bigna Another often-overlooked aspect of classical research is the inherent subjectivity within scientific practice, despite its objective goals. Science is conducted by humans, who inevitably bring their perspectives, biases, and experiences into the process. Personal interests, cultural context, and societal priorities often shape the topics researchers pursue, the questions they ask, and the methods they use. Even in structured experiments, subjective judgment influences data interpretation, follow-up questions, and how results are communicated. In psychology and neuroscience, bias arises not only from researchers but also from the participant samples, which often come from WEIRD populations - Western, Educated, Industrialised, Rich, and Democratic (Henrich et al., 2010). While "male" wasn't specified in that term, many disciplines, especially medical science, have long overrepresented male participants, leading to misdiagnosis and inadequate treatment for women. As a psychology student, I had to participate in studies for credit, yet as a left-handed woman, I was often excluded because many experiments focused solely on right-handed men. This was justified by avoiding variables like hormonal cycles or brain organisation differences. But such selective sampling undermines the validity of findings and limits our understanding of human behaviour by failing to reflect the diversity of lived experience.

Helen Yes, there have been powerful feminist critiques of science that acknowledge these kinds of methodological issues, for example the "situated" nature of scientific knowledge - its dependence on the very particular and located circumstances under which it is produced (Haraway, 1988). On another tangent, Susan Oyama and Evelyn Fox Keller have written extensively on the role that similes and metaphors have played in the perpetuation of largely unexamined assumptions in the biological sciences, some of which have overt gender biases (Keller, 1995; Oyama, 2000). Oyama points out that oppositions such as "autonomy versus connection, central control versus distributed control, and nucleus versus cytoplasm have rich metaphorical associations that are not scientifically or socially inert" (Oyama, 2000, p. 126). It is also interesting to think about subjectivity in artmaking, and modes of assessing the "success" of artworks, that operate so differently compared to science. As I have described above, when I'm making work my initial attempts often feel lacklustre or flat. But at some point, there will be a sudden small insight or spark: something will speak to me and I'll know it's interesting, but it would be hard to define why it's interesting - it somehow excites my nervous system and I feel excited, engaged and present, like disparate or misaligned elements have somehow snapped into alignment and are now speaking clearly to me. That becomes a direction to follow, then at some stage I'll realise, "this language is working". The following stages then become about crafting and refining the language rather than creating it, which is a more straightforward, but never-the-less an intricated process.

Bigna I'm a bit curious: You say that you know when it "works." Is that true for you, personally? Or do you think that if it works for you, it works for others as well?

Helen I think that if it works for me, it usually works for others as well, with the caveat that people have different tastes - some people will connect with my work and others not. But if I know a piece I've made is 'working' then it's likely to connect with audiences too. I imagine successful artworks offer some kind of satisfying calibration and alignment between the stimulation of cognition (through ideas) and our senses (the sensorial and perceptual). However there are still large terrains of subjectivity in the assessment of "quality" in artworks, and connecting with some works depends on familiarity with the disciplinary or cultural discussions underlying them.

Bigna The question of how we assess quality - and how this differs between art and science - is a fascinating one. In art, as you have described, there's often a subjective yet intuitive sense of whether something "works." This feeling, while personal to the artist, often aligns with how audiences respond. It reflects a paradoxical mix of subjectivity and objectivity. Science, by contrast, relies on more formal evaluation methods - like the p-value to assess statistical significance and determine whether a hypothesis is supported. Though seemingly more objective, the p-value has faced widespread criticism, raising doubts about its reliability as a marker of success. Part of the difference may lie in the relationship between creator and creation. Art is often deeply personal and visibly tied to the artist's voice and style, while scientific papers are designed to appear detached and objective. You might instantly recognise an artist through their work, but rarely a scientist through their paper.

SCIENTIFIC SPECULATION AND IMAGINATION

Helen I once had a conversation with a Director at a Max Planck Institute where I was working, who reflected on changes in scientific practice since the 1960s. She commented that in her early career there was much more room for speculation in scientific papers, which had much lengthier discussions, whilst the emphasis today is much more on methodology and results. She felt that PhD students now, with their access to complex analytic tools in molecular biology, are more like technicians than speculative thinkers, focused on getting these complex tools to function as needed. She even wryly commented that the introduction of GFP (Green Fluorescent Protein), so ubiquitous as a tool in molecular biology, may have actually hindered scientific imagination by shifting the focus to technological tools at the expense of creative thinking. There is a lot of pressure on early career scientists to produce results and publish, which may have also contributed to this trend.

Bigna Yes, I completely agree. Much of this issue stems from how the system is structured and the intense pressure on students and early-career scientists. The scientific process is often messy and unpredictable, yet the system prioritises efficiency and measurable outcomes over exploration and creativity. We need more space for curiosity-driven and speculative thinking in both training and professional practice. I love the example of my mentor, Peter Brugger, a brilliant neuropsychologist, who as a PhD student would spend one day a week in the library reading a random book from any discipline for inspiration. His approach shows how randomness and serendipity can fuel science - yet such opportunities are rarely encouraged today. There's generally less time for broad, imaginative, or interdisciplinary thinking.

TRANSITIONAL STATES: METHODOLOGIES IN LIMINAL SPACES

Bigna I believe exploratory and speculative thinking is especially important in research that challenges conventional understanding - such as transitional states like out-of-body experiences (OBEs) and near-death experiences (NDEs), which we've both studied. For me, it's crucial to uphold scientific rigour while staying open to alternative ideas, even those that may initially seem "unscientific." For example, while the notion of a "soul" leaving the body during an OBE lacks scientific support, my own research has linked such experiences to altered brain activity and disrupted multisensory integration (Lenggenhager et al., 2007). Still, I believe we shouldn't dismiss alternative views outright, especially when current methods can't definitively disprove them. Acknowledging the limitations and subjectivity of our tools helps us stay open-minded while exploring these phenomena within a scientific framework.

Helen I admire your openness in taking a position of "agnosticism," with respect to questions that can't be definitively answered with scientific tools, whilst also bringing scientific methods to questions that can, even in speculative areas like OBEs. To me, your stance expresses a humility about science's limitations that scientists don't always exhibit. Many scientists argue that if a phenomenon can't be substantiated scientifically, then it mustn't exist - which I think is very unscientific. It may simply reflect the fact that we don't yet have the tools.

My practice explores the materiality of human and non-human bodies, especially ambiguous border zones such as life-death, organ transplantation, prosthetics, and human/non-human subjectivity. I use living and semi-living entities - cells, organs and biomolecules - often collaborating with scientific institutions and using scientific technologies and methodologies to address philosophical questions. For example, works like *The Body is a Big Place* (Figure 2) and *The End is a Distant Memory* (Figures 3, 4) examine the boundaries of life and death, using techniques like heart perfusion and tissue culture to challenge our perceptions of life and mortality. Trained in cell and molecular biology, my "bioart" practice is influenced by pioneers in the field such as Oron Catts and Ionat Zurr, focusing on the actual "presentation" of living entities rather than their representation in traditional art forms. My work uses living entities to prompt ethical and ontological reflections on the complexities of life, death and existence, in ways that more traditional representational approaches could not.

One question I've asked myself is whether this attachment and commitment to exploring and presenting the "real" capacities of living entities is a vestige of my science training. This aspect fascinates me more than working with "representations" of life, despite the additional freedoms representational modes offer. This isn't an attachment to

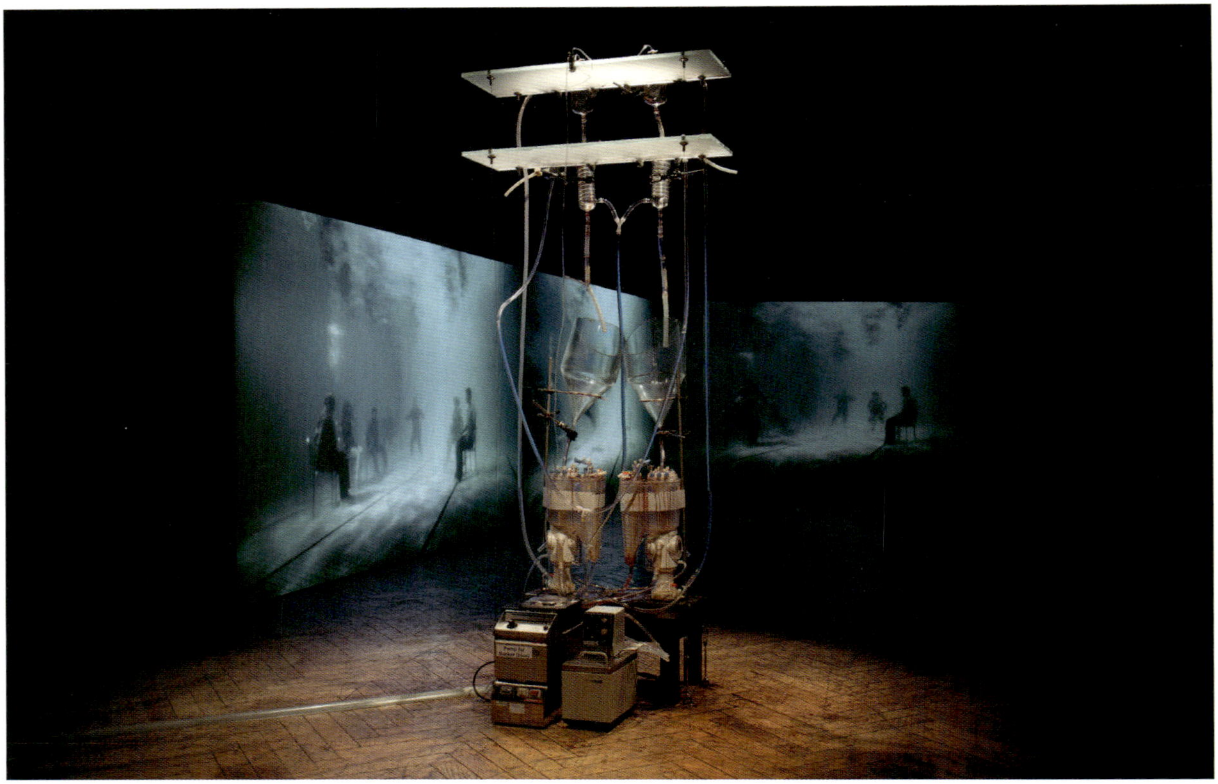

Figure 2: *The Body is a Big Place.* Pynor, H. and Clancy, P. (2013). 3-channel video projection, heart perfusion device, live heart perfusion performance, single-channel video on monitor, soundscape by Gail Priest.
Photo: Miha Fras.

the empirical, which is an epistemological issue. It's closer to a commitment to ontological enquiry - what is the actual nature of living entities? - a question shared by scientists.

Bigna On my side, there's perhaps a mirror effect - my scientific work has been shaped by interactions with artists. In studying transitional states, such as the fluid boundaries of self-other distinction (Roel Lesur et al., 2020), I've found that engaging with the lived experience of these states can greatly enrich the research process. While firsthand experience isn't always necessary, this experiential, exploratory element often leads to new insights. At my former lab at the University of Zurich, we created a "phenomenological playground" - a space for free experimentation outside formal protocols. We tested virtual reality, multisensory stimulation, hypnosis, and other techniques on ourselves, simply to explore what felt most intriguing. These playful sessions helped refine our research questions and often sparked unexpected ideas - closely connected to the "night science" phase of research.

<u>Helen</u> I find your "playground" methodology fascinating and inspiring. It parallels how many artists work, and I wonder whether it could apply to other branches of science too? Mycologist Merlin Sheldrake describes a Cambridge University study on the effects of psychotropic drugs such as LSD on scientific problem-solving. Scientists were asked to consider a difficult problem in their own research whilst under the influence of LSD. Sheldrake, who was grappling with a complex issue around plant-fungal relationships, participated. Although the experience didn't lead to any direct scientific insights, it immersed him in a vivid, sensorial "experience" of soil's complexity. This altered perspective helped him approach his problem more dynamically, rather than through rigid, mechanistic models. Sheldrake emphasises the value of scientific imagination, where subjectivity can lead to insights that complement traditional, systematic scientific methods (Kanowski and Sheldrake, 2021).

<u>Bigna</u> As mentioned earlier, scientific practice has evolved, with growing emphasis on individual differences and recognition of heterogeneity. Traditional studies focused on group averages, but newer statistical methods now support more individualised analyses, renewing interest in subjective measures - especially in psychology. Tools like neurophenomenological interviews prioritise individual experience, and I've increasingly integrated qualitative methods alongside psychometric and psychophysiological tools. I'm particularly drawn to co-design, especially when transparently documented in publications. In an ongoing project, I'm collaborating with researchers in psychiatry, neuroscience, and human-computer

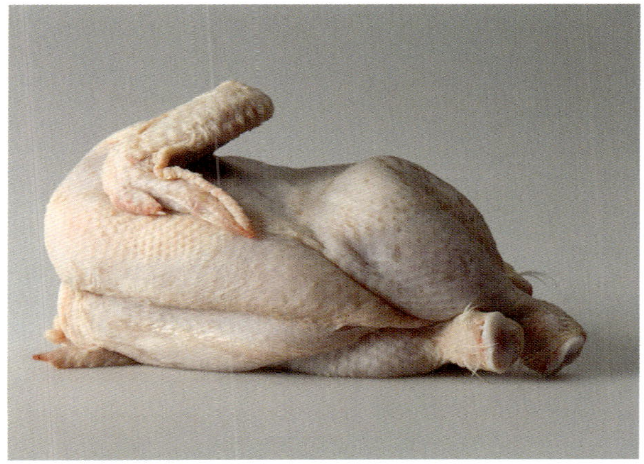

Figure 3: *The End is a Distant Memory*. Pynor, H. (2016). Archival pigment print, 80 x 120cm. Installation: 6 single-channel video with sound (various durations), photographs, glass. Sound by James Brown. Image courtesy of the artist and Dominik Mersch Gallery, Sydney.

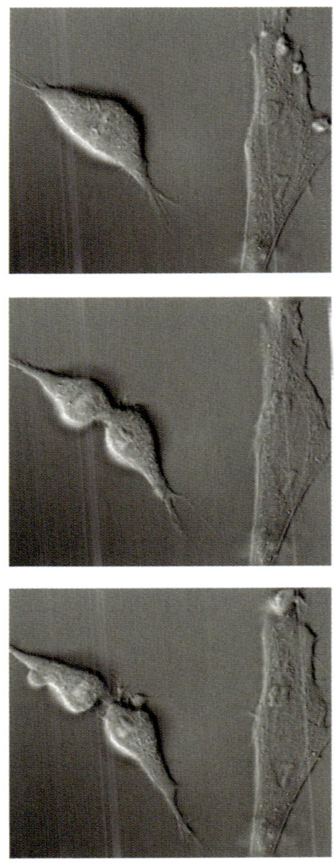

Figure 4: *The End is a Distant Memory*. Pynor, H. (2016). Video stills, time-lapse microscopy images of chicken fibroblast cells, growing and dividing in culture. Cells were extracted from chicken meat bought at a supermarket, and subsequently grown in culture using tissue culture techniques. Installation: 6 single-channel videos with sound (various durations), photographs, glass. Sound: James Brown. Image courtesy of the artist and Dominik Mersch Gallery, Sydney.

interaction to develop a clinical intervention using generative AI and virtual reality. It allows participants to engage in embodied self-dialogue with their younger selves, shifting perspectives to foster self-compassion. We used an iterative co-design process involving patients, clinicians, and our interdisciplinary team, and documented it in detail (see *Power of Two:* https://poweroftwo.me (Figure 5). Such approaches enhance transparency and help bridge subjective experience with scientific rigour, enriching the research process.

ASYMMETRIES IN ART-SCIENCE PRACTICES

Helen Having collaborated extensively with scientists and knowing many other artists who also have, it's rare for scientists to acknowledge that artistic methodologies have anything directly useful for them in terms of concrete scientific outputs. I think scientists generally love the stimulation to thought, and I'm sure some of these conversations have influenced their thinking and may have led to less tangible outcomes. Nicola Triscott's concept of co-inquiry offers an inspiring model for how artists and scientists might "co-investigate" the same problem or subject using different tools, with the osmosis between these parallel inquiries offering insights across disciplinary divides (Triscott, 2017). But generally, there's an asymmetry: artists often gain core conceptual and practice-based content that they need and deploy for the production of artworks, whereas for scientists, it's usually viewed as an optional, nice-to-have extra, rather than something that would foundationally affect their methodology or publishing outputs. There are notable exceptions such as artist/scientist Brandon Ballengée who publishes extensively in scientific literature.

Bigna I completely agree with your observation. In one of our studies on alternative embodiment in VR, we conducted experiments using artistic tools in a museum setting. In this paper, we also discussed the challenges, hierarchies, and asymmetries that can arise in such collaborations (Roel Lesur et al., 2020). Recognising and addressing these dynamics will be crucial for future art-science partnerships. From my own experience, collaborating with artists has fundamentally shifted my perspective on scientific research. It has deepened my interest in the "interindividual" and the subjectivity of phenomena – areas often underexplored in traditional scientific methodologies. I believe there's immense potential for science to benefit from artistic approaches – not just in terms of inspiration, but to challenge and expand our methods and frameworks. These collaborations can serve as a feedback loop, where artistic outputs not only stimulate curiosity but also inform scientific processes in meaningful ways. By integrating artistic tools and perspectives, we might uncover new ways to approach research questions, interpret data, and engage with the complexity of human experience.

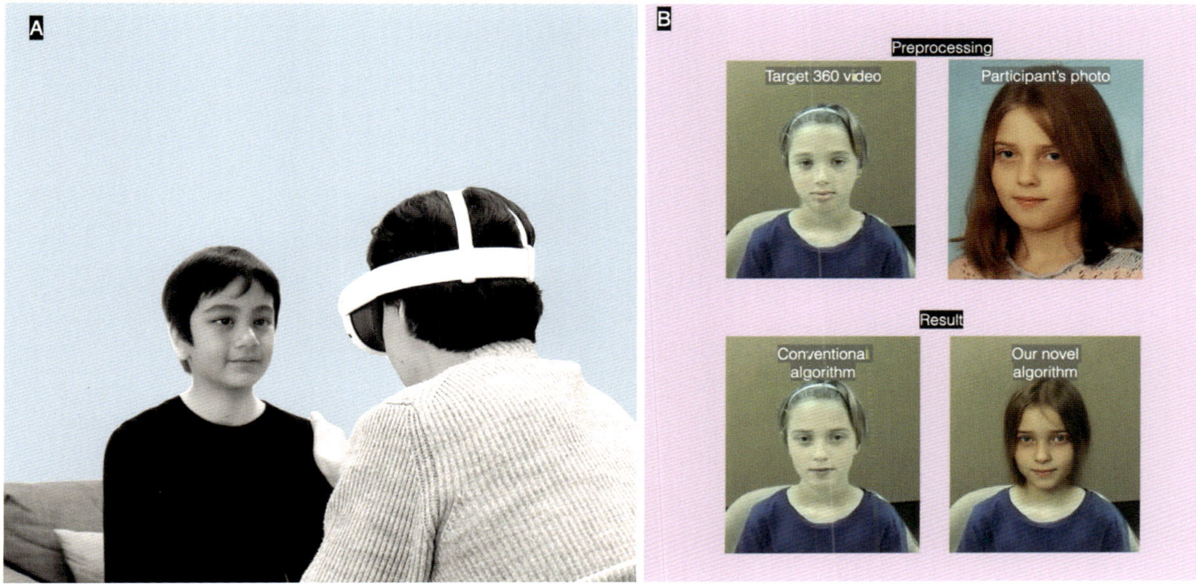

Figure 5: Shows the setup of the AI and VR based self-compassion intervention which was developed in a co-design process with researchers, artists, psychotherapists and a patient in a joint initiative between the University of Zurich and the ZHdK. (see https://poweroftwo.me/ for further information).
A. depicts a participant wearing a VR headset comforting a younger version of himself. Later, the participant will see his adult self comforting him while the touch is mimicked by the experimenter.
B. shows the new algorithm developed to apply the *Deepfake* on the video of a child, based on the participant's childhood picture. Where traditional *Deepfake* techniques only replace the face and leave the hair, head shape, and facial expression unchanged (left side), this new approach completely regenerates the head from scratch based on the input image as well as text cues (right side). The result is a hyperrealistic replica, offering full control over its facial expression.

Acknowledgements

Bigna Bigna would like to thank all her amazing collaborators and co-authors - far too many to list individually - for going with her through both the messy and the shiny parts of the research process. A special thanks goes to Marte Roel Lesur and Paulina Zybinska, the principal investigators of the ME^2 project, for the inspiring collaboration on this ongoing art-science exploration.

Helen Helen wishes to thank all collaborators on the projects discussed in this chapter.

Collaborators and funding partners:

Habitation - Display cabinet design: Anna Tregloan. An Experimenta Commission. Funding partners: Creative Australia; City of Joondalup, Perth, Australia.

The Body is a Big Place - Collaborating scientists and clinicians: Professor John Headrick and Dr. Jason Peart, Heart Foundation Research Centre, Griffith University, Queensland, Australia; Professor Michael Shattock, Cardiovascular Division, King's College London; Dr. Kumud Dhital, Dr. Arjun Iyer and Jonathan Cropper, St Vincent's Hospital, Sydney, and the Victor Chang Cardiac Research Institute, Sydney; Dr. Gorazd Drevensek, Institute of Pharmacology, University of Ljubljana, Slovenia. Funding partners: Creative Australia; ANAT (Australian Network for Art and Technology); Create NSW.

The End is a Distant Memory - Collaborating scientists: Dr. Jochen Rink, Dr. Britta Schroth-Diez and Dr. Jan Peychl, Max Planck Institute of Molecular Cell Biology and Genetics, Dresden. Performance co-devising: performers, Branch Nebula (Lee Wilson and Mirabelle Wouters), Alejandro Rolandi and Rohan Thomas. Funding partners: Creative Australia; FACT (Foundation for Art and Creative Technology), Liverpool, UK.

LASERZURICH Sharing common themes brings art and science together in Zurich. Switzerland. These authors met at *LASERZURICH* and their conversations continue! *Can Both Art and Science Explore the Limits of Out-of-Body or Nearly-Dead Experiences?* (2018) Prynor H. and Lenggenhager B. Moderation: Prof. Dr. Jill Scott. https://www.laserzurich.com.

References

- Haraway, D. 1988, 'Situated Knowledges: The Science Question in Feminism and the Privilege of Partial Perspective', Feminist Studies, 14(3), pp. 575-599, available at: https://philpapers.org/archive/harskt.pdf
- Henrich, J., Heine, S.J. & Norenzayan, A. 2010, 'Most people are not WEIRD', Nature, 466(7302), p. 29, available at: https://doi.org/10.1038/466029a
- Jacob, F. 1995, The Statue Within: An Autobiography, Cold Spring Harbor Laboratory Press, Plainview, New York, pp. 296-297.
- Kanowski, S. & Sheldrake, M. 2021, 'Fascinating fungi - the intelligent kingdom' [podcast], Conversations, available at: https://www.abc.net.au/listen/programs/conversations/merlin-sheldrake-the-world-of-fungi-wood-wide-web/13490878 [Accessed 14 April 2025].
- Keller, E.F. 1995, Refiguring Life: Metaphors of Twentieth-Century Biology, Columbia University Press, New York.
- Lenggenhager, B., Tadi, T., Metzinger, T. & Blanke, O. 2007, 'Video ergo sum: Manipulating bodily self-consciousness', Science, 317(5841), pp. 1096-1099, available at: https://doi.org/10.1126/science.1143439
- OPEN SCIENCE COLLABORATION 2015, 'Estimating the reproducibility of psychological science', Science, 349(6251), p. aac4716, available at: https://doi.org/10.1126/science.aac4716
- Oyama, S. 2000, Evolution's Eye: A Systems View of the Biology-Culture Divide, Duke University Press, Durham, pp. 126.
- Pynor, H. 2024, 'Tooth Fairies for Adults: Performing Ritual', in Bouchard, G. & Mermikides, A. (eds.), The Routledge Companion to Performance and Medicine, Routledge, London and New York, pp. 431-441.
- Replifate 2025, 'A European-based multidisciplinary, multi-institution consortium of researchers exploring epigenetic regulation of DNA replication, including three artists-in-residence', available at: https://replifate.eu/ [Accessed 14 April 2025].
- Roel Lesur, M., Lyn, S. & Lenggenhager, B. 2020, 'How Does Embodying a Transgender Narrative Influence Social Bias? An Explorative Study in an Artistic Context', Frontiers in Psychology, 11, available at: https://doi.org/10.3389/fpsyg.2020.01861
- Stenner, P. & Zittoun, T. 2020, 'On Taking a Leap of Faith: Art, Imagination, and Liminal Experiences', Journal of Theoretical and Philosophical Psychology, 40(4), pp. 240-263, available at: https://psycnet.apa.org/doiLanding?doi=10.1037%2Fteo0000148
- Triscott, N. 2017, Art and Intervention in the Stewardship of the Planetary Commons: Towards a Curatorial Model of Co-inquiry, PhD Thesis by Published Work, University of Westminster.

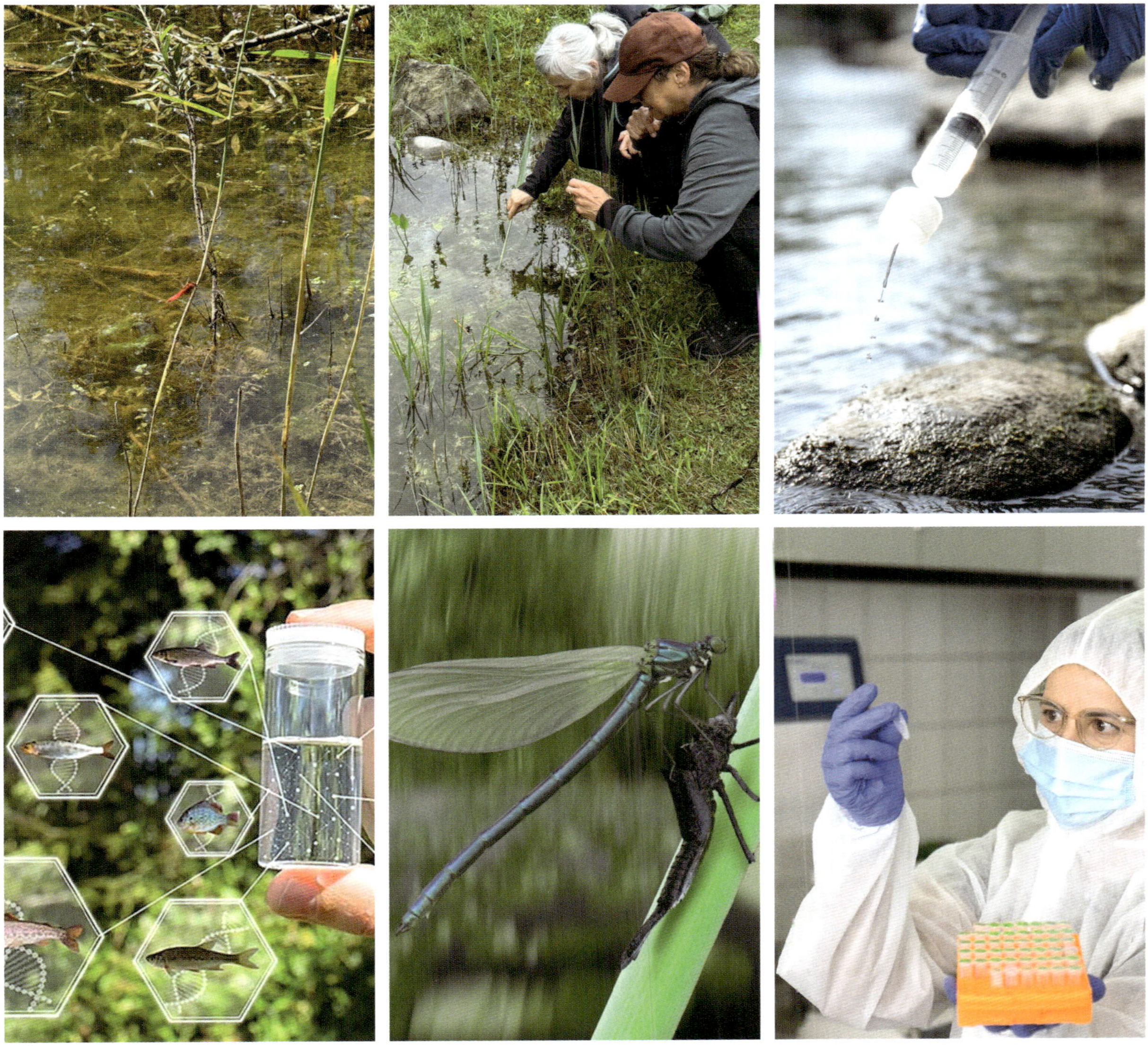

Workshop: *Biodiversity Lives Here: The Sampling of eDNA.* Scott, J. and Rust, D. with Deiner, K. from SimplexDNA, Winterthur, Switzerland. (2025). (See page 41).

THE BODY POLITICS OF A CYBERFEMINIST FROM SINGAPORE

Margaret Tan and Kathleen Ditzig

This chapter presents an interview conducted in Singapore between Margaret Tan and Kathleen Ditzig, focusing on Tan's evolution as a cyberfeminist artist in relation to the introduction of feminist theory in Singapore's art education and the nation's art history of critically engaging with technology. Cyberfeminism, coined in the early 1990s, describes feminists theorising, critiquing, exploring and re-making the Internet, cyberspace and technology (Seu, 2022). Tan's emergence as a noted cyberfeminist (since 1999) coincided with state investment in contemporary art, exemplified by the Renaissance City Plans (2000 – 2012), which sought to develop the cultural "hardware" and "software" positioning Singapore as a global arts city (National Library Board, n.d.). Associated with the "Lasalle School" – contemporary art practices rooted in critical theory from Lasalle-SIA College in the 1990s – Tan credits her relationship with scholars and curators, Professors Irina Aristarkhova and Gunalan Nadarajan, as instrumental in developing her feminist and new media art practice. In 2001 Vehicle Magazine identified Tan as an avant-garde artist advancing critical thought and interdisciplinary practice rooted in performance. Collaborators, including Faith Wilding on "Double/Shift: Maintenance Performance" (2001), saw Tan extend the critique of cybernetic technologies and neoliberalism in works like "Virtual Bodies in Reality" (2001) and "Smart Apron" (2004). This interview charts Tan's critical engagement with feminism, technology and globalisation, outlining the development of a cyberfeminist perspective in Singapore.

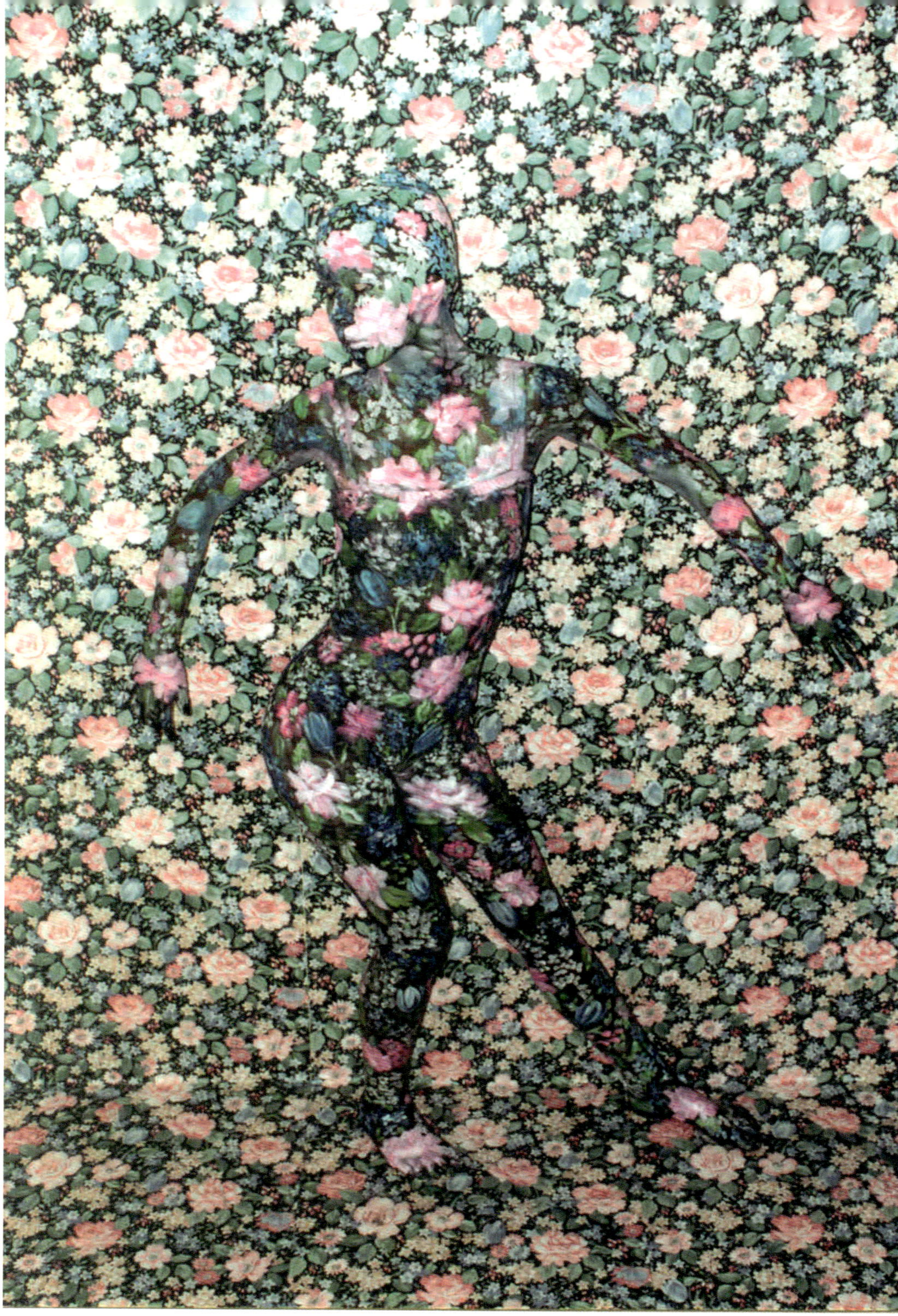

Figure 1: *Restless*. Tan, M. (1999). Performance, performed by Samantha Hutton. Image courtesy of the artist.

Interview: Feminism and Collaboration

Kathleen Margaret, you are known as one of Singapore's feminist artists to pioneer a robust interrogation of technology. You've said that your education at Lasalle-SIA College of the Arts (1996-2000) was pivotal in the formation of your practice as a feminist artist. In particular, you've spoken about the influence of Professor Irina Aristarkhova, and a *Feminist Art* workshop she ran in 1999 at the school that culminated in an exhibition and one-day symposium *A Self of One's Own*. Aristarkhova has mentioned that a key part of the class was to collaboratively engage with the concept of "woman" and its redefinition by thinkers and artists. Coming out of this workshop, the artwork that you presented at the exhibition was the 5-minute performance *Restless* (1999). It was a collaborative performance with Samantha Hutton. From this formative moment, how has collaboration been a refrain in your practice? How did you and how do you define your practice as feminist?

Margaret I was drawn to collaboration as a feminist strategy to subvert modernist art's positioning of the artist as a lone (white, male) genius. Historically, collaboration has also been a way to overcome limited resources and/or build camaraderie and solidarity. It has the potential to encourage openness, generosity and self-reflexivity. With *Restless*, I asked Samantha if she would allow me to paint her in the same print as a wallpaper that I had chosen and to perform with the wallpaper based on a simple script I provided (Figure 1).

With my later *Double/Shift: Maintenance Performance* (2001) with Faith Wilding, the collaboration was very enriching for my practice (Figure 4). Wilding generously shared her earlier scripts and was open to me making amendments and suggestions. She was also very sensitive to local contexts as I acted as an interlocutor of local culture. Our collaboration was that of equals even though she was an established artist, and I had just graduated from art school. It taught me the virtues of being humble and generous in collaboration.

When it comes to my cyberart works, such as *Virtual Bodies in Reality* and *The Smart Apron*, collaboration was essential. I don't think I would have been able to create both works without the Cyberarts and Cyberculture Research Initiative (CCRI), organised by Aristarkhova at the National University of Singapore and the Artists-in-Labs (AIL) project in Zurich, organised by Professor Jill Scott at the Zurich University of the Arts (ZHdK). Collaboration is key in such works because of the different and specialised skill sets necessary to undertake the making of the artwork.

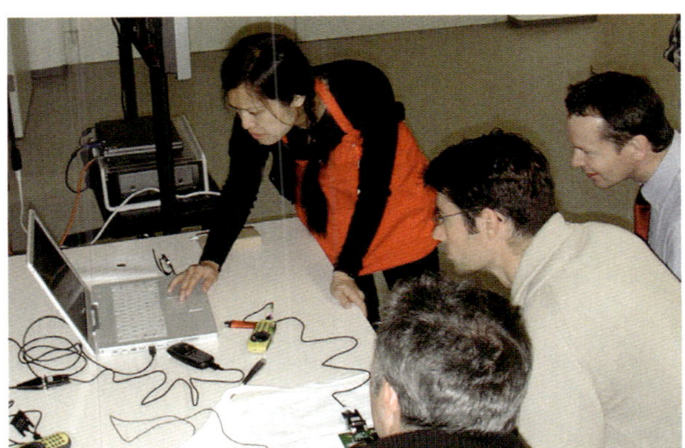

Figure 2: *The Smart Apron*. Tan, M. (2004). Demonstrating to the CSEM team. Image courtesy of the artist.

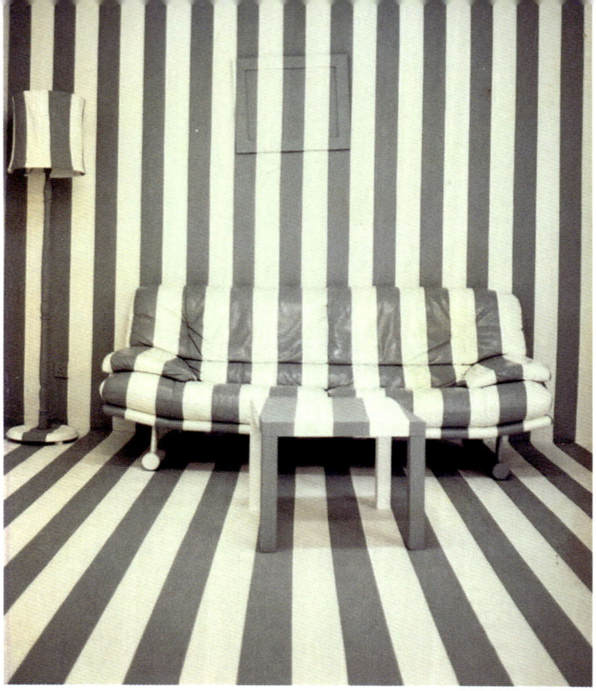

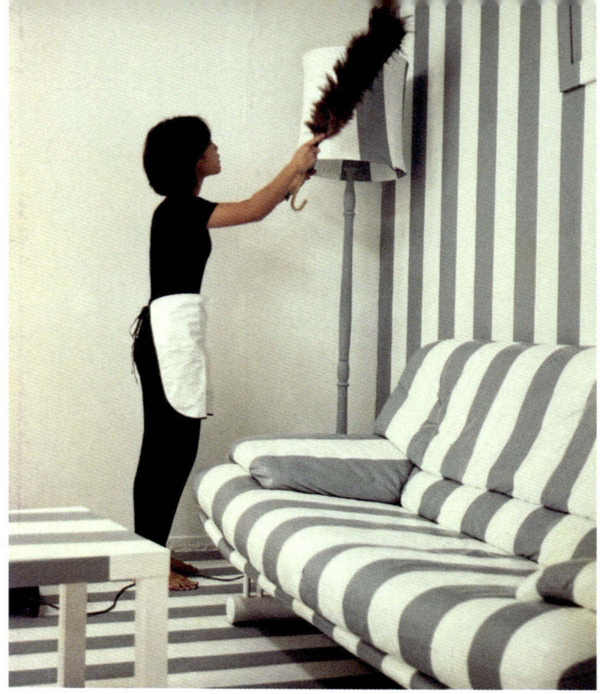

Figure 3a: *Picture Perfect.* Tan, M. (2000). Installation with performance. Image courtesy of the artist.

In this regard, beyond just the refrain of collaboration, I believe that the site of the university as a space for collaboration has also been integral to my practice. For artists keen to work with innovative technologies, universities are best placed to provide such opportunities as they have the necessary research, expertise and equipment. Hence, programmes such as CCRI and AIL are invaluable for providing a collaborative platform among artists, scientists and engineers, encouraging a culture of art appreciation, interdisciplinary research and innovation.

As for Lasalle-SIA, this was really a fecund space for artistic experimentation and intellectual development when I was a student there. I believe it fundamentally boiled down to the people involved and if the institution supports their endeavors. I know because I was Co-director (2012-2015) of the NUS Art/Science Residency Programme, together with Associate Professor Lonce Wyse. It was really a lot of work and time to organise, find funding and coordinate the artists, students, researchers and funders, on top of our regular jobs. We did it because we strongly believe in the benefits of such programmes. But when our efforts were not fully recognised by the larger institution working through a strict Key Performance Index (KPI), it made it hard for us to keep going.

Kathleen Beyond the university, your work has evolved through collaborations with civil society. In the catalogue for *A Self of One's Own*, you share that "Feminism is not just about getting things done" or simply a historical event, but that it was a "way of life - how we see ourselves, understanding how others see and frame us but, most of all, how we relate to others" (Aristarkhova, 1999, p. 14). The works that you made during this time such as *Picture-Perfect* (2000) but also *Restless* (1999)

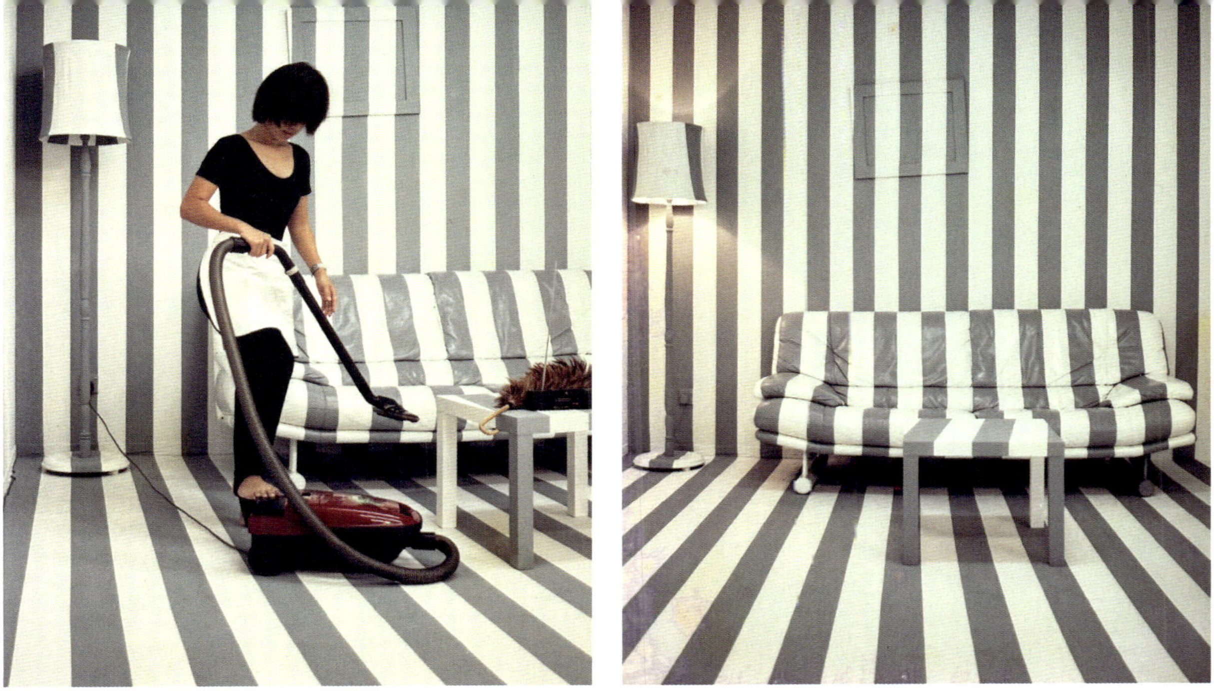

Figure 3b: *Picture Perfect.* Tan, M. (2000). Installation with performance. Image courtesy of the artist.

privileged the woman as an agent, drawing her out of the background and where her labour was one that unsettled, but also made the image. Interestingly, you also applied these to promotional material like flyers and posters for events organised by the Association of Women for Action and Research (AWARE), such as in 2001 when *Picture Perfect* (1999) was used to frame AWARE's *women@work* forum. When did you begin working with AWARE? How do you see the circulation of your artwork beyond the exhibition?

Margaret I see my artworks as political projects, so I am very happy to lend my works to causes that I care about. *Picture Perfect* was one of several artworks in the slide-deck used during the opening performance for AWARE's *women@work* forum. I strongly believe that art can make a difference in society, and I see such circulation of my artworks as an important way to share my concepts and concerns beyond the conventional art world. My association with AWARE started from Aristarkhova's *Feminist Art* workshop as part of a B.F.A. course at Lasalle-SIA where I was a student. There were several feminists and AWARE members, particularly Dana Lam and Shirley Soh, who joined us, and we have since become very good friends. Soon after the symposium, I signed up as an AWARE member and have worked with them in several ways. Apart from contributing money during fundraisers, I have also painted a mural for their center at Dover Road. It was a mural showcasing the silhouettes of AWARE's founding members. *Restless* was performed again during the opening of that space. As several AWARE members were also members of The Working Committee 2 (TWC2), I subsequently also became involved in their advocacy work on improving the welfare of migrant workers in Singapore.

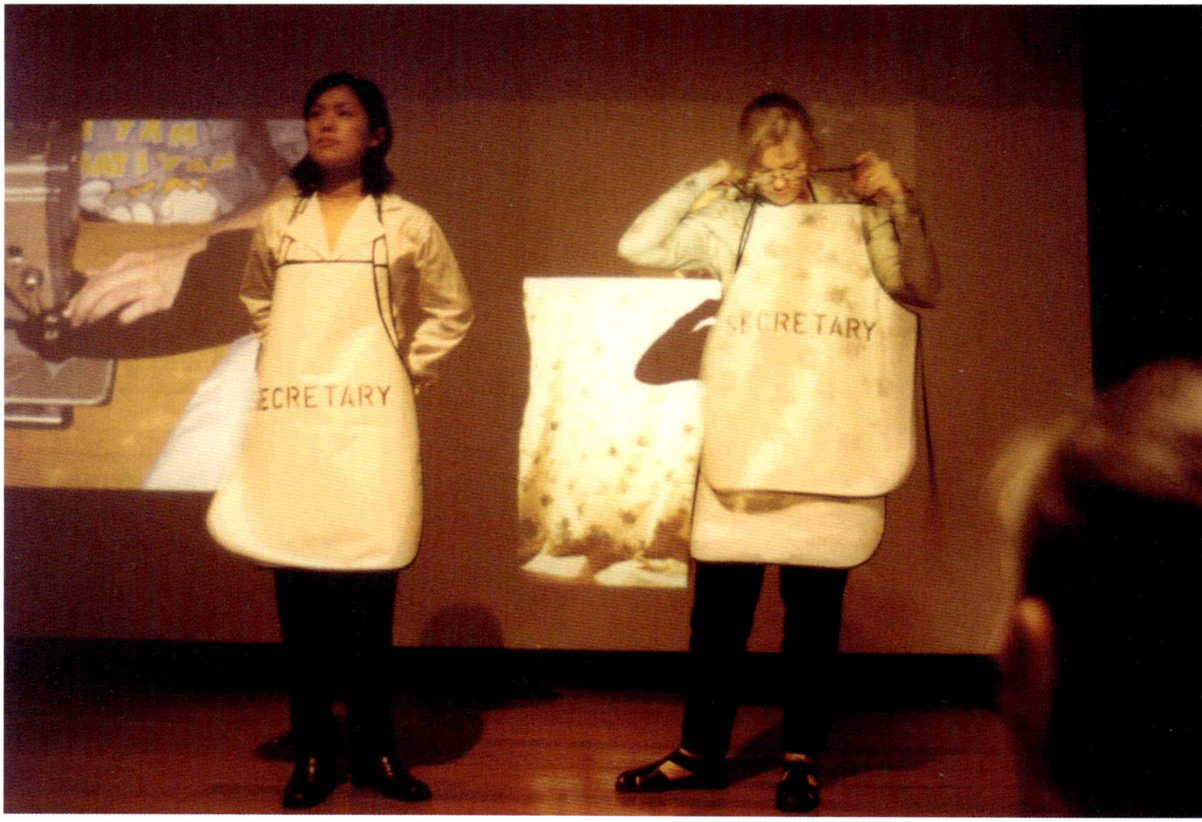

Figure 4: *Double Shift: Maintenance Performance.* Tan, M. and Wilding, F. (2001). *Picture Perfect.* Tan, M. (2000). (Singapore/USA). Multimedia performance. Image courtesy of Margaret Tan.

Kathleen Your education at Lasalle-SIA seems formative in part due to the intellectual kinship you developed with Aristarkhova and Nadarajan, and the scholarly and curatorial projects you collaborated on. How did these collaborations and mentorship lend to your engagement with an international art world and community of feminist artists? How did you end up collaborating with the feminist artist Faith Wilding (Wilding, 2017) in 2000, which you wrote about as being significant for women in Singapore (Figure 4)?

Margaret Aristarkhova and Nadarajan both played instrumental roles in my development at Lasalle-SIA and beyond the art college. Not only did they inspire me intellectually to go beyond my comfort zone, but they were also very generous in providing me opportunities both locally and internationally to showcase my works. As their student, I was exposed to many western philosophies and theories, including feminist thoughts and art practices. But there were also concerted efforts on their parts to encourage local and regional connections, such as through the *Feminist Art* workshop and forum, and the *18oKG* exhibition in Jogjakarta where I collaborated with Indonesian artists, such as Nerfita 'Popi' Primadewi. So, in many ways, through their influences, my practice has always straddled both local and global discourses, looking at issues that are not limited to Singapore, yet based on situated knowledge. I was introduced to Wilding through Aristarkhova, who proposed we could work together during the former's first visit to Singapore. I was very excited with this opportunity because I admire Wilding's works. I thought our collaboration would be a good opportunity to look at challenges women faced across our two countries. I believe a comparative approach could serve to highlight the predominance of patriarchal culture across borders. Hence, while acknowledging differences, it is also good to look at commonalities, and what we can learn from each other. This is what I like about feminism, that it allows for plurality and solidarity. Apart from comparative approaches, one noteworthy aspect of the performance is the undercurrent of how technology in the new economy has shaped and impacted women's work.

So, besides highlighting the invisible, endless maintenance work, the performance also touches on the tedious, repetitive labour harnessed to the speed of electronic technology.

Kathleen Your collaboration with Wilding expanded into an itinerant project with *subRosa* known as *Matrixial Technologies*. How did your investment in situated knowledge and comparative approach to feminism change with these projects?

Margaret Wilding and members of the cyberfeminist art collective *subRosa* visited Singapore in January 2003 and collaborated with Adeline Kueh, Aristarkhova, and me for the project *Matrixial Technologies*. The project was largely about mapping the movement of human tissues, specifically embryonic stem cell lines and umbilical cord blood stem cells, in the global bioinformatic economy and thereby raise critical awareness on this issue. Singapore was racing to position itself as a biotechnological hub at the time. My role included researching embryonic stem cell and cord blood research in Singapore, the bioethics advisory committee's position and public opinions (if any) on the topic, as well as giving feedback on the initial proposal. Together with Kueh, we also contributed in terms of introducing local cultural elements, such as some silver capsules we bought in Chinatown to encase messages that were to be distributed during the performance. *subRosa* also brought their ideas and experiences to the project, having worked in this area for some time. Through this project, I was grateful to discover an aspect of Singapore that was not on my radar, and to learn from other cyberfeminists about critical interventions. However, I had my reservations too on certain more radical or oppositional approaches. Having observed how civil societies work here vis-a-vis a powerful state with low tolerance for strong criticisms, along with our conservative public, I thought such approaches would be counter-productive in the context of Singapore. So global discourses and collaborations are rewarding, but they must be coupled with situated knowledge and sensitivities toward local contexts and ties.

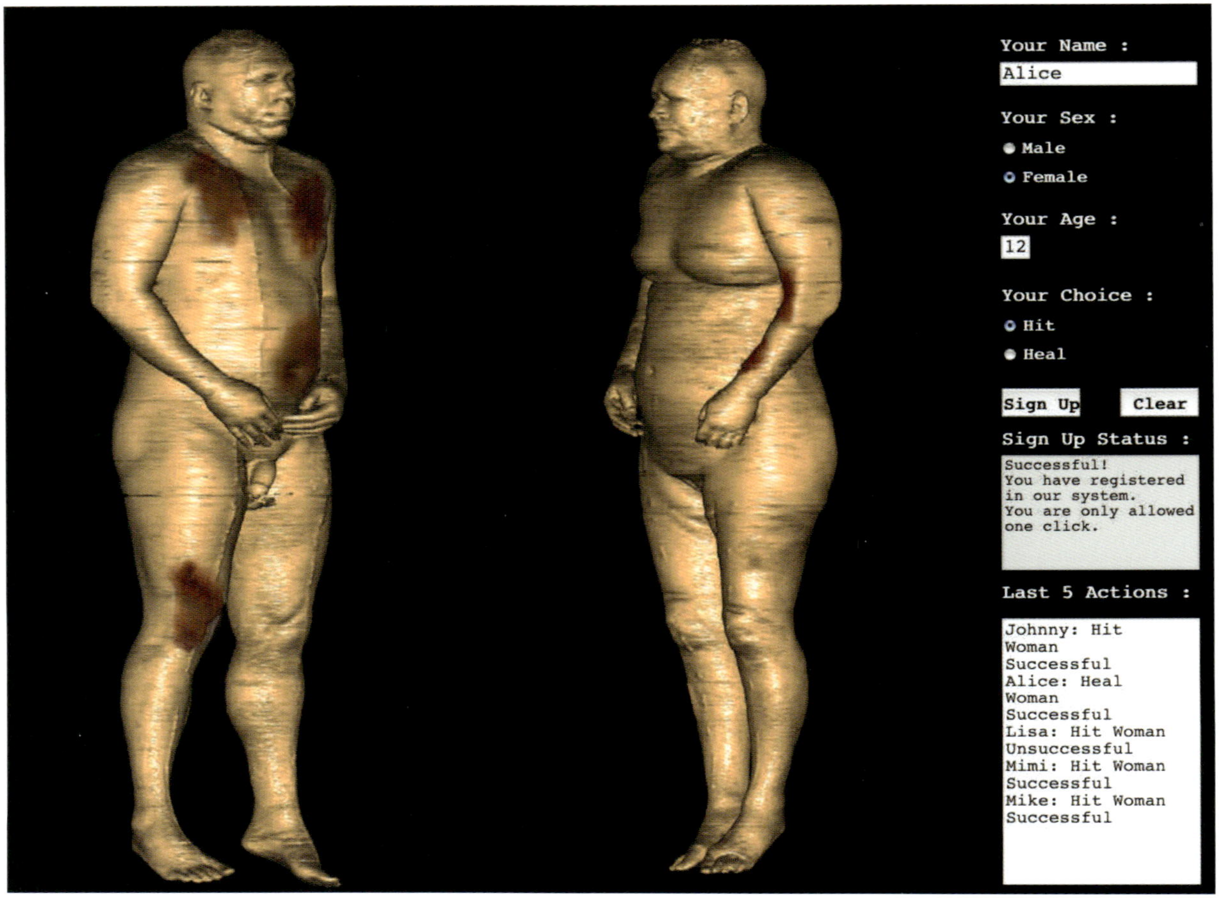

Figure 5: *Virtual Bodies in Reality.* (detail), Tan, M. (2001). Interactive media. Image courtesy of the artist.

Towards locating Singapore in a global Cyberfeminism

Kathleen You were part of several seminal programmes in Singapore's digital art history including *Cyberarts* (2001), supposedly the first web art exhibition in Southeast Asia curated by Nadarajan. In 2004, Nadarajan, then Dean, Office of Research and Creative Industries at Lasalle-SIA curated the exhibition *The Lasalle School*, in which he included your work *Virtual Bodies in Reality* (Figure 5). The exhibition intended to suggest that the college captured a zeitgeist of contemporary art practice in Singapore. In particular, he noted that *Virtual Bodies in Reality* (2001) which had been presented in *Cyberarts* (2001) "has the distinction of being the first virtual reality artwork produced in Singapore" (Nadarajan, 2004, p.14). From your perspective, what was the significance of *Virtual Bodies in Reality* (2001)?

Margaret *Virtual Bodies in Reality* was produced in the context of the Cyberarts and Cyberculture Research Initiative (CCRI), overseen by Aristarkhova, with the aim of being showcased at the Cyberarts exhibition, curated by Nadarajan. Both were ground-breaking projects in supporting artists in creating and showcasing works at the intersection of art, science, and technology. *Virtual Bodies in Reality* was the first artwork in Singapore using data from the Visible Human Project and to critically reflect on the military-scientific-industrial complex. While it doesn't fit neatly into the conventional notion of virtual reality (VR), commonly associated with simulation technology and special gadgets, such as data gloves and headsets, the artwork is grounded on the use of two real bodies that can only exist in virtual space. The digitisation of these bodies has made them manipulable and reproducible, and one can only interact with them through digital technology, in this case the computer screen and mouse.

Kathleen Later in *Contemporary Art in Singapore* (Nadarajan, Storer and Tan, 2007) one of the first books to historise contemporary art practices in Singapore, Nadarajan wrote an essay that sets up a connection between *Virtual Bodies in Reality* (2001), and *Picture-Perfect* (2000) and *Restless* (1999), wherein your feminist perspective played out in your research interest in *Virtual Bodies in Reality* (2001). He reported that you were interested in how audiences might be more willing to "virtually" harm the female body as opposed to the male body. Did *Virtual Bodies in Reality* (2001) change your ideas around the body in art?

Margaret I was very intrigued by the feminist critique (Cartwright, 1998) of the *Visible Human Project*, demonstrating how scientific knowledge and discourse can be gendered, as the male and female bodies were treated as virtual Adam and Eve, while the female body was disparaged for being menopausal. In terms of audience participation, I did consider how gender might impact the interactions with the work, not just in terms of whether the male or female body would be chosen, but also whether participants would heal or wound the bodies. More importantly though, I wanted the work to surface how our actions and sense of violence and responsibility might change, when mediated through digital technology.

Kathleen In 2004, you and Shirley Soh, participated in an art residency organised by the Zurich University of the Arts (ZHdK). You worked at the Swiss Center for Electronics and Microtechnology (CSEM) and with the group director Max Erick Busse-Grawtiz over 5 months to develop *The Smart Apron*. It was based on a proposal for a wearable computer that could improve the working conditions of migrant domestic workers. How did the invitation to the residency come about?

Margaret The Artists-in-Labs Project, founded by Professor Jill Scott in the Zurich University of the Arts (ZHdK), in 2002, was set up to facilitate artistic research through residencies in scientific laboratories and research institutes in Switzerland. In the inaugural run, it was an open call where artists from all over the world could apply. Since then, it has become a national programme. It was Scott who informed me of this opportunity and I, in turn, informed Soh. For the proposal, you had to describe the concept of your work and identify the laboratory, from a list of participating laboratories, you wanted to work with. It was a very competitive process as, Soh and I found out later, many established new media artists applied as well. Soh and I were delighted we were both selected, although we were placed in different laboratories in Switzerland. There was also an artist from India, one from Australia, one from the USA, and several from Switzerland/Germany who made the cut. My idea, the *The Smart Apron*, was based on an initial proposal I submitted to the UNESCO Digital Arts Award at IAMAS, Japan, which received an honorable mention.

Kathleen Did the use of aprons in the *Double/Shift: Maintenance Performance* (2001) with Wilding anticipate your later work *The Smart Apron* (2004)?

Margaret The use of aprons first appeared in the performance with Wilding. In our preparation for the *Double/Shift*: *Maintenance Performance* (Figure 2), Wilding and I had an extended exchange on how we might perform, and dress, use statistics and slides. She brought up how dressing up in housemaid uniforms while typing at the computer could be humorous. I suggested rubber gloves and aprons as alternatives, since housemaid uniforms are more a signifier of American culture and not a popular practice in Singapore. The apron appeared again during the housework project. I suppose it is an easy signifier for domestic space and work. But with *the Smart Apron*, I was thinking of the apron not only as a metaphor, but also a form of wearable technology that can empower migrant domestic workers. Wearable computing then was an innovative technology that only the rich could afford, and I wanted a functioning apron dedicated to the migrant domestic workers. In terms of the metaphorical value, the apron's features - heat sensor, tilt sensor, communications capability and fall detector - speak to the challenges faced by these workers, such as their abuse by the iron, long hours of work, isolation, and falls from Singapore's high-rise buildings.

Kathleen How did your Ph.D project grow out of the development of *The Smart Apron* (2004)? You have described your Ph.D as a performative act. How so?

Margaret When I embarked on my Ph.D at the Communications and New Media (CNM) Department, National University of Singapore, the residency in Switzerland was still fresh in my mind. I thought I could build on top of what I had done, but with a twist. I was not thinking about the body as an art medium; rather, I was interested in making technology "non-western". I think having spent time in London and then Switzerland made me want to connect back with my Asian roots. I remembered being very surprised when the secretary at the Swiss lab I was attached to shared how she could claim from her insurer treatment performed by Traditional Chinese Medicine (TCM) practitioners, something we could not do in Singapore at that time. TCM was then regarded as "folk medicine" and non-scientific by western medical practitioners and the government in Singapore. So, my Ph.D research proposal was to create a wearable computing piece, based on Asian notions of the body, bridging in effect, this disparity. In particular, I was interested in drawing on TCM philosophies of meridian points, and how that might change the way we design wearable pieces, and therefore, their functions. Unfortunately, the department did not have a laboratory then to support prototyping, and I could not find an engineering co-supervisor to see me through the project. I eventually switched my Ph.D to a full research paper on pervasive computing, in the context of Singapore and its Masterplan called the Intelligent Nation 2015 (iN2015). I did, in the end, write *The Smart Apron* into one of the chapters. It became a node for me to unpack art production and immaterial labour in the context of a neoliberal, technologised political economy. It was a critical and self-reflexive piece touching on complicity and how technology is empowering or disempowering depending on where you are on the technological ladder. In a sense, the Ph.D articulated and extended what I was already doing as a performance artist.

Kathleen Technologies both govern and extend the body, as seen through your interest in the mouse constituting the body or being an extension of the body in *Virtual Bodies in Reality* and in the cybernetic loop of mobile technologies in the making of *the Smart Apron*. As a performance artist, did you see your role as collaborating with machines? Or was technology a tool for making your work?

Margaret Technology (both analogue and digital) permeates our lives. They extend and augment our bodies in increasingly pervasive ways. I see technology as something empowering and disempowering, depending on where one stands on the technological ladder (following Haraway), but necessary to be engaged with, especially in the context of a highly technologised society like Singapore. I also see technology as having a life of its own, in Winner's (1980) sense of artifacts having politics and Virilio's (2007) sense of "the Accident". So, the use of technology in my earlier works really functioned as a tool for me to critically highlight social issues and the aesthetics/politics of the technology. I believe we shape technologies as much as they shape us and that we can never fully control. Today, with the predominance and capabilities of AI, the potential for such technology as collaborative machines has taken on new meanings. For me, I would be more interested in thinking about the ethics of AI.

Kathleen At the OBN *(Old Boys Network)* Conference, Hamburg, December 13-16, 2001, where cyberfeminism was defined as "feminism in relation to digital media" (Pierce et al., 2022, p.154), Aristarkhova called for "a more ethical relationship between 'local' and 'global Western' players within the cyberfeminist community...[so as to avoid] claiming 'subaltern' or 'otherness' status on the part of 'local' cyberfeminist communities in relation to the West [that] often obscures power relations with local contexts" (Pierce et al., 2022, pp.145-148). You and Aristarhova extended this discourse on this disparity at the *ISEA2008: The 14th International Symposium on Electronic Art* held in Singapore from 25 July to 3 August 2008. Both of you participated in *Locating Cyberfeminism in Singapore: A Dialogue* (Aristarkhova and Tan, 2008) where you discussed the collaboration with *subRosa* in Singapore and the dissonances between feminist perceptions and overcoming the perception of Singapore being a "Disneyland with death penalty". When you look back on this period, was there a sense of a global community of cyberfeminists that you were part of? What did OBN represent to you and how do you see your place in a global cyberfeminism?

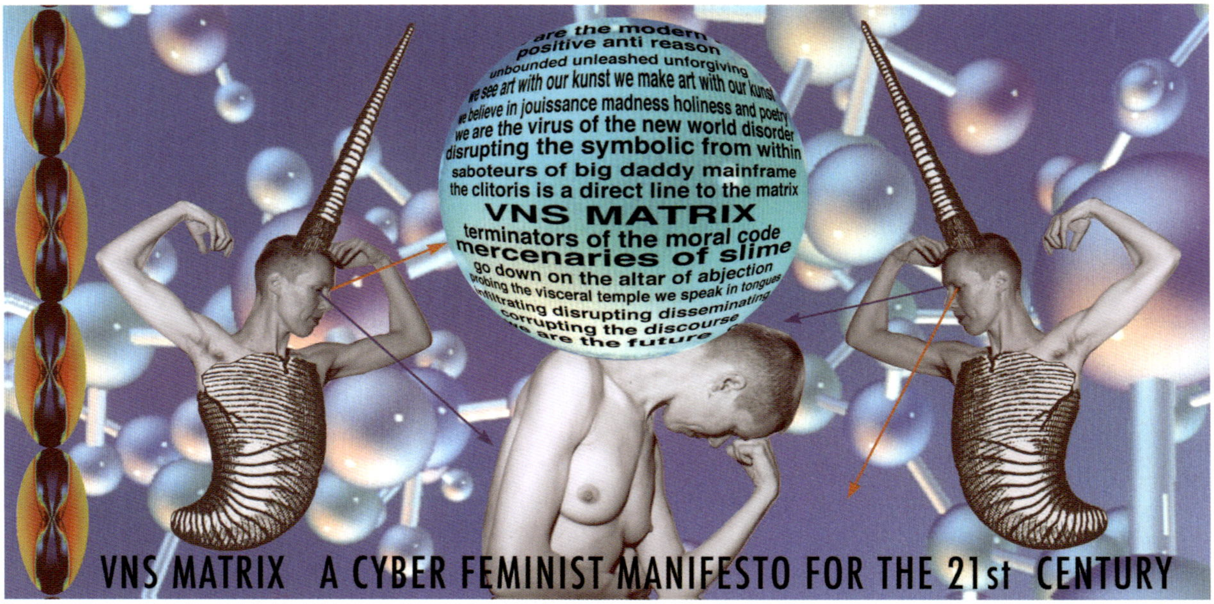

Figure 6: *Cyberfeminist Manifesto for the 21st Century. VNS Matrix.* (1991). Billboard, Digital Image. Image: Courtesy the Artists. https://vnsmatrix.net

Margaret I think I was a small node in the global community of cyberfeminists, providing an alternative voice at strategic moments. The 2001 *Very Cyberfeminist International OBN Conference* in Hamburg, Germany, was my first encounter with cyberfeminists, like *VNS Matrix*, from all over the world under one roof (Figure 6). I was there to present on a panel with Aristarkhova, Wilding and Fernández. I remembered it was a tough crowd, and at one point the conversation turned to issues of race. Subsequently, I was invited to join the listserve *Undercurrents*, an online community where cyberfeminists could introduce themselves and their works, start discussions on pertinent issues, and plan and connect physically when they travel. The listserve, renamed *Faces*, is still active and I am still on it, but inactive. I think the OBN conference was a useful experience for me to see differences amongst the cyberfeminist community, but also to network. It was there where I first met Jill Scott who came up to me after the session to introduce herself and left some encouraging words. She subsequently informed me of the *Artists-in-Labs* Project open call. We became close friends after my residency in Switzerland. In 2023, Aristarkhova, Wilding, Fernández and I were on the *Cybercultures and Cyberfeminisms* panel convened by Jeanine Tang. In 2025, I joined one of the founding members of *subRosa*, Hyla Willis, on another cyberfeminist panel, *Cyberfeminist Legacies in New Media Art*, chaired by Aristarkohva in New York. We were joined by another panelist, Nat Mengist, and Fernández was the discussant. So, to return to your question, I think I am part of a small selective group within a global community of cyberfeminists.

References

- Aristarkhova, I., 1999. A Self of One's Own (Exhibition Catalogue). Singapore: Lasalle-SIA College of the Arts, p. 14.
- Aristarkhova, I. and Tan, M., 2008. 'Locating Cyberfeminism in Singapore: A Dialogue'. Presentation at ISEA 2008, Singapore. Available at: http://www.refugia.net/irina/MTIADialogue.pdf [Accessed: 21 August 2025].
- Cartwright, L., 1998. 'A Cultural Anatomy of the Visible Human Project', in Treichler, P., Cartwright, L. & Penley, C. (eds.) The Visible Woman: Imaging Technologies, Gender and Science. New York University Press, pp. 21-43.
- Nadarajan, G., 2004. Exhibition Catalogue, The Lasalle School: 20 years of Fine Arts from Lasalle-SIA College of the Arts. Singapore: Lasalle-SIA College of the Arts, p. 14.
- National Library Board, n.d. Renaissance City Report. Singapore: National Library Board. Available at: https://www.nlb.gov.sg/main/article-detail?cmsuuid=d0504b41-06f4-4f4b-80d2-f7d84aa2086d.
- Pierce, J. et al., 2022. Cyberfeminism Index. Edited by M. Seu. Inventory Press, p. 154.
- Pierce, J. et al., 2022. Cyberfeminism Index. Edited by M. Seu. Inventory Press, pp. 145-148.
- Plastique Kinetic Worms, 2001. 'vehicle: Contemporary Visual Arts Issue 03'. Singapore: Plastique Kinetic Worms.
- Seu, M., 2022. Cyberfeminism Index. Los Angeles: Inventory Press.
- Virilio, P., 2007. 'The Invention of Accidents', in Rose, J. (trans.) The Original Accident. UK: Polity Press, pp. 9-14.
- VNS matrix (http:VNSmatrix.net)
- Wilding, F., 2017. Faith Wilding papers in the Getty Research Institute Special Collections: Wilding: Contracts and grants 1986-2001 (M.8, Box 8). Print.
- Winner, L., 1980. 'Do artifacts have politics?', Daedalus, 109 (1), pp. 121-136.

INVESTIGATIONS

ART AS EVIDENCE: THE FUTURE IS NOT WHAT IT USED TO BE!

Inês Montalvão

Once viewed through the lens of boundless potential and endless opportunity, the future now carries the weight of uncertainty and apprehension. The relentless march of climate change has reshaped our perceptions of what lies ahead, casting a shadow of doubt and fear over the prospects of tomorrow. In the face of overwhelming evidence, denialism has emerged as a formidable obstacle in the fight against the climate emergency. Despite mounting scientific consensus and undeniable proof of environmental degradation, some still refuse to acknowledge the reality of our changing world. This denialism, fuelled by vested interests and ideological biases, perpetuates a dangerous narrative of complacency and inaction. The consequences are dire and far-reaching. From extreme weather events to ecological collapse, climate change is already claiming lives, displacing communities, and irreparably damaging ecosystems. The link between climate change and death is becoming increasingly clear, underscoring the urgent need for decisive action. Yet amidst the gloom, there is hope. The growing movement for climate justice demonstrates our collective capacity for change. From youth-led protests to grassroots initiatives, momentum is building towards a more sustainable future. By harnessing evidence-based policy, innovative technology, and community-driven solutions, we can chart a course where environmental stewardship and social equity go hand in hand. The future may be uncertain, but with determination and solidarity, we can ensure hope prevails over despair.

Evidence-Based Practice in Art-Science

Art-science, as a dynamic field, thrives on the integration of evidence and creativity, forging new pathways for knowledge production in a non-hierarchical way. It is rooted in both creativity and curiosity and therefore bridges scientific rigour with artistic exploration. My experience in the realm of art-science has led me to emphasise the pivotal role of evidence in this collaborative space, where the objective nature of empirical data meets the subjective realms of artistic interpretation. By grounding art-science in evidence-based methodologies, we ensure that these collaborations not only foster scientific inquiry but also open broader avenues for creative exploration, addressing societal and environmental issues in innovative ways.

Beyond highlighting the significance of evidence-based approaches in art-science collaborations, it is imperative to acknowledge the role of feminism and the contributions of women in shaping this dynamic field. Historically, women have faced systemic barriers in both the arts and sciences, yet their influence and innovation have been instrumental in pushing the boundaries of traditional disciplines. As an art-science practitioner, I recognise the importance of amplifying the voices and perspectives of women in this space, particularly those who have been historically marginalised. Women have played a central role in advancing interdisciplinary inquiry and challenging conventional modes of thinking. By celebrating their contributions and advocating for greater inclusivity and equity, we can foster a more vibrant and diverse art-science community, one that is better equipped to address the complex challenges of our time.

Art-science collaborations led by women frequently demonstrate this ethics of care by exploring themes that are not only grounded in empirical evidence, but also sensitive to the experiential and affective dimensions of ecological relationships. Projects that integrate sensory experiences, such as installations and soundscapes, invite audiences to engage with the environment in ways that transcend conventional scientific data, making them feel the impacts of climate change, biodiversity loss, or habitat degradation on a visceral level. This empathetic approach is designed to provoke a deeper awareness of the fragility of ecosystems and the urgency of preservation. One of the core aspects of feminist art-science practice is an ethic of care, which emphasises mutual support, co-responsibility, and interdependence across species. This approach is especially pertinent in ecological and environmental work, where the interconnections between humans, other species, and the natural world become essential to the practice itself.

Transdisciplinary Fusion of Evidence and Expression

In art-science, transdisciplinary practice is important to foster novel insights. By intertwining artistic and scientific processes, art-science practitioners are able to investigate complex issues like climate change, species extinction, and ecological resilience through a dual lens that makes these topics accessible and emotionally resonant. Evidence, in this context, serves as both a grounding and a transformative element, guiding the creative process while enabling new forms of scientific and artistic expression. Feminist perspectives in art-science collaborations are deeply enriched by the contributions of women whose innovative practices have shaped the field's interdisciplinary character. Figures like Beatriz da Costa, whose critical explorations of technology and activism have profoundly influenced my own curiosity and endeavours, exemplify the power of blending empirical research with artistic inquiry. Her work serves as a foundation for understanding how art-science can bridge gaps between activism, data, and creative engagement, inspiring a generation of practitioners to challenge traditional boundaries.

Inspired by da Costa's fearless interrogation of limits (da Costa, 2008), I have embarked on a path to explore the intersections of art and science. This exploration manifests both in my work in exhibitions and experience design for international museums and science centres, as well as in my own art-science practice. As both a practitioner and curator, I strive to create immersive and complex narrative environments, diverse in form and purpose (Austin, 2020), that transcend disciplinary constraints, inviting audiences to confront complex issues and engage in meaningful dialogue. By using empirical data as a foundation for creativity, art-science practitioners invite audiences to engage with the evidence itself through unique sensory experiences.

For instance, in *Lingua Plantae*, a project that I co-created with Finnish sound designer and composer Auri Antinranta, biodata sonification translates plant responses into sound, allowing audiences to "listen" to the plants whilst fostering a sense of connection across species boundaries. With *Lingua Plantae* we wanted to not only question, but also raise awareness and engage people in a multisensory experience that challenges the established norm and dichotomy of human/non-human spheres, bringing in a connection that bridges people, space and nature. Through biodata sonification, a process to translate complex real-time sensor data into musical notes and controls, we explore the auditory sensory modality to provide insights into an invisible phenomenon. This process consists of a narrative environment, sound design, tech development, the interface and the installation. The final outcome aims to engage the audience to interact with the plants and share a recording of this unique experience. These "sound postcards" enable a democratic spreading of a message produced by and through a plant, acting also in the process of finding a common language with humans. This project exemplified how evidence, when coupled with artistic interpretation, can lead to insights that traditional scientific communication might not achieve.

In 2023, I joined *Artists with Evidence* (AwE) as Program Director. AwE is a non-profit organisation that believes that we need multidisciplinary conversations to address multidisciplinary problems. Art-science does this by placing artists, scientists, and the public in conversation on equal footing to think through climate problems and develop new ideas for workable social solutions. At *Artists with Evidence*, we are committed to gender equity and therefore, in our programming and content, we highlight women-identifying creatives in art-science at the helm, recognising their unique insights and contributions to these critical dialogues.

As demonstrated by our carefully curated programme, with themes such as Climate & Death, Climate Security and War & Environment, amplifying women's voices in art-science ensures a diverse and inclusive representation of perspectives, enriching our understanding of these complex topics. Other creative works mentioned in this essay will emphasise an evidence-based approach grounded in careful observation and intimate, multisensory engagement with the environment, challenging the boundaries between scientific investigation and artistic expression. This fusion of empirical observation and artistic immersion exemplifies how transdisciplinary work can generate novel insights into ecological and social issues, shaping meaningful, reflective experiences that deepen public understanding.

Feminist Perspectives in Art-Science

By engaging with traditionally marginalised subjects such as non-human life and ecological degradation, women practitioners have pioneered unique impactful approaches that blend ethics of care, environmental consciousness, sensory-based research and relationality. This theme resonates with the idea that women in art and science have historically been instrumental in expanding the field and integrating marginalised knowledge, bringing transformative approaches to the field by centering on collaborative, multispecies engagement that questions dominant, anthropocentric frameworks. Feminist perspectives involve a commitment to interdependence and mutual responsibility, positioning art-science as a domain where humans are collaborators, not dominators, of the natural world. An example of this feminist approach is found in projects that transform scientific evidence into immersive experiences, allowing viewers to interact directly with the living processes and relationships within ecosystems. Women art-science practitioners often experiment with sound, installation, and new media to render invisible ecological phenomena visible or tangible. This mode of working goes beyond simply presenting data; it seeks to make complex systems, like climate change, accessible and personally relevant, creating a bridge between the observer and the observed, and fostering a profound empathy for non-human life.

Contributions to Art-Science

Women in art-science have profoundly shaped the field, offering critical insights into multispecies' futures, body politics, and ecological preservation. Alongside creatives such as post-disciplinary artist and researcher Mari Keski-Korsu and interdisciplinary artists Eeva-Liisa Puhakka, Joanna Rajkowska and Majella Clarke in collaboration with Mareike Dobewall, exemplify how feminist perspectives influence and define art-science practices. Their projects, from sound installations to participatory rituals, highlight the importance of embodied experiences and sensory engagement in fostering empathy and care.

Finnish creatives Mari Keski-Korsu and Eeva-Liisa Puhakka participated in the *Climate & Death* programme, organised by *Artists with Evidence* and partners, in April 2024. They took part in the public conversation *Transcending Boundaries: An Evening of Art-Science*, where they addressed critical ecological and existential themes present in their work. Their presentations emphasised the interconnectedness of life and death in the Anthropocene, positioning their work within the broader discourse of ecofeminism. Both Keski-Korsu and Puhakka are also members of the creative network at *Artists with Evidence*, which includes over 60 individuals. The network fosters thought exchange and collaboration, key aspects of my role in curating the programme. The full conversation is available on YouTube (Artists with Evidence, 2024).

Mari Keski-Korsu

Mari Keski-Korsu's participatory explorations of permafrost thaw and microbial life in *Permafrost Bathing* (2023) and *Cryospheric Steams Repository* (2024) highlight the intersection of ecological transformation, rituals, and art (Keski-Korsu, 2022).

Permafrost, defined as ground that remains frozen for at least two consecutive years, covers approximately 15% of the Northern Hemisphere. Due to the climate crisis, it's rapid thaw releases microbes that have been frozen since prehistoric times. These microbes include viruses that pose potential risks to contemporary ecosystems and human health (NASA, 2024). Beyond microbial threats, the thawing of permafrost is a significant contributor to climate change, releasing vast amounts of CO_2 and methane into the atmosphere - greenhouse gases that exacerbate global warming (Nature World News, 2024).

Keski-Korsu's *Permafrost Bathing* transforms these alarming data points into a participatory ritual, integrating microbial life from permafrost into the traditional Nordic practice of sauna and peat folk healing. In this performance, participants are immersed in waters and peat that contain microbial traces from the thawing permafrost. This act becomes both a cosmological and corporeal engagement with the climate crisis, where participants physically and symbolically encounter the past lives of microbial ecosystems. In the ritual, there are samples collected that form an archive installation called *Cryospheric Steams Repository* (2024), where the encounters of permafrost microbial life, sweat and peat continue living (Figure 1). This sauna becomes a space for embodied understanding - a cosmological technology for facing the uncertainties of a warming world.

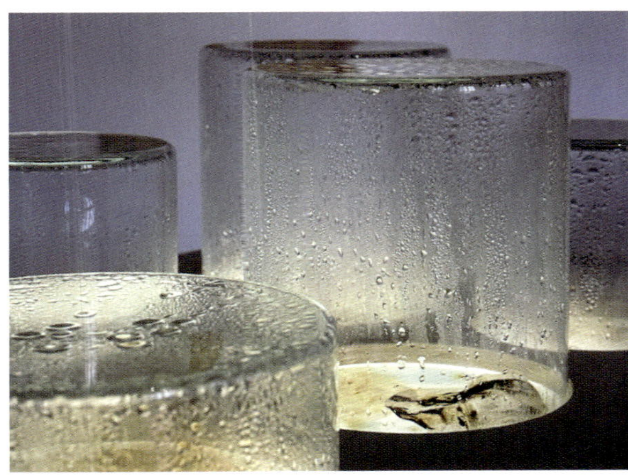

Figure 1: *Cryospheric Steams Repository*. Keski-Korsu, M. (2024). Installation. Photo: Katri Naukkarinen. https://www.artsufartsu.net/cryospheric-steams-repository/

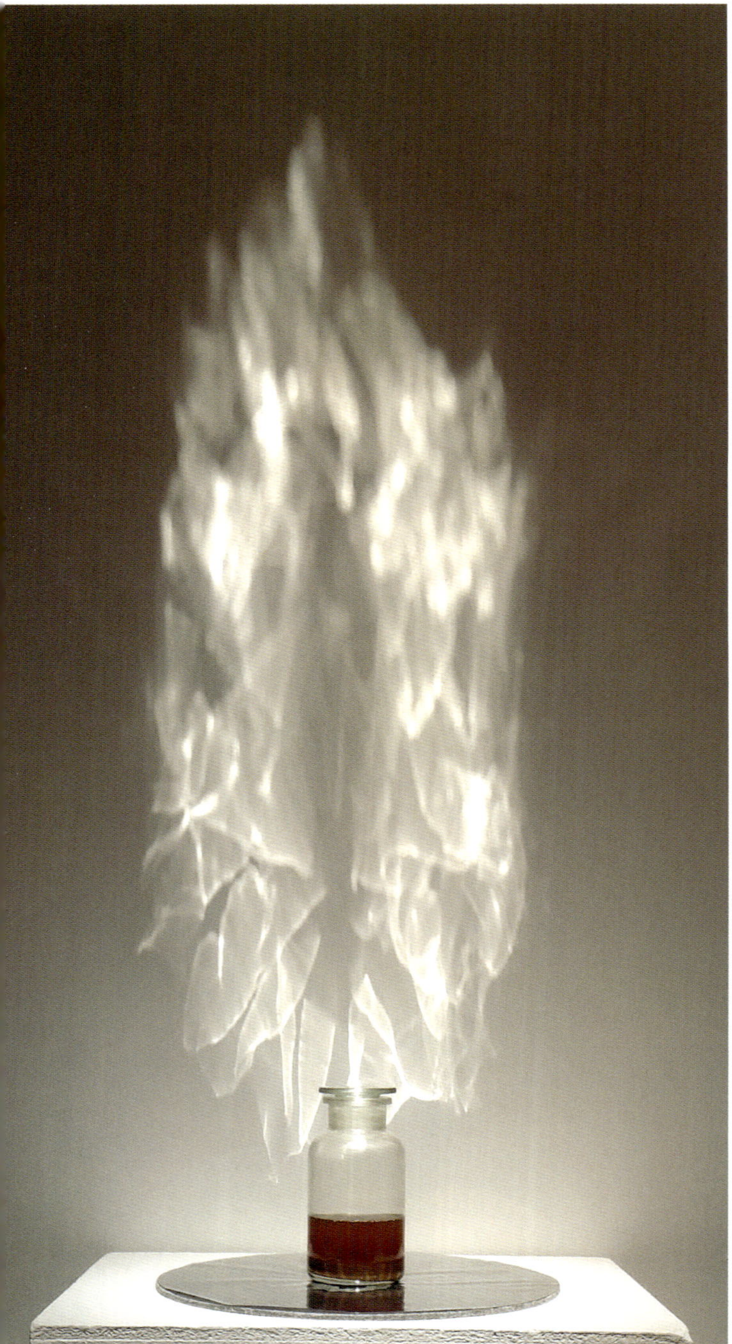

Figure 2: *Leave the Body, Leave the Mind.* Puhakka, E-L. (2024). Installation. Photo: Eeva-Liisa Puhakka. https://www.eeva-liisa.net/project/leave-the-body-leave-the-mind/

Eeva-Liisa Puhakka

Puhakka's interdisciplinary practice exemplifies the sensory and relational dimensions of art-science, bringing an embodied awareness to ecological and societal concerns. Through mediums such as olfactory art, installations, and bio-based materials, her work explores themes of interspecies dependence, rural depopulation, and the profound connections between life, death, and time. Central to her approach is the use of scent as a conduit for memory, empathy, and care - qualities deeply rooted in feminist ethics and body politics.

In projects such as *Smell of Death* (also known as *Leave the Body, Leave the Mind*, 2019-2024), Puhakka employs olfactory art to evoke visceral emotional responses, using scent as a medium to confront audiences with the fragility of ecosystems and the shared vulnerabilities of human and non-human life (Puhakka, 2023).

By engaging the sense of smell (Figure 2), which is intimately tied to memory and emotion, her work transcends cognitive understanding, fostering an embodied empathy that resonates with feminist principles of interconnectedness and care.

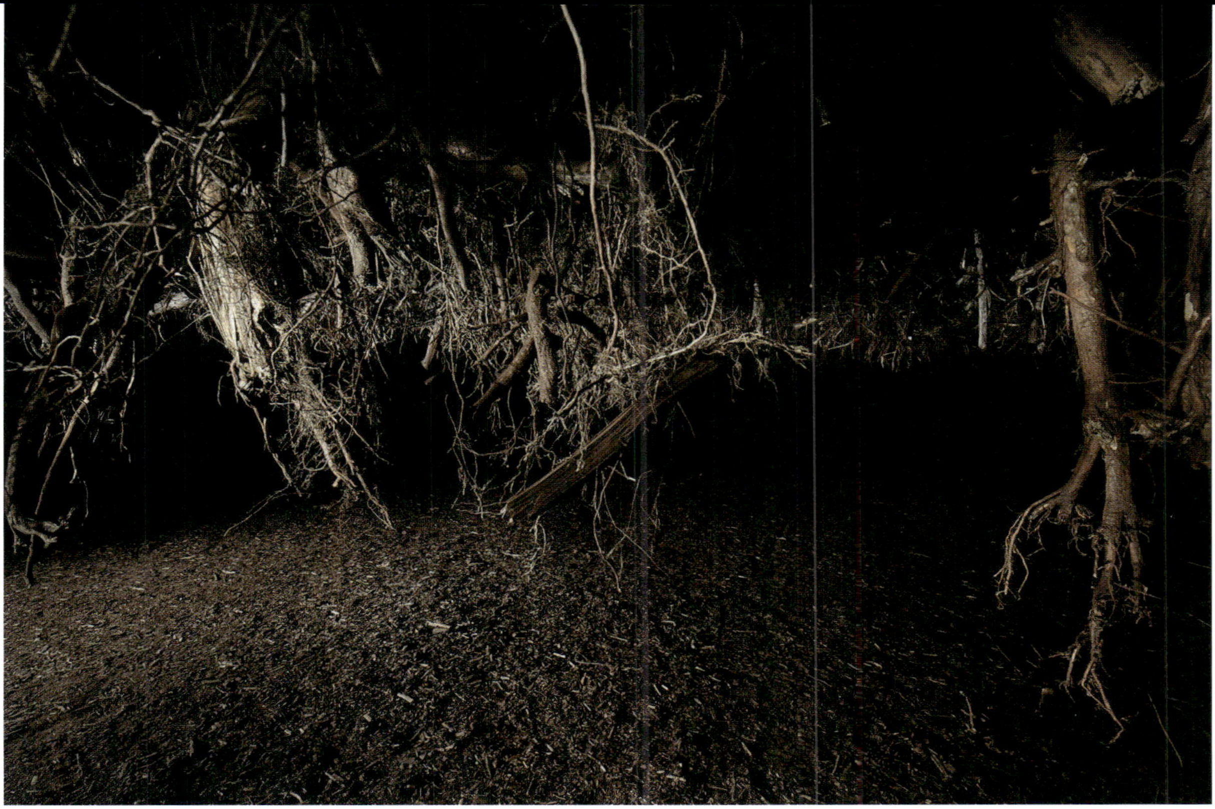

Figure 3: *Rhizopolis*. Rajkowska, J. (2021). Installation. Photo: Jędrzej Sokołowski. https://www.rajkowska.com/en/rhizopolis/

Joanna Rajkowska

In *Rhizopolis* (2021), Rajkowska created an immersive subterranean installation crafted from tree roots and stumps (Figure 3). It served as a profound example of evidence-based art-science. Inspired by ecological evidence of environmental degradation and deforestation, *Rhizopolis* constructs an alternative, post-Anthropocene sanctuary or refuge for all species (Sliwinska, 2023). Through the physical embodiment of ecological evidence, the installation invites audiences to confront the impacts of human activity on biodiversity, while challenging the boundaries between science, art, and public engagement.

The engagement with natural elements, such as roots and soil, as physical evidence of ecological collapse encourages viewers to reconsider their connection to the environment, fostering a space for empathetic response grounded in both sensory and intellectual exploration.

Much like in Rajkowska's work, Puhakka transcends conventional scientific narratives by inviting audiences to perceive the fragility of life from an embodied perspective, thus demonstrating the potential for art-science to cultivate deep, sensory-based knowledge grounded in feminist ethics.

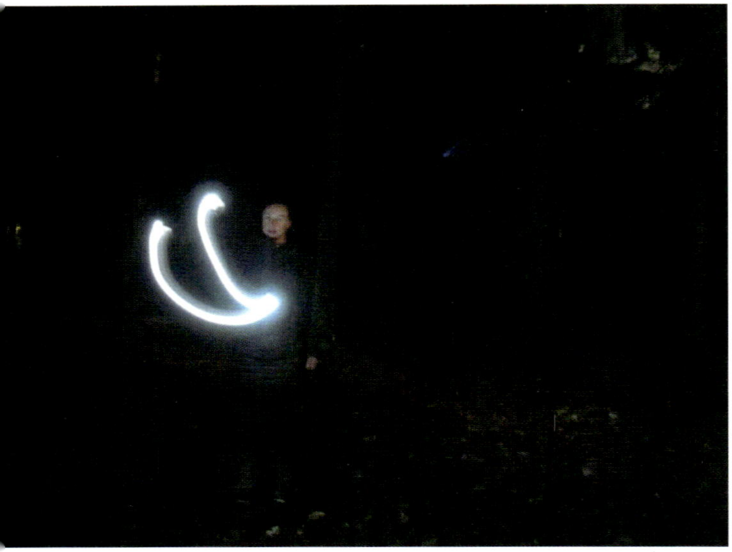

Figure 4: *Receptaculum.* Clarke, M. and Dobewall, M. (2024). Performance. Photo: Timo Sarpola.
https://www.majella-clarke.com/
https://www.mareikedobewall.com/

Majella Clarke & Mareike Dobewall

Expanding on the above topics, it is worth exploring the interdisciplinary project *Receptaculum*, by Australian conductor Majella Clarke and German director, scenographer, and composer Mareike Dobewall. Their work reimagines the concept of refuge through contemplative soundscapes, offering immersive spaces for reflection and resilience. The project's innovative score, composed by Dobewall, breaks away from traditional musical notation by incorporating unique spatial-temporal and gestural elements. Designed to be read top to bottom rather than left to right, the score challenges conventional auditory and temporal practices for conductors like Clarke, requiring imaginative engagement to interpret and perform it effectively.

Receptaculum (2024) integrates nature-inspired visual forms, such as gestures derived from pine needle shapes (Figure 4), and combines them with text and graphic scoring techniques. This approach emphasises the materiality of sound and gesture, fostering an experimental interaction between time, space, and auditory perception. The resulting performance transcends traditional musical boundaries, embodying the spirit of refuge as a conceptual and sensory space that connects performers and audiences with nature and imagination.

The afore mentioned works parallel the themes of *Refugium for a Dream*, the sound installation I am curating for *Artists with Evidence*, where sound becomes a medium for addressing the topics of Climate & Death, as further explored in *Refugium for a Dream: Hacking the Future!*

These creatives exemplify how feminist art-science practices transform our engagement with pressing ecological and existential challenges, offering innovative pathways to understanding and resilience through interdisciplinary collaboration. Their works provide profound insights into the potential of *refugium* as a concept and practice - spaces of sanctuary and regeneration that align with feminist ethics and the broader goals of environmental and social justice.

Refugium for a Dream: Hacking the Future!

The concept of *refugium* - a sanctuary for species amid ecological crisis - is a powerful theme for feminist art-science, symbolising the need for protected spaces that support biodiversity and ecological resilience. In both ecological and metaphorical terms, refugia represent sites of safety, recovery, and regeneration, offering a model for how humans might coexist with non-human life in sustainable, respectful ways. These sanctuaries foster the resilience of species impacted by climate change, habitat destruction, and pollution, providing vital grounds for the continuation of life and evolution.

The notions of climate and death are explored through immersive environmental encounters that urge individuals to reflect on planetary vulnerability and survival. The concept of *Refugium* connects these themes to a broader context of survival and interdependency. This notion resonates with the sound journey *Refugium for a Dream*, inviting a meditative, sensory engagement with the environment that underscores the importance of sanctuary and resilience in the face of ecological crisis.

The concept of *Refugium*, particularly within the context of Climate & Death, resonates as a powerful call to action for earth workers (Barca, 2024) - those who defend the biosphere at a time when the potential for collective extinction has, alarmingly, become a profit model within fossil capitalism. Rather than merely seeking to preserve fragments of nature from destruction, a vision of *Refugium* insists on the need to confront and dismantle the systems responsible for the ecological crisis. As Johanna Oksala argues, our environmental politics must go beyond protecting an imagined nature isolated from capitalism; instead, we must challenge the capitalist structures that commodify and destroy life on Earth (Oksala, 2023). This philosophical stance lays a foundation for a united feminist and ecological resistance against environmental and social injustice, exposing the capitalist logic that drives both environmental destruction and gender oppression. In this framework, refugium becomes more than a sanctuary; it symbolises a radical and collective rejection of biocapitalism - a system that not only exploits natural resources but also intensifies precarity for human and non-human communities alike.

The feminist dimension of *Refugium* emerges as a response to systemic crises, offering a vision for the future that prioritises empathy, relationality, and multispecies' solidarity. Women have long been at the forefront of imagining and building such spaces, drawing on traditions of care and collaboration to reimagine what sanctuary means. In the context of *Refugium for a Dream*, the idea of "hacking" the future involves reclaiming spaces of survival and regeneration - not only for humans but for entire ecosystems. Feminist thinkers like Donna Haraway and Johanna Oksala remind us that to challenge these structures of exploitation requires both imagination and collective effort.

Embracing Oksala's framework, *Refugium* emerges as both a literal and metaphorical space of resistance, a sphere of life where all beings can persist and regenerate in defiance of exploitative systems. In envisioning refugia, earth workers from diverse backgrounds - scientists, artists, activists, and stewards of ecosystems - are united in an effort to rebuild and sustain a biosphere that honors the interconnectedness of all life.

Practitioners like Marietta Radomska and Mari Keski-Korsu have integrated feminist frameworks into their work, emphasising multispecies' coexistence and the necessity of ecological sensitivity in art-science practices. Radomska, through her work on feminist posthumanities, addresses ecological vulnerability and mortality, viewing art-science as a means to cultivate what she calls "the ethics of non/violence" - a framework that respects the life cycles of both human and non-human entities in a shared, interconnected world (Lykke, Mehrabi, and Radomska, 2021).

Mari Keski-Korsu's work also contributes to this dialogue by investigating ways to "hack" ecological futures. Through her participatory and community-oriented projects, she explores the potential of art to transform how people understand their roles within ecosystems, advocating for a regenerative approach to both environmental and social care. This feminist hacking of the future reclaims *Refugium* as a space of collaborative agency, where species survival becomes a shared responsibility.

Refugium for a Dream (Figure 5) embodies the intersections of *Climate & Death*, refugium, and feminist art-science by creating a sensory experience that reflects on the precarity of life in the face of ecological collapse. The concept of *Refugium* resonates deeply with these themes, positioning the work as a meditation on survival, loss, and resilience. The soundscapes evoke the fragility of natural habitats, inviting audiences to confront the impacts of human-driven climate change on both vulnerable ecosystems and human communities. Featuring contributions from visionary artists including: The Mourning School, Linda O'Keeffe, Ondi, Eline Gaudé and Sarah Bachinger, *Refugium for a Dream* offers a requiem for the old ways, heralding a new era of multispecies symbiosis and environmental stewardship.

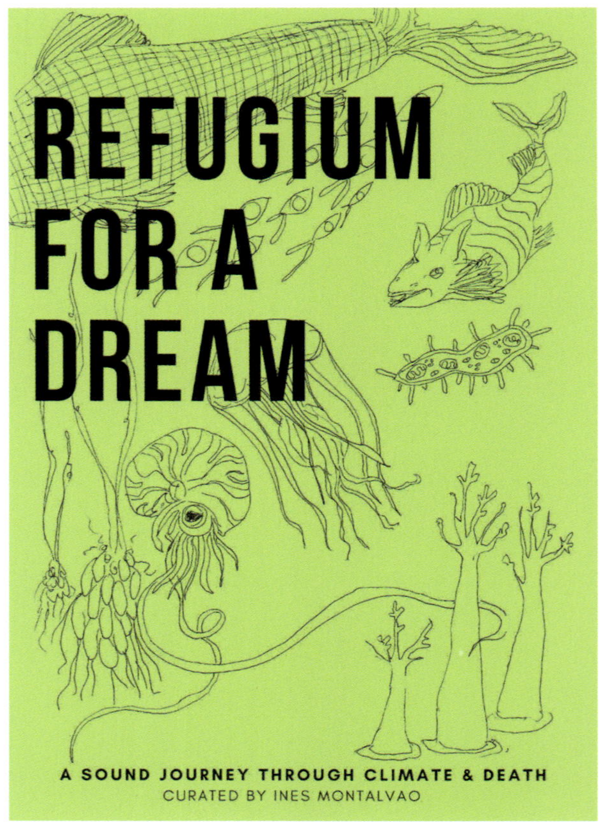

Figure 5: *Refugium for a Dream.* Montalvão, I. (2024). Poster illustration and design by the author. https://linktr.ee/inesmontalvao

Embodied Knowledge and Hybrid Spaces

How can the combination of evidence-based art-science collaborations and feminist approaches create spaces that inspire empathy, innovate beyond conventional boundaries, and elevate women's roles in shaping interdisciplinary fields?

Through the focus on multispecies' interdependencies, the creative endeavours and reflections in this essay exemplify how art-science spaces can foster embodied knowledge, moving beyond traditional, segmented understandings of science or art alone. This aligns with my experience as a hybrid practitioner, emphasising that art-science can inspire fresh understandings through immersive, sensorial interactions in narrative environments (Austin, 2020). It suggests that bridging empirical and artistic realms can catalyse innovative problem-solving and collective adaptation, reflecting the concept of *Refugium for a Dream* as an emotional, psychological refuge amid environmental challenges.

Evidence-based, feminist art-science provides an invaluable framework for addressing the ecological and social challenges of our time. Through interdisciplinary collaboration, feminist ethics, and a commitment to relationality, practitioners are forging new ways of thinking and creating that are responsive to the complexities of the Anthropocene. By grounding their work in both empirical evidence and immersive experience, art-science practitioners can inspire audiences to engage with pressing environmental issues in ways that foster empathy and ethical responsibility.

Feminist contributions to art-science have enriched the field with a unique sensitivity to care, connection, and awareness. By creating *refugia* - sanctuary spaces that nurture both human and non-human life - these practitioners offer a model for resilience and coexistence in a world increasingly shaped by environmental crisis. As we move forward, the lessons of feminist art-science will continue to guide us toward a future where art and science collaborate not only to understand the world, but to nurture and protect it. These connections - between curiosity, imagination, evidence, and feminist praxis - form the backbone of my essay and practice. Together, they underscore the transformative potential of *Refugia* as both a concept and a call to action, inviting us all to participate in hacking the future toward a more inclusive and resilient world.

References

- Austin, T., 2020. Narrative Environments and Experience Design - Space as a Medium of Communication. Routledge.
- Barca, S., 2024. Workers of the Earth: Labour, Ecology and Reproduction in the Age of Climate Change. 1st ed. London: Pluto Press.
- da Costa, B., 2008. 'Reaching the Limit: When Art Becomes Science'. Available at: https://nideffer.net/shaniweb/files/limit.pdf
- da Costa, B., and Philip, K., 2008. Tactical BioPolitics: Art, Activism and Technoscience. MIT Press.
- Keski-Korsu, M., 2022. 'On the edges of consciousness: Messaging between species'. Technoetic Arts, 20(1), pp. 39-50.
- Lykke, N., Mehrabi, T., and Radomska, M., 2021. Routledge Handbook of Queer Death Studies. London: Routledge.
- Oksala, J., 2023. Feminism, Capitalism, and Ecology. Evanston: Northwestern University Press.
- Puhakka, E.-L., 2023. 'The Bouquet of Death and Decay'. Research in Arts and Education, 2023(2), pp. 45-52.
- Sliwinska, B., 2023. Joanna Rajkowska's Rhizopolis, 2021: A rhizomatic refugium for caring commons. IT online, 2023, n. 37, pp. 1-25. Available at: https://www.rajkowska.com/wp-content/uploads/2023/11/i-t-37-article-18-sliwinska-1.pdf.

Links

- Artists with Evidence, 2024. Artists with Evidence. Available at: https://www.artistswithevidence.org/
- Artists with Evidence, 2024. Climate & Death programme. [online] Available at: https://www.saferclimate.org/program
- Artists with Evidence, 2024. Transcending Boundaries: An Evening of Art-Science. [video] Available at: https://youtu.be/KNt8qe5ak5M?feature=shared
- Intersectional Environmentalist, 2024. Ecofeminism. Available at: https://intersectionalenvironmentalist.com/toolkits/ecofeminism-and-environmental-liberation
- Lingua Plantae, 2021. Instagram. Available at: https://www.instagram.com/lingua.plantae/
- NASA, 2024. Thawing permafrost could leach microbes, chemicals into the environment. [online] Available at: https://www.jpl.nasa.gov/news/thawing-permafrost-could-leach-microbes-chemicals-into-environment
- Nature World News, 2024. Permafrost exacerbates global warming. Nature World News. Available at: https://www.natureworldnews.com/articles/60517/20240202/arctic-rivers-risk-losing-permafrost-releasing-carbon.htm
- Puhakka, E., 2019. Smell of Death (also known as Leave the Body Leave the Mind). [online] Available at: https://www.eeva-liisa.net/project/leave-the-body-leave-the-mind/
- Rajkowska, J., 2021. Rhizopolis (2021). [online] Available at: https://www.rajkowska.com/en/rhizopolis/

Additional Resources

- Alley, R.B., Marotzke, J., Nordhaus, W.D., Overpeck, J.T., Peteet, D.M., Pielke, R.A. Jr., Pierrehumbert, R.T., Rhines, P.B., Stocker, T.F., Talley, L.D. and Wallace, J.M., 2003. Abrupt climate change. Science.
- Berger, E., Keski-Korsu, M., Radomska, M. and Thastum, L. (eds.), 2023. State of the art: Elements for critical thinking and doing. Helsinki: SOLU / Bioart Society.
- Classen, C., Howes, D. and Synnott, A., 1994. Aroma: The cultural history of smell.
- Douglas, M., 2001. Purity and danger: An analysis of concepts of pollution and taboo. Available at: https://monoskop.org/images/7/7d/Douglas_Mary_Purity_and_Danger_An_Analysis_of_Concepts_of_Pollution_and_Taboo_2001.pdf
- Rogers, H.S., Halpern, M.K., Hannah, D. and de Ridder-Vignone, K. (eds.), 2021. Routledge handbook of art, science, and technology studies. Abingdon, Oxon: Routledge, Taylor & Francis Group.
- Scent of Death, 2022. Death scent. Available at: https://deathscent.com/2022/01/12/odour-of-sanctity/
- Vass, A.A., 2012. Odor mortis. Forensic Science International, 222(1-3). Available at: https://www.sciencedirect.com/science/article/abs/pii/S0379073812002824

PERFORMING THE AESTHETICS OF SENSEMAKING: SHEDDING LIGHT ON THE RELEVANCE OF THE BODY AS A FEMINIST APPROACH TO DESIGNING CYBER-PHYSICAL-SYSTEMS

Claudia Schnugg, Daniela Brill, Christian Stary

This chapter presents the Digital Sensemaking project, which introduces the relevance of the body in processes of sensemaking within digital transformation – particularly in fields such as communications engineering, where research focuses on Cyber-Physical Systems (CPS) for work processes. Sensemaking refers to the collaborative process by which people interpret information and develop shared understanding. It acknowledges that individuals bring different interests and perspectives, and may interpret information in diverse ways. Sensemaking involves meaning, mindful engagement, and the connection of social, technological and ecological clues, where the body and senses play a central role. Sensemaking is not logocentric; it includes embodiment, temporality, and the nexus between action and sense. Integrating the body into increasingly digitised environments is key to participation, diversity and accessibility. Two female researchers working with art, science and feminist approaches were invited into the Institute of Business Informatics/ Communications Engineering to introduce methodologies that incorporate the body into scientific research. By inviting female artists to develop performances aligned with scientists' research questions, the project revealed the role of the body in sensemaking with CPS from a feminist perspective.

Introduction

Several recent studies have identified the lack of a suitable methodology for CPS design as a major obstacle in engineering labs. The recommended extensions of current systems engineering methods include: the integration of agile methods, the integration of methods for stakeholder collaboration, and both rapid and virtual prototyping. In this project, we propose to approach this lack of methodology by drawing from feminist research to include the body into CPS design. How do we create meaningful interactions with CPS in the digital transformation of workplaces? Inspired by female researchers, we approached this main research question by working with artists. Inspired by feminist theories and studies that have contributed to understanding the body and embodiment in sensemaking over the past few years (e.g., de Rond et al., 2019), the body needs to be seen as aesthetically involved and situated for a holistic understanding of the role of embodiment in sensemaking. Studies in collaborative work or production, such as Zhang et al. (2023) and Luo et al. (2022), focus on the role of the body - particularly for practical purposes - in digital transformation.

We did this by researching the role of the body and aesthetics in "digital sensemaking," through a collaboration with performance artists, drawing on feminist methodologies used to investigate aesthetics of organisational life (Biehl, 2017). Performance art is inherently a bodily practice, and performance artists are trained to work with and be aware of their body (Spatz, 2015). Performance art also connects to the four core constituents: as a relational practice (Greil, 2021), performance artists engage with others and the spaces and contexts in which they perform ("being-in-the-world"); it is an ephemeral art form that evolves over time ("temporality"); and it is deeply embodied ("embodiment"). Furthermore, performance artists, their audiences, and collaborators such as choreographers, also communicate through language to verbalise what is seen, experienced, or envisioned ("language").

This research was conducted at an Institute of Business Informatics - Communications Engineering (CE institute), where several research projects on CPS, digital twins, process digitalisation, tangible interfaces in digitised business processes, and IoT elements were underway. This environment provided the research team with the necessary hardware, software, and theoretical background to empirically investigate the role of the body and aesthetics in sensemaking with CPS.

To explore digital sensemaking through artistic approaches and feminist performance methodologies, a principal investigator and a research assistant, both experienced in artistic research, art-science collaboration, and organisational aesthetics were invited to work with the team at the CE institute, which had no prior experience in working with art or feminist approaches. The research built upon the existing environment at the CE institute, and a methodology was developed to address the needs and open research questions arising from the intersection of these disciplines. With approximately 10 years of experience in curating and researching at the intersection of art, science and technology, this track record guided the mediation of interdisciplinary collaboration. It helped bridge gaps in organisational structures, needs, and disciplinary jargon (Schnugg, 2019: 217ff.), while a mixed background in organisation studies, organisational aesthetics, and artistic research in new media and technologies facilitated the alignment of artistic development with the scientific research questions and the research setting.

Theoretical Orientation: Aesthetics, the Body, and Sensible Knowing in Sensemaking

Since the 1990s, organisational aesthetics has gained attention in understanding organisational life, focusing on how sensory experiences and aesthetic knowledge influence members' work processes and environments (Strati, 1992; Taylor, 2002). Scholars have explored aesthetic judgments, materiality, and the role of sensory cues in organisational sensemaking, emphasising the body's role in how people engage with their surroundings (Höllerer et al., 2019; Stigliani & Ravasi, 2018). Recent perspectives categorise aesthetics in organisations as a directed stimulus, a knowledge tool, and an open-ended outcome, each highlighting the intersection of the individual, their senses, and their environment. In sensemaking theory, there is a growing emphasis on how bodily and sensory experiences shape decision-making and collective sensemaking processes, especially in the context of organisational change (Baldessarelli, 2022). With digital transformations, the role of the body and aesthetic cues in making sense of digital environments becomes a critical area of exploration, as embodied practices are often overlooked in automated, algorithm-driven work. Empirical research is focused on understanding how embodied knowledge and aesthetic experiences contribute to sensemaking in digitised work processes, helping workers navigate increasingly complex and abstract systems (Zhang et al., 2023, Gemeinboeck & Saunders, 2022).

Performance Art: Performers' Kinaesthetic Knowledge and Performance in Organisation-research

In line with feminist theorists and researchers, we decided to work with performance artists in the empirical setting to investigate digital sensemaking. Our focus on the body and sensible knowledge aligns with research into (a) the body in organisations through performance (Biehl, 2017) and (b) the research on the body in HCI and Human-Robot Interaction (HRI) through engagement with performance art, choreography and dance (LaViers et al., 2018), to harness performance artists' kinaesthetic awareness (Gemeinboeck & Saunders, 2016). Performance artists are trained to work with their body, to listen to their body, focus on their sensory perception and are familiar with concepts like proprioception and embodiment (Brill et al., 2022; Spatz, 2015). Another argument is that dancers and choreographers can organise meaningful encounters and thus enrich HCI and HRI research through this capacity (LaViers et al., 2018). In the same vein, dancers and performance theorists argue that performance art is a relational practice, developing relations between actors and audience, spaces and objects including The Internet of Things (IoT) elements (Greil, 2022, Cuan et al., 2019).

In organisational research, dance and performance studies as methodology and theoretical perspective for analysing organisational processes and situations have gained attention for accessing embodied knowledge, skills and understanding of organisational contexts (Biehl, 2017), gesture theories have also become valuable resources for organisational researchers (Ruprecht, 2015). Laban movement analysis (Reynolds, 2007) has been used by HCI and organisational researchers to investigate the movements of their research subjects (LaViers et al., 2018, Reinhold et al., 2018). Aside from analysing embodied interaction with a focus on rhythms and disruptions, such as breaks in rhythm (Chandler, 2012: 876), dance in space and time through gestures and movement has been employed in research when people move in relation to each other (Biehl-Missal, 2016). Performance or "performing a space" and rhythm analysis connects to making sense of spaces and places (Nash, 2020). In terms of embodiment and sensemaking, the lens of dance studies can provide access to tacit knowledge, ideas of repetition and routines, or how spontaneous movements occur in organisational life (Slutskaya & de Cock, 2008).

Methodology and Data Collection

Guided by sensemaking theory, the methodological design for exploring the role of the body and sensible knowledge in digital sensemaking was structured into three phases. In phase one, we worked with two performers to access their kinesthetic knowledge, reflecting on embodiment and aesthetic aspects of interacting with digital technologies unfamiliar to them. Phase two tested insights from phase one in a consistent setting with test subjects, incorporating moments of sensebreaking and sensegiving (Vitry et al., 2020; Gioia & Chittipeddi, 1991). In phase three, we returned to a collaboration with two artists to explore digital sensemaking amid changing interface functionalities, focusing on the body as a change agent - drawing on Weick's (2011) concept of "change poets" based on the insights and findings from phases 1 and 2 (following a Design Science approach (Hevner et al., 2004).

We employed a mixed methodology inspired by prior research in sensemaking, organisational studies through performance, art, and HCI/HRI work to evaluate data. The methodology combined ethnographic work with participatory observation, interviews, informal conversations, and written materials, such as sketches and reflections from the performers. We also used video-based analysis, guided by de Rond et al.'s (2019) methodology, and worked with performance artists to record and analyse their artistic explorations and rehearsals. By integrating performance art into our research, we aimed to address aesthetic awareness and explore the role of the body in organisational processes. The data collected, including video recordings, sketches, and interviews, was analysed using qualitative research software like MAXQDA and supplemented with manual categorisation. The analysis led to the creation of "thick descriptions" of each case, detailing the processes by which artists made sense of digital technologies, ensuring that our approach aligned with previous studies in performance art and organisational research methodologies.

Research Phases and Data Gathered

Over the course of 1.5 years we worked with five artists in the research setting.

Phase 1: Artistic Exploration and Mimicry

For the first phase, we invited performance artists Laura Stoll and Marko Markovic to explore the digital technologies provided by the CE institute. The artists were selected for their interest in exploring embodiment in contemporary performance, with a focus on cognitive, behavioural, and social dimensions of meaning making. Moreover, we chose them because they are not engaged in new media art nor with topics of digital transformation, beyond average use of mobile phones and laptops.

The goal was to investigate the two performance artists' sensemaking process throughout their engagement with IoT sensors M5 Stacks and there robot with a 3D scanner as payload. The visual representation of the sensors and functionalities also formed a digital twin. They needed to learn how to interact with the sensors and the coding language in a self-guided process to make sense of the provided digital technology - both individually and collectively.

We asked the artists to focus on bodily sensemaking - exploring technology through and with the body - and to report on physical changes, embodied knowledge, and aesthetic experience. We complemented their self-reflection by asking the artists to break down their interactions into micro-movements and create micro-performances that embodied their sensemaking with the technologies. In the evaluation of the video material, we focused on repeated movements, sequenced the interaction in micro-movements, and compared how movements changed or became more precise throughout the duration of the artists' engagement with the technologies.

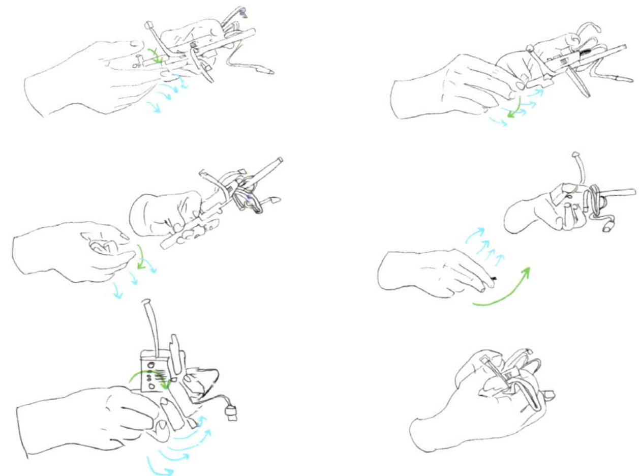

Figure 1: Trying to make sense of provided instructions, with the performers' fluent movements using sensors. Stoll, L. (2022). Drawings: Daniela Brill.

This sequencing took place by creating image sequences from stills from the videos and comparing stills from different moments in the artists' exploration. Additionally, drawings of hand movements including directions and sequential information was added to enrich the visual information for analysis (Figure 1).

The artists sought to extend their exploration into a performance, resulting in the work *Mimicry*, developed through their sensemaking processes with and from the body with the robot. It was presented in two versions: outdoors at the university's

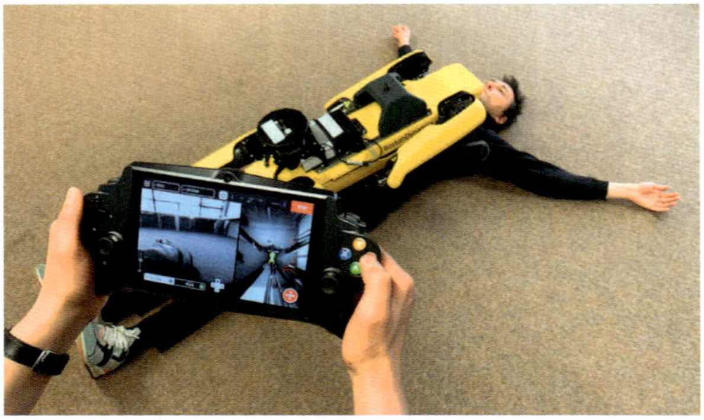

Figure 2: *Feeling the weight of the robot.* Markovic, M. and Stoll, L. (2022). Exploring another bodily aspect to understand it. Photo: Daniela Brill.

Long Night of Science, and indoors at an art gallery in Vienna. The performance continued their investigation of the CE robot through focused, individual bodily movements. Throughout the development of the performance, these movements and interactions became increasingly refined and were attributed with additional meaning. For example, the artists started by imitating the movements of the robot to interact and understand its capacities. This developed into a language, with meaning attributed to certain movements of the human and robot bodies, rather than a pure imitation (which was not possible, as the joints and limbs of the robot differ from those of the human body). The artists created situations to make sense of the robot by feeling its movements and weight, for example by lying beneath the robot (Figure 2). This action was first perceived as strange at the CE institute but made sense when explained. Data was collected from video recordings, interviews, and diaries. The weight, physical feel, and capacity to move softly or stomp are part of making sense of the technology, handling it, designing interactions, and making sense of possibilities and dangerous situations.

Phase 2: An Interface to Draw with the Body and an Exploration of Space with Sound

For the second phase, we invited new media artist Antoni Rayzhekov to investigate sensemaking through the body in the context of visual and sound feedback. The task emerged from insights from Phase 1. The goal was to create a situation that allows empirical research with a group of test subjects. The artist decided to develop two performative installations, in which the audience became performers by interacting with the installation. The interaction was designed as a sensemaking process of the installation. The first artwork, *Drawing Exercises,* invited pairs of test subjects to make sense of the interaction and functionalities through a series of tasks guided by visual feedback. The second artwork, *The Distance Between Us Is Music* invited the audience to explore a space in relationship to other audience members guided by sound feedback.

Research into the role of visuals and objects has been explored in studies on multimodal sensemaking (Höllerer et al., 2018) and the role of materiality in individual and collective sensemaking (Stigliani & Ravasi, 2012). In the context of the digital, and drawing from insights from Phase 1 - where the performance artists began to feel and move differently in response to visual input, robot movements, or feedback from sensors or their digital twins - we sought to further explore the visual, material and other aesthetic aspects of sensemaking in relation to the body. This exploration was extended to a larger cohort of test subjects.

Drawing Exercises offers a full-body interaction with digital technology, moving beyond gestures or touch. Sensors on the performers track body orientation, stress level, and heart rate (Figure 3). Performer 1 controls vertical lines and performer 2 horizontal ones, allowing them to draw collaboratively through movement.

Early tasks involve drawing lines and circles to explore the interface and coordinate their actions. In task four, the line starts to jitter as the stress sensor interferes, disrupting the flow and prompting reinterpretation. In task five, the heart rate sensor alters the drawing behavior again, requiring the performers to adapt their movements to the new feedback.

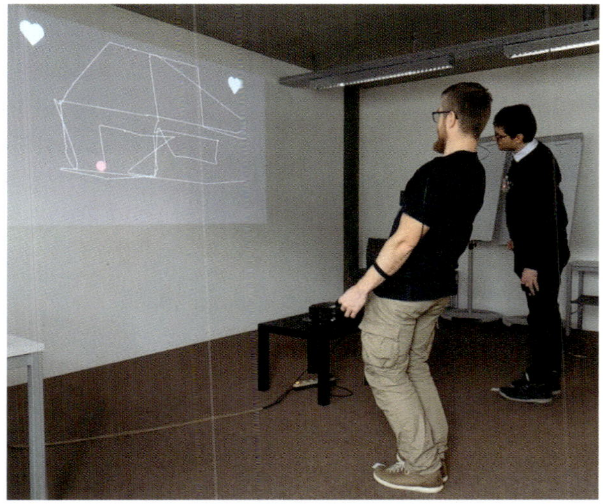

Figure 3: *Test phase two*. Rayzhekov, A. (2023). Subjects performing the cycle with sensor sets mounted on their bodies. Photo: Daniela Brill.

The performative installation was staged at the CE institute, with 26 test subjects taking part. Data was collected from video recordings and questionnaires (an overview of the answers can be found here: https://drive.google.com/file/d/1aJKvAy7jj8HAitO33M8HUsihBTybeTjF/view?usp=drive_link).

Students being introduced to business engineering, business engineering specialists, 2 artists, and middle-aged visitors (16 male, 10 female) entered the performative installation without any prior knowledge of its functionality. Putting on the sensors, their function was explained, and they were informed that they had to work together to draw - this was the first clue to help them figure out how to solve the tasks presented in the projection.

The Distance Between Us Is Music. This second performative installation investigates the relationship between sound, listening, bodily movement and sensemaking processes. It invites the audience to become performers, moving together and adjusting their distances while exploring the emerging group dynamics and the available space in different rhythms. This act of listening and moving is part of sensemaking of space - both physical and relational - and the creation of sound. As they filled the space together, the performers navigated it by making sense of their positions, distances, velocities, and the physical group dynamics. In this artistic attempt to focus on the joint sensemaking process of the distance between individuals who become a group within a space, the artist translated these distances into sound.

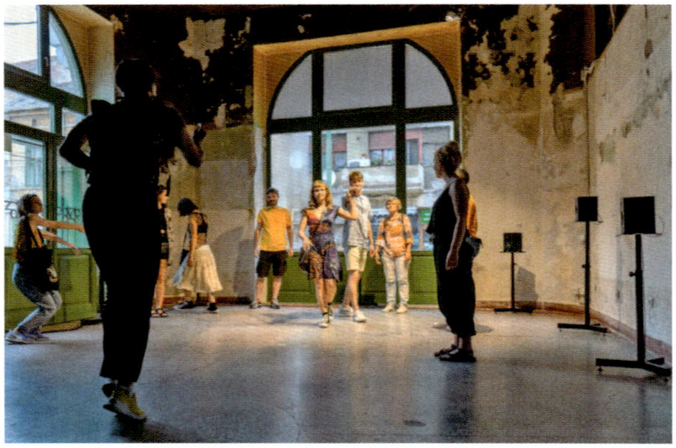

Figure 4: *The Distance Between Us Is Music*
Still from performance in Timisoara. (2023). Photo: Marginal.

The sound heard in the space served as guiding aesthetic feedback for the actively listening performers. Based on a sample derived from a piano piece, the artist generated sounds for each performer moving in the space, relating to others, and fusing sounds into music (Figure 4).

Eight speakers were positioned in the corners and sides of a room, creating a spatial sound experience of the space and the performers. The performers were tracked by a camera that calculated distances on an ongoing basis. The sound algorithm added layers of complexity, rhythms and sounds to the sound experience, depending on the number of performers, their distances, and position in the space.

After the premiere of the performative installation, one of the researchers engaged in participatory observation, interviewing four initial participants of the performative installation about their experience and gathering feedback from the exhibition team (5 people). One staged performance with four Romanian professional performers took place, in which additional 6 people from the audience took part. Data was collected from video recordings.

Phase 3: The Body as Change Agent

In the third phase of the project, we invited new media artist Klemens Kohlweis and dancer Andrea Vezga to develop a performance that addresses change in digital transformation or a digitised CPS. Two aspects became pillars for this task, both important for the CE institute and for the digital sensemaking research: (a) included a Digital Twin in the system they created, and (b) investigated the role of the body as a change agent, as an embodied analogy to Weick's (2011) poets of change. The two artists were also provided with theoretical background in sensemaking and the main insights from the analysis of Phases 1 and 2, specifically to test the insights concerning the connection of aesthetic feedback and the body in the sensemaking of digital technologies.

Key questions addressed in the project were: What role does the body and aesthetic feedback play to cope with change in digital environments? What is the interplay of bodily movements and aesthetic feedback in overcoming challenges posed by a changed gesture vocabulary, which is difficult to describe in words or abstract representations, such as in instruction booklets?

Starting from these central questions, the two artists collaborated over three months to create a performance in which the dancer bodily explores sensemaking with interactive technology. She responds live to changes in an established gesture vocabulary (Aigner et al., 2012) while steering a

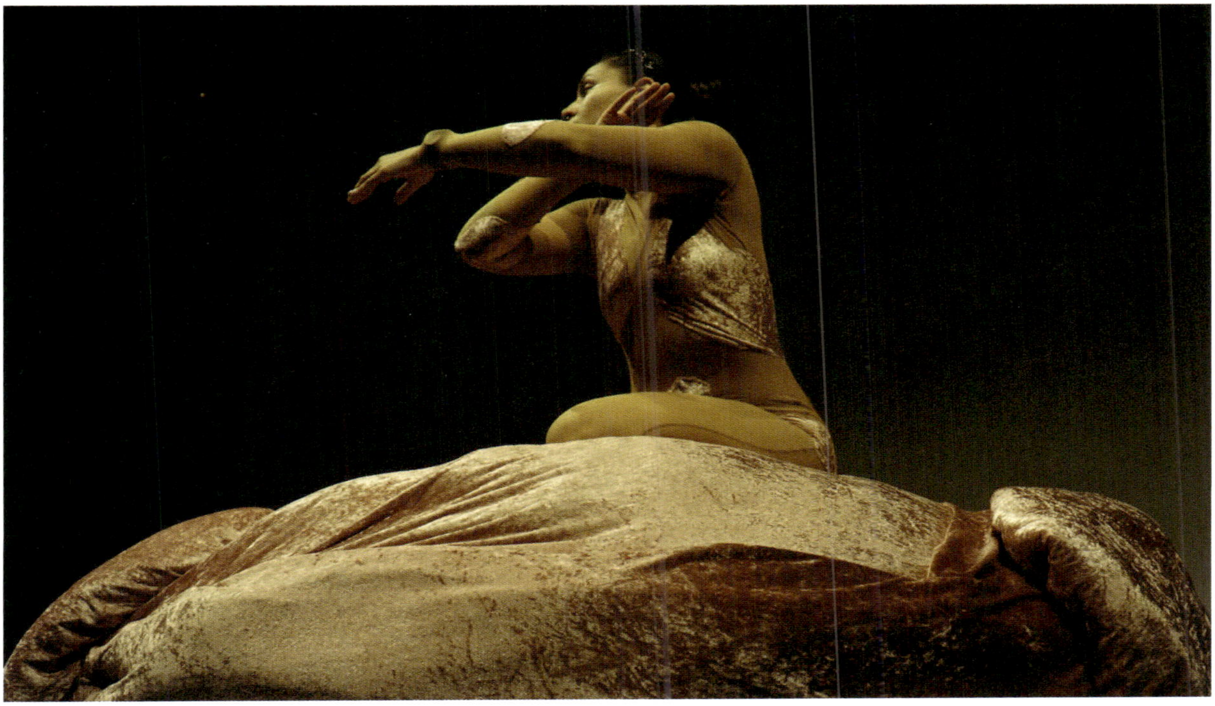

Figure 5: *Sync with Change.* Vezga, A. and Kohlweis K. (2023). Performance. Photo: Daniela Brill.

moving platform using sensors on her hands, head, and left foot. A sound-based digital twin provided feedback and supported her perception, especially as the platform's movement disrupted her direct bodily experience.

The performance lasted between 12 and 16 minutes. While the performance followed a dramaturgy, the gesture vocabulary was slightly different each time it started, as it was newly configured by the media artist. The performance started with the dancer lying on the platform at rest. Slowly, the dancer started to explore the gestures required to move the platform, eventually standing up and moving more freely (Figure 5). Midway through the performance, the media artist changes the gesture vocabulary required to control the platform's movement. The dancer was now confronted with a change in the functionalities of digital technology, but the sound digital twin helped her orientate herself and make sense of the new gestures. She then left the platform and performed her way off-stage, making sure that through her gestures and movements the platform could not follow her.

One of the researchers worked closely with the artists for participatory observation in the process. Data was collected from research diaries, in-depth reflection sessions, and qualitative interviews after the performance.

Analysis

In the analysis of the first phase, we looked for moments where aesthetic cues played a central role in the performers' sensemaking of the technologies that they encountered for the first time and learned to use. Additionally, we were interested in the interplay between the performers' embodiments and the increasingly fluid micro-movements that are mediated in space or by aesthetic cues. To this end, we brought together the video data, body language, spoken words in the video, research diaries, interviews, and individual reflections. Coding resulted in 514 coded moments throughout the sensemaking process relevant for evaluation.

General insights regarding aesthetics and sensemaking from the first phase are as follows:

- Aesthetic feedback helps the performers to make sense of the technologies and supports their process in becoming fluent in while interacting with the technologies.

- Aesthetic cues provided by others (e.g. instructions) tended to make sense only retrospectively, once the performers had already made sense of the technologies and developed their own embodied way of interacting with them. Some of the aesthetic cues in these instructions were found to be confusing. Additionally, the tangible quality of the IoT sensors, perceived as "cheap plastics", irritated the performers when they began to make sense of the sensors and their functionality. Nevertheless, both female and male artists had similar issues.

- An interplay of the aesthetic properties of the technologies and the performers' bodies could be identified, not only in the performance of mimicry, but also as they became "more fluent" in the operation of the technologies.

In analysing the visual installation from Phase 2, we focused on how participants collaboratively made sense of the tasks and embodied the interaction principles to produce the desired visual output (Brill et al., 2023). Coding the performance yielded 205 distinct moments. The primary feedback for the performers was the visual line representing their combined movements. They had to make sense of how their actions influenced the line and jointly decide whether the result met the task requirements before progressing.

The main insights were:

- The visual data gathered from the videos and interviews often differed: the way the person moved and behaved in the video differed from the latter description of the movements in the interview or questionnaire. For example, when participants touched each other or held hands in the video, they later claimed not to have done so in the performance. Their retrospective descriptions did not match their actual actions!

- The participants were frequently stuck in incorrect movements, repeating them even when they knew they weren't producing the desired outcome. New movements were difficult to embody, especially when they needed to adjust the velocity or stop moving for the line to appear.

- The movements that were a result of cognitive processes frequently did not result in the desired results. They often used movements that they were used to from interaction with mobile phones or imagined gesture interaction between one person and the digital device. In the test cohort, more women than men were more easily stressed when they could not immediately interact correctly.

- However, movements driven by the feeling of the other person - leading to fluidity and synchronicity - resulted in correct lines. For example, coordinating movements by counting instead of "feeling" each other's movements, or moving in a more "fluid" way, resulted in a square instead of a circle.

The analysis of the sound installation in phase 2 was limited due to the limited data. The most important takeaways were that the audience entering the installation took some time to become aware of their body in the space, following an initial surprise at what was happening. This then created a new kind of awareness of their body and helped them to focus on the sound, the space, and the group dynamics in space in a new way. Mostly participating women reported being surprised how this made them feel part of something, relating to others, and the space. Exploring the physical space guided by sound helped them to focus on their body in relation to space, others and the changes in the crowd. This is an important aspect because, in the development of digital systems for organisational processes, the question of how to deal with spaces in VR and AR and to make them experienceable, along with the relation to movement and other sensory cues such as physical objects, is still being discussed (Luo et al., 2022; Zhang et al., 2023).

The goal in phase 3 was to find out if the body could be considered an agent of change and understand the role of aesthetic feedback in this context. The analysis focused on juxtaposing video analysis with the analysis of the interviews, research diaries and reflective sessions (151 coded moments). The dancer identified two keyways of making sense of the interaction with and through the technology. First, there was a moment of synchronicity with the technology, during which she could bodily sense the platform, and move accordingly to perform. Second, there was a moment of switching to a more conscious, less instinctive way of moving when she felt she needed to make deliberate decisions about her movements.

In both cases, the trigger for movement was aesthetic, embodied, and sensed through her body, limbs, muscles, etc.: "I felt like I had to listen to the technology in a sense, my body had to listen to the technology, it became more felt internally like a negotiation."

The incorporated sound digital twin was partially perceived by the dancer as aesthetic feedback guiding her movement in a particular direction. She explained in her final interview: "The sound [...] was a signal for me to know that the sensor was properly working. So if I could hear the sound being synchronised with my movements, I knew that the signal was being picked up correctly and that I could trust my body to move," and: "If the sound had a certain tonality, it told me I move softer, or to move faster, [...], but in an aesthetic sense, I would go by the feeling of what the sound transmitted."

In this way, she learned to make sense of her movement and digital interaction through sound, which helped her stay focused. In critical moments where something wasn't working correctly or she felt out of control, she needed to switch to a more conscious mode of decision-making to prevent falling or crashing. As soon as the gesture vocabulary that she had embodied in the first half of the performance was "updated", with changes or new functionalities added, critical moments became inevitable. In such moments, the sound digital twin immediately signalled to her when the movement was not working, helping her to act swiftly. After this update, she again needed to focus and "listen" to the system with her body to embody the new gesture vocabulary in order to finish the performance.

Contribution and Discussion

Our contribution is twofold:

a) We included different aspects of sensemaking, we could show how the body (and embodiment) and the physical (and digital) context (or "being-in-the world" and "sense-action nexus") are intertwined through aesthetics.

b) We valued the importance of acknowledging the body in digital transformation through aesthetics.

A The Role of Aesthetics and Body in Sensemaking

Although language and cognitive processes are important in sensemaking, descriptions and abstractions of what one is supposed to experience or the complexities of physical contexts cannot substitute for the actual experience. The interplay of experiencing the world and the embodiment is often mediated by aesthetics - whether through aesthetic cues, sensory information, or sensible knowledge. In that sense, all three different perspectives on aesthetics in organisational studies, as described by Baldessarelli et al. (2022), play a role: directed stimulus, knowledge tool, and open-ended outcome.

Moreover, as the performances show, time - temporality - also plays a part, as the body needs time to explore and embody knowledge, movement, or to react to aesthetic cues. As each phase of empirical exploration reveals aesthetics can be a directed stimulus that informs the sensemaking individual. At a certain point, aesthetics and embodied sensible knowledge become a knowledge tool for navigating processes. Once individuals become deprived of their learned, embodied knowledge, they are at a loss!

This is something that many workers experience during digital transformations or after the introduction of new or altered systems. Aesthetics in sensemaking is also an open-ended process, as new ontological aesthetics emerge, which in turn help individuals navigate new situations (e.g., gesture vocabularies for digital interaction). In times of change, it is not only the final articulation of the sense being made that supports the change process or making sense of the change, but also the body which can be mediated by aesthetic feedback. This aesthetic feedback can be more helpful than verbal descriptions of how to move as the combination of the sound digital twin with the movement of the platform has shown. Adding this component to the often-logocentric approach to designing CPS is an important contribution raised by predominantly female researchers and feminist approaches.

B Awareness of Aesthetics in Digital Transformation

Movements such as gesture vocabularies become part of embodied practices, so simply changing them for a new update can lead to problems, misunderstandings, and misuse of the digitised systems. In digital transformation, it is necessary to be aware of aesthetic cues and embodied practices that inform the workers, allowing them to continue making sense of processes and emerging situations in digitised or semi-digitised environments. To design valuable systems, we must also include feminist ideas regarding the importance of aesthetics, sensible knowledge and the body, or finding representations and other ways to integrate them digitally. This goes beyond the idea of "embodied provenance" or considering analogue aspects when designing digitised work processes (Luo et al. 2022; Zhang et al. 2023).

It is not only the material elements that support the sensemaking, but the objects and spaces in relation to the body, its position, and the environment, eventually supported with additional aesthetic feedback. The latter can culminate in a digital twin that provides (in)direct information to the performer, particularly when focusing on the visual representation of combined information about bodily movements.

Issues such as *video conference fatigue*, (experienced by many during the Covid-19 pandemic lockdowns and still affects some today), which assumes workers are merely eyes, ears, and brain, or the need for furniture in AR collaborative processes, understanding the role of the body, movements, embodiment, and aesthetics in organisational life will help design systems for digital transformation that allow workers and organisational members to cope more effectively.

C Role of the Project at the CE-Institute

Right from the beginning of the DIGI-Sense project, the translation between the disciplines was a central issue. Core themes such as "art, aesthetics, and performance" were difficult to grasp for the team at the institute and the participatory observation showed this in the first weeks and months of the DIGI-Sense project. Over the time of the project, the team members of the CE institute shifted from a superficial understanding of these concepts to a more complex understanding and the ability to relate them to their own work. Experiencing the work with the artists and regular reflection on the results helped to do so, as a logocentric explanation of these concepts at the beginning of the project were rather confusing for the CE researchers.

Conclusion and Further Questions

From the perspective of sensemaking as something collective, it is worth exploring the ontological potency of aesthetics (González Valerio, 2023) in digital transformation and the sensemaking of digital technologies, with different behaviour sequences and interpretations for women and men. Which strategies could enrich digital transformation in work and everyday life by adopting a feminist approach that recognises the importance of the body in CPS (Cyber-Physical Systems)? This remains to be researched and in addition, it could be insightful to compare such research across different work cultures and disciplinary backgrounds.

Funding

The authors acknowledge financial support from the Linz Institute of Technology.

Acknowledgements

The authors thank María Antonia González Valerio for feedback on aesthetics, Scott de LaHunta for feedback on video analysis strategies, artists Sougwen Chung, Alexandra Murray-Leslie, Aisen Caro Chaicin and Merritt Moore for discussion on performers' kinesthetic knowledge in preparing the empirical work. Thanks to Markus Jahn for building the wearable sensor set for *Drawing Exercises*, to Marginal for providing support for *The Distance Between Us Is Music*.

References

- Aigner, R., Wigdor, D., Benko, H., Haller, M., Lindbauer, D., Ion, A., Zhao, S. and Koh, J., 2012. Understanding Mid-Air Hand Gestures: A Study of Human Preferences in Usage of Gesture Types for HCI. Microsoft Research TechReport MSR-TR-2012-111, 2, pp.30.
- Baldessarelli, G., Stigliani, I. and Elsbach, K., 2022. The Aesthetic Dimension of Organizing: A Review and Research Agenda. Academy of Management Annals, 16, pp.217-257.
- Biehl, B., 2017. Dance and Organisation. New York: Routledge.
- Biehl-Missal, B., 2016. Filling the empty space: site-specific dance in a techno club. Culture and Organization, 25, pp.16-31.
- Brill, D., Schnugg, C. and Stary, C., 2022. Digital Sensemaking: Sensemaking as a Driver of Transformation. Proceedings IFKAD'22 - Int. Forum on Knowledge Asset Dynamics, Lugano, Switzerland, pp.652-672, ISSN 2280-787X.
- Brill, D., Schnugg, C., Stary, C. and Rayzhekov, A., 2023. Researching the body and movement through artistic performative installations for collaborative digital sensemaking. Proceedings KUI '23. https://doi.org/10.1145/3623462.3624629
- Chandler, J., 2012. Work as dance. Organization, 19, pp.865-878.
- Cuan, C., Berl, E. and LaViers, A., 2019. Time to Compile: A Performance Installation as Human-Robot Interaction Study Examining Self-Evaluation and Perceived Control. Paladyn: Journal of Behavioral Robotics, 10, pp.267-285. https://doi.org/10.1515/pjbr-2019-0024
- De Rond, M., Holeman, I. and Howard-Grenville, J., 2019. Sensemaking from the body: An enactive ethnography of rowing the Amazon. Academy of Management Journal, 62, pp.1961-1988.
- Gemeinboeck, P. and Saunders, R., 2022. Moving beyond the mirror: relational and performative meaning making in human-robot communication. AI & Society, 37, pp.549-563. https://link.springer.com/article/10.1007/s00146-021-01212-1
- Gemeinboeck, P. and Saunders, R., 2016. Towards Socializing Non-Anthropomorphic Robots by Harnessing Dancers' Kinesthetic Awareness. In: Koh, J., Dunstan, B., Silvera-Tawil, D., Velonaki, M. (eds.), Cultural Robotics. Lecture Notes in Computer Science, Vol. 9549, pp.85-97. Cham: Springer. https://doi.org/10.1007/978-3-319-42945-8_8
- Gioia, D.A. and Chittipeddi, K., 1991. Sensemaking and sensegiving in strategic change initiation. Strategic Management Journal, 12, pp.433-448.
- González Valerio, M.A., 2023. Life in Medium: Rethinking the Possibilities of Art and Bio-Media from an Aesthetic Ontology. In: González Valerio, M.A. and Tratnik, P. (eds.), Through the Scope of Life: Art and (Bio)Technologies Philosophically Revisited, pp.3-32. Cham: Springer.

- Hevner, A.R., March, S.T., Park, J. and Ram, S., 2004. Design science in information systems research. MIS Quarterly, 28, pp.75-105.
- Höllerer, M., Jancsary, D. and Grafström, M., 2018. 'A Picture is Worth a Thousand Words'. Organization Studies, 39, pp.617-644. https://doi.org/10.1177/0170840618765019
- LaViers, A., Cuan, C., Maguire, C., Bradler, K., et al., 2018. Choreographic and Somatic Approaches for the Development of Expressive Robotic Systems. Arts, 7, 11. https://doi.org/10.3390/arts7020011
- Luo, W., Lehmann, A., Widengren, H. and Dachselt, R., 2022. Where Should We Put It? Layout and Placement Strategies of Documents in Augmented Reality for Collaborative Sensemaking. Proceedings of the 2022 CHI Conference on Human Factors in Computing Systems, pp.1-16.
- Nash, L., 2020. Performing Place: A Rhythmanalysis of the City of London. Organization Studies, 41, pp.301-321. https://doi.org/10.1177/0170840618789161
- Reinhold, E., Schnugg, C. and Barthold, C., 2018. Dancing in the office. A Study of Gesture as Resistance. Scandinavian Journal of Management, 34, pp.162-169. https://doi.org/10.1016/j.scaman.2018.05.001
- Reynolds, D., 2007. Rhythmic subjects: Uses of energy in the dances of Mary Wigman, Martha Graham and Merce Cunningham. Alton, UK: Dance books.
- Ruprecht, L., 2015. Gesture, Interruption, Vibration: Rethinking Early Twentieth-Century Gestural Theory and Practice in Walter Benjamin, Rudolf von Laban and Mary Wigman. Dance Research Journal, 47, pp.23-42.
- Schnugg, C., 2019. Creating ArtScience Collaboration: Bringing Value to Organizations. Cham: Palgrave Macmillan, Springer. https://doi.org/10.1007/978-3-030-04549-4
- Slutskaya, N. and De Cock, C., 2008. The Body Dances: Carnival Dance and Organization. Organization, 15, pp.851-868.
- Spatz, B., 2015. What a Body Can Do: Technique as Knowledge, Practice as Research. New York & London: Routledge.
- Stigliani, I. and Ravasi, D., 2012. Organizing Thoughts and Connecting Brains: Material Practices and the Transition from Individual to Group-Level Prospective Sensemaking. Academy of Management Journal, 55, pp.1232-1259.
- Stigliani, I. and Ravasi, D., 2018. The Shaping of Form: Exploring Designers' Use of Aesthetic Knowledge. Organization Studies, 39, pp.747-784. https://doi.org/10.1177/0170840618759813
- Strati, A., 2009. 'Do You Do Beautiful Things?': Aesthetics and Art in Qualitative Methods of Organization Studies. In: Buchanan, D. and Bryman, A. (eds.), The Sage Handbook of Organizational Research Methods, pp.230-245. London: Sage.
- Strati, A., 1992. Aesthetic understanding of organizational life. Academy of Management Review, 17, pp.568-581.
- Taylor, S.S., 2002. Overcoming aesthetic muteness: Researching organizational members' aesthetic experience. Human Relations, 55, pp.821-840.
- Vitry, C., Sage, D. and Daintly, A., 2020. Affective atmospheres of sensemaking and learning: Workplace meetings as aesthetic and anaesthetic. Management Learning, 51, pp.274-292.
- Weick, K.E., 2011. Reflections: Change agents as change poets–On reconnecting flux and hunches. Journal of Change Management, 11, pp.7-20.
- Zhang, Y., Ens, B., Satriadi, K., Yang, Y. and Goodwin, S., 2023. Defining Embodied Provenance for Immersive Sensemaking. Extended Abstracts of the 2023 CHI Conference on Human Factors in Computing Systems, pp.1-7.

ENGAGING ART, SCIENCE, AND EMPATHY (EASE): LESSONS FROM INTERDISCIPLINARY, CARE-CENTERED RESEARCH ON THE WICKED PROBLEM CHRONIC PAIN

Jane Prophet, Afton Hassett, Rahbel Rahman-Tahir

This chapter extends the authors' individual and collective research on interdisciplinary, community-engaged inquiry by examining how an Ethics of Care can shape collaborations across art, design, social work, and STEM fields. We share insights from a research initiative involving thirteen academic researchers and nine advisers, focused on the "wicked problem" of chronic pain and health inequities. Through six interdisciplinary teams, we co-designed arts-informed studies with over 100 participants living with chronic pain to support well-being, advocate for systemic change, and foster thriving. We examined the research that led to a Photovoice study co-developed with patients identifying as women of colour to illustrate how creative methods, relational accountability, and community engagement can challenge extractive research norms. Our findings underscore the importance of navigating disciplinary differences, building trust, and recognising lived experience as expertise. We propose that adopting an Ethics of Care approach to research design and team practices can lead to more inclusive, patient-centred inquiry. By reflecting on those approaches, we aim to promote equity in health research and support broader institutional transformation.

An Ethics of Care Approach to Chronic Pain

Chronic pain is an umbrella term that emerged in the 1970s to describe any pain that recurs or lasts longer than three months (Treede et al., 2015). Now classified as a separate condition, chronic pain is experienced by around 20% of adults globally, and by 100 million (over 20%) American adults (Dahlhamer et al., 2018; Simon, 2012). Unlike acute pain, which typically has a clear cause and resolution, chronic pain is highly individualised and there is no single practical standardised test or "cure." The need to balance evidence-based guidelines and patient-specific needs is now better understood. Still, diagnosis and treatment remain inequitable, with studies showing disparities in the experience and treatment of chronic pain, and age, race, gender, sexuality, and income linked to differences in the prevalence of pain (Breivik et al., 2006; Fejer, Kyvik, and Hartvigsen, 2006; Haukenes et al., 2015; Stubbs et al., 2010). Gender significantly influences how patients are treated in clinical settings, with those who identify as women or as gender-diverse individuals more likely to have their symptoms dismissed or pathologised as psychological or imagined (Johansson et al., 1996; Ware, 1992). A person's race and ethnicity significantly shape how their pain is interpreted by medical professionals (Edwards, Fillingim, and Keefe, 2001), with well-documented racial disparities in U.S. healthcare including the underdiagnosis of chronic pain and insufficient pain management among racially and ethnically minoritised patients (Hoffman et al., 2016; Wakefield et al., 2018). While patients presenting as White women are more likely than those from racially and ethnically minoritised groups to have their pain acknowledged by healthcare providers, they too are often subject to what has been termed the "gender pain gap" (eClinicalMedicine, 2024). These disparities underscore the urgent need for research that centres the voices of those most affected by chronic pain, particularly women or gender-diverse individuals from racially and ethnically minoritised backgrounds.

An Ethics of Care (EoC) approach is well-suited to understanding chronic pain health disparities and addressing treatment inequities because it emphasises attentiveness, responsiveness to lived experience, and relationality - principles frequently absent in biomedical models that prioritise objectivity and standardisation. In her key work on the EoC in 1984, the American philosopher Nell Noddings described EoC as "rooted in receptivity, relatedness, and responsiveness" (Noddings, 1984, p.2). Noddings' focus was on relations between people, which is highly relevant to chronic pain and its treatment, where one group of people (medical professionals) has often treated people from another group (patients) differently depending on each patient's intersectional identity. Noddings was not using "relational" as Donna Haraway inferes as a more-than-human relational network, which accounts for nonhumans such as plants, ecosystems, animals, technologies and immaterial entities such as ideas and practices. However, within a decade, Joan Tronto's definition of EoC came closer to Haraway's more-than-human relational network concept when Tronto described caring as "a species activity that includes everything we do to maintain, continue and repair our 'world' so that we can live in it as well as possible. That world includes our bodies, ourselves, and our environment, all of which we seek to interweave in a complex, life-sustaining web" (Tronto, 1993, p.103). Living with chronic pain unfolds within a more-than-human relational network in which the environment - both built and natural - can shape experiences of suffering and relief. Inaccessible architecture, noise pollution, or extreme weather can intensify pain or limit mobility. At the same time, elements such as soothing landscapes, animals, or adaptive technologies can offer comfort, mitigate symptoms, and foster a sense of connection beyond the human - contributions which point toward the need for more inclusive, patient-centred research and sustained advocacy, as evidenced in the image-text pieces produced by participants who identify as women of colour living with chronic pain, discussed later in the section on the *Photovoice* research study.

Carelessness in Medical and Academic Research Settings

At the British Pain Society's 2012 Special Interest Group for Philosophy and Ethics annual meeting, titled *The Ethics of Care*, participants analysed systemic failures in healthcare at the time. These shortcomings were attributed to a "loss of an ethos of care - not because their practitioners are essentially uncaring, but because of financial, organisational pressures, as well as the challenge of reconciling biomedical science with holistic approaches to healing and caring for the "whole person" ("The Ethics of Care," 2012, p.3). Subsequent speakers reinforced the importance of treating the whole person, acknowledging their place within chronic pain's more-than-human relational network. One speaker noted that "Medicine's preoccupation with the biology of the disease risks distracting us from the biography of the person that is both the essential context of the biological problem and essential to its solution" ("The Ethics of Care," 2012, p.17). Care work extends beyond formalised tasks, encompassing institutional and everyday acts of care. Indeed, care work is broadly defined as the relational, emotional, and practical labour involved in supporting others, especially in contexts of vulnerability, dependence, or interdependence.

It would be disingenuous to discuss academic research and EoC without acknowledging what has been termed the "carelessness" in academic life. Like medical practitioners, academics operate under heavy institutional scrutiny, where auditing and organisational priorities frequently undermine genuine care despite pervasive rhetoric that superficially champions it. In academia, care is increasingly instrumentalised as a managerial tool, appearing in diversity statements, wellness programmes, and mentorship policies, while being disconnected from lived, relational ethics. Applying an EoC lens to academic research practices reveals how institutional inequities shape who bears the burdens of care within research teams. These disparities span institutional hierarchies and career stages, with graduate students and early-career researchers often burdened by emotional, administrative, and relational labour with little recognition or support. This lack of care, or academia's broader "moral status" of carelessness, is especially prevalent in research-intensive universities, where Lynch (2010, p. 59) argues that "the pursuit of unbridled self-interest (rationalised in terms of a "career") has not only been normalised, but it has also attained status and legitimacy." To counter academia's pervasive carelessness, an EoC ought to be structurally embedded within institutional frameworks. This requires formally recognising and rewarding relational labour, such as mentoring, emotional support and collaborative work, through hiring practices, promotion criteria, and workload distribution changes. Key steps include fostering relational accountability through cooperative research models, implementing inclusive decision-making, and establishing mechanisms for repair when harm occurs. Care ethics should inform research practices, particularly in community-engaged or trauma-informed work, with deliberate attention to the well-being of both participants and researchers. Institutional success metrics should be redefined to prioritise equity, well-being, and collaboration over narrow productivity measures. Structural inequities, particularly across institutional types (e.g., R-01 vs. research-focused) and career stages, must be addressed to ensure that care is not merely performative but systematically enacted. While institutional transformation remains inadequate, individual scholars and research teams can proactively model EoC principles through collaborative structures.

Care-full Team Building to Solve Wicked Problems

Writing on EoC, Carol Bacchi reminds us that "how we talk about or theorise care means examining critically the concepts we use–asking what they allow us to see and what they (may) leave out" (Bacchi, 2024). How care is understood and applied in research (ie., by whom; whose voices are heard and whose are silenced) leads to partiality of knowledge and perpetuates inequities. It is therefore essential to critically examine how chronic pain research unfolds and to develop, test, and advance models of inquiry that intentionally amplify marginalised voices. Bringing together diverse perspectives is also central to studying "wicked problems," a class of complex, contentious problems that defy complete definition and resolution, and for which there is no single solution (Rittel and Webber, 1974). To solve them requires thinking beyond any one discipline, necessitating interdisciplinary teams of individuals with "interpersonal and professional skills that allow them to collaborate successfully within diverse teams of researchers and other stakeholders" (Kawa et al. 2021, 2). Chronic pain is known to be a wicked problem, and our approach was to build an interdisciplinary team to consider it from new angles and to ensure that perspectives of people living with chronic pain were central - not only as "subjects" to be studied but as participants in the research itself.

The overall project began after Jane Prophet, an interdisciplinary visual artist whose collaborations with scientists bridge art and science (Prophet, 2016; Prophet and d'Inverno, 2004), met with an anaesthesiologist and expert in translational science, Dr. George Mashour, an advocate for team science (Kabo and Mashour, 2019) and for the contributions that the arts can make to the clinical sciences (Dittman Stanich and LaPensee, 2022). He introduced Dr. Prophet to Dr. Hassett, a pain researcher who develops tailored and innovative approaches to support people living with chronic pain in ways that enable them to thrive (Hassett and Gevirtz, 2009; Nicol et al., 2016). Dr. Mashour sourced funds for Drs. Hassett and Prophet to explore chronic pain using arts-informed methods through collaborations that adapted team science approaches ("Team Science," 2016) to a team art and science model. After a scoping review of arts-informed approaches to ameliorating chronic pain, they contacted colleagues to see who might be interested in joining the team. Our initial academic research team comprised twelve core individuals from the University of Michigan: six faculty members from art, design, and music; one from social work; two clinical researchers from pain research and psychology; and two paid graduate research assistants from design and social work. Later, Dr Rahbel Rahman-Tahir joined in, bringing her expertise in race and community-based participatory research (Rahman et al., 2023; Pinto et al., 2021). They began with in-person meetings to build trust and understanding among team members with different disciplinary backgrounds. Creating a safe space for team members to describe their situation, aspirations, and motivations was key. During these gatherings, team members described their professional roles and situations and revealed much about their personal lives as they built trust. Four team members disclosed that they had lived experience of chronic pain - slightly above the U.S. national prevalence of 21% - which aligns with expectations for a group self-selecting to engage in research on a personally relevant topic. All were committed to and had experience in community-engaged research using various methods. This team brought a wide range of positionalities across race, ethnicity, gender, sexuality, and disability, shaping there intersectional perspective and informing our research approach.

Our Perspective

In early meetings, we showcased our research and creative work. We described our preferred research production and dissemination methods, which included deeper dives into methods that were arts-informed, such as *Discursive Design* (Tharp and Tharp, 2019), and those that had a creative component from social work, like *Photovoice* (Wang and Burris, 1997). The primary question guiding our discussions was, "How might creative practices with participants who live with chronic pain increase well-being, advocate for changes to healthcare, and enable those living with chronic pain to thrive?" In our first team meeting, we considered the different needs of team members, their individual goals and how they were situated. This discussion was one we returned to repeatedly throughout our work together. By the end of our collaboration, we had identified ten significant differences that mattered to us as we scoped how we might work together and then embark on interdisciplinary research in an academic setting with an EoC. These are not exhaustive, but they were essential to our project. Intentionally discovering our differences helped us begin learning how to conduct caring research that divided effort more equitably and would enable us to advocate for institutional change whilst supporting one another.

We learned from first-hand accounts from our teammates that:

1. Allocated research time varies, with individuals on research contracts having more time than colleagues on research/teaching or teaching-only contracts.

2. There are significant differences in teaching loads between different schools/departments within a university and between research-intensive and teaching-intensive universities.
3. Remuneration varied based on colleagues' employers, contract type, rank and disciplines.
4. The pressure on STEMM colleagues and colleagues with research-only contracts to secure grants often exceeded the expectations placed on art colleagues. However, colleagues from art and design had fewer opportunities to access external funding, and their funding was of lesser amounts.
5. Access to university facilities differed significantly, with artists and designers frequently bearing personal expenses for external studio space. At the same time, STEMM and social science researchers often have space allocated by their universities.
6. The range of qualitative and quantitative research varied, with STEMM researchers generally being more familiar with quantitative methods than researchers from art and design backgrounds.
7. We had different traditions and norms associated with working with community participants.
8. There was a wide variety in accepted and preferred forms of dissemination, from exhibitions to papers.
9. Our team comprised people at all career stages, from graduate students to early career researchers to full professors, with associated hierarchies and power differentials.
10. Each team member's life situation and position affected the time and energy they had for research.

To foster a caring collaborative environment, we agreed that involvement would be voluntary, with members able to step back or leave anytime. Given the small grant, graduate students and community participants would be compensated, but salaried faculty and researchers would not. We co-designed clear objectives, in line with team effectiveness studies, showing that clear goals and committed individuals are critical for predicting the overall success of joint projects (Poulton and West, 1999).

Distributed Leadership and Co-Designing Research with Community Participants

In our large-group meetings, potential research projects emerged, with people drawn to specific methods and groups living with chronic pain. Instead of voting for the most popular, we formed smaller interdisciplinary teams, each co-researching with participants to help people thrive despite living with chronic pain. We disrupted the often-instrumentalist structures of STEAM collaborations (Halpern and Rogers, 2021), where artists frequently serve scientists. Each of our six research teams, consisting of 2-6 members led or co-led by art and design researchers, fostered an inclusive leadership structure, based on an EoC commitment of mutual respect and engagement. Periodic group meetings allowed discussion and sharing about practices that worked well, helping one another develop ways to overcome barriers, and reminding one another of how we could best balance individual interests and career goals throughout the research process. Each project used arts-informed methodologies designed to centre participants whose expertise stemmed from living with chronic pain with intersecting health disparities. One team comprising two designers and a pain researcher developed reflective tools, including mindset collages and relationship maps, to empower chronic pain sufferers who identified as women. Another team, consisting of a musician and a pain researcher, worked with African American elders to gather data and explore how music could soothe and express pain, then develop online "social prescription" playlists. An artist and pain researcher co-designed collage kits for patients to create layered translucent lightbox works to express their pain. Another team, composed of an artist and psychologist, co-designed an augmented reality app for youth living with sickle cell anaemia, enabling them to express their wishes for change in healthcare support. Through the collaboration of an artist-designer and psychologist, a team explored the integration of wearable technology for youth living with pain to help them self-soothe and distract from their pain. Lastly, through a partnership with an artist (Prophet), pain researcher (Hassett) and a *Photovoice* expert from the University of Michigan (Kattari) and a social work expert from Fordham University (Rahman-Tahir), we designed a *Photovoice* study that empowered participants identifying as women of colour living with chronic pain to share their perspectives and experiences through photos and texts.

Photovoice is a well-established and rigorous "participatory action research method that involves placing cameras in the hands of participants so that they may visually represent and communicate to others their lived experiences" (Wang and Burris, 1997, p. 13). The *Photovoice* approach offers unique insights into patients' experiences living with chronic pain. During this process, participants respond to prompts by taking photographs and then reflect on and discuss these photos in a facilitated group setting. The structure offered opportunities for critical reflection on both individual and communal levels. This approach has been used to investigate the complexities of living with chronic pain (Wheeler and Early, 2018; Wallace et al., 2014). However, few studies have explicitly examined how gender, ethnicity, and race intersect to shape health disparities in chronic pain populations. *Photovoice* positions participants as experts in their lived experiences, empowering them to use photography and narrative to inform and advocate for changes in clinical practices, health strategies, and policy-making. This participatory approach has proven valuable for working with under-represented and vulnerable populations because it is "relatively unobtrusive and has the capacity to be empowering" (Wilkin and Liamputtong, 2010). Numerous *Photovoice* projects have effectively highlighted areas requiring systemic change (Drew, Duncan, and Sawyer, 2010), and aligns with our team's experience using art-based methods to bridge scientific research and patient experience. Our approach emphasises meaningful engagement with science rather than one-way dissemination (Gubrium, Hill, and Flicker 2014), a principle that underpins this project. *Photovoice* has been utilised in many studies to explore complex or sensitive topics, including intersectional healthcare disparities, while fostering collaborative knowledge production (Padgett et al., 2013; Wang, Cash, and Powers, 2000). Through the iterative process of taking photographs, group discussion, and narrative development, participants document, analyse and reflect upon their personal and collective experiences, captured in their visual representations that are accompanied by short texts.

Co-designing a Photovoice Study

To improve our study design, we engaged in community feedback to refine our approach. The Michigan Institute for Clinical Health Research (MICHR) facilitated a 90-minute Community Engagement Studio, where two research team members presented proposals for the *Photovoice* study and related reflective tools study. Nine participants, all women with lived experience of chronic pain, recruited from MICHR's UMHealthResearch.org registry, provided input to improve the study's responsiveness to their needs. These participants were compensated with a meal and a $20 cash card for their advice. MICHR staff facilitated the session, and our role was to listen actively and answer questions concisely, reflecting EoC's principle of the wisdom of embodiment. The Community Engagement Studio took place in 2019, before the COVID-19 pandemic. Initially, we planned in-person sessions. However, respondents suggested that the study be conducted via Skype or Blue Jeans due to concerns about exhaustion, pain, and stress. At the time, *Virtual Photovoice* had no precedent, making it hard to get approval from the Institutional Review Board. However, after COVID-19 disrupted in-person plans, we secured ethics approval to conduct the study online, pioneering *Virtual Photovoice* (Chen, 2022). One participant, who used art therapy for self-care, emphasised physical comfort and suggested flexible seating, movement breaks, and individual comfort preferences. We applied them to our virtual format, encouraging participants (n=20 across two groups) to prioritise their well-being (e.g., turning off the camera when needed). Remarkably, only one participant dropped out. The twenty others who stayed were likely able to adjust more easily if they experienced pain or discomfort. Other practical recommendations included scheduling sessions in the evening, as many pain sufferers need extra time in the morning to manage their condition. Expert opinions were divided on whether caregivers should be included in the sessions. Some felt uncomfortable with caregivers present, while others wanted them to be excluded in order to speak truthfully. We decided to offer caregivers a space with compensation, but no one took it up. Advisers also suggested broader recruitment criteria, so we used the clinical definition of chronic pain lasting more than three months and did not require a clinical diagnosis.

The financial burden of chronic pain is as high as $635 billion annually in the US (Muneer 2015). In addition to social costs, individuals and families face lost earnings and increased medical and self-care expenses. Given this, it was unsurprising that advisers questioned participant compensation, suggesting $25 to $50 per session. We settled on offering a $50 gift card per session. Advisers also inquired about the *Photovoice* approach, asking if participants could take pictures of anything they chose. They believed this freedom could encourage creativity. We confirmed this, with the condition that participants could only photograph people if they obtained consent and signed permission forms. Some participants did take images of others with the necessary consent. The overall sentiment from the Engagement Studio was that: "this *Photovoice* group could help others and empower them to express themselves and advocate and communicate using their art" (Anonymous participant).

Participants' Insights into More-than-Human suffering and thriving from our Photovoice Study

Subsequently, our study *Deepening Public Engagement with Chronic Pain Research: A Photovoice Project: Using Art and Design for Translational Medical Research with Pain Researchers and Patients* received ethics approval from the University of Michigan Health Sciences and Behavioural Sciences Institutional Review Board (approval # HUM00166379). The study, which involved twenty people who self-identified as women of colour working in two groups, facilitated by Dr. Rahman-Tahir with Dr. Prophet acting as technical assistant, was completed in the summer of 2021. We detailed how we adapted *Photovoice* using arts-informed methods and incorporating asynchronous videos to introduce participants to foundational concepts from art and photography theory on interpreting images and image-text works. We also explained practical art-based techniques such as lighting, scene composition, and the intentional use of colour in a separate paper (Prophet, Rahman and Hassett, 2023). In summary, the participants took photographs, created short narratives to accompany each photograph, and sorted this data into groups, defining categories. Each group reached a consensus about how to share the publications to advocate for changes in healthcare. The two groups shared their connected publications as printed books and eBooks. One group chose the title *Journeying beyond pain: our truth as women of colour*, and the title of the other group's work was *The Invisible Struggle* (20 Anonymous Participants, 2022).

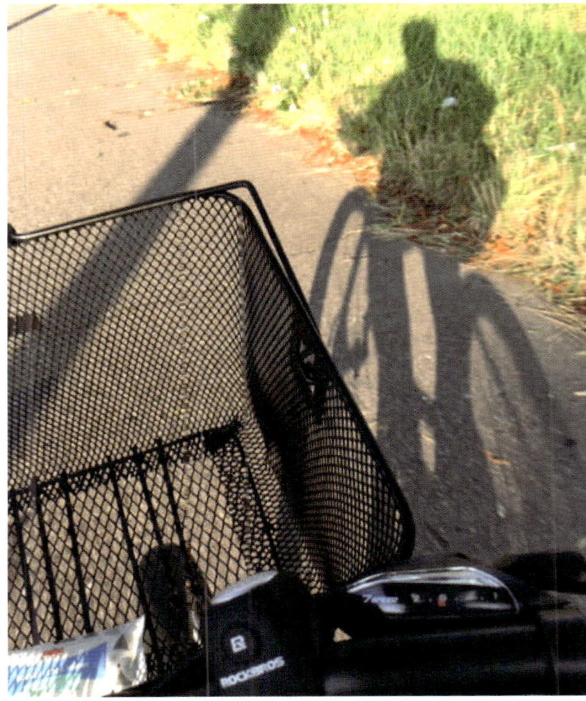

Figure 1: "This shows more of me on the bike. It's like proof of proof of life. It's like I'm really riding this bike. It's not me talking about riding the bike. The bike itself is not important. It's the process of riding it that's important, and so this is me, in flight." (Jan, *Photovoice* piece from the 2021 study). Reproduced with permission.

Pain is more than a physical sensation; it is becoming understood as a whole-person experience that can cause suffering (Siler, Borneman, and Ferrell, 2019). As a more-than-human relational network, the pain humans feel is not solely a human experience but a complex interplay of biological, psychological, and social factors extending beyond individual bodies and encompassing relationships with other beings and the environment.

Studies that compare pain and suffering suggest that suffering is a separate but related experience that can be significantly impacted by the individual's perception and coping mechanisms. Hassett's research explores the key role that the human brain plays in processing pain and how small, simple actions can make profound changes in how we experience chronic pain, showing that it is possible to find ways of thriving despite living with chronic pain (Hassett, 2023). Positioning humans as part of a more-than-human relational network invites a shift in perception that understands the environment, plants, and animals not as passive backdrops or resources, but as active participants in interconnected systems of meaning, care, and mutual influence.

Photo-text pairs and how each group categorised them reveal individuals' fluctuating movement across a spectrum of suffering and thriving, illustrating how seemingly simple environmental interactions can alleviate or intensify pain. In (Figure 1), Jan depicts her embodied entanglement with the riverside landscape through cycling, describing it as liberating and affirming, "It's the process of riding that's important, and so this is me, in flight." In contrast, the interlacing staircases of a train station (Figure 2) were perceived as overwhelming. The group categorised them as an "everyday activity that can be difficult," under the broader theme of "obstacles."

These examples reflect an EoC orientation, where well-being is understood as emerging through relational, contextual, and embodied engagements with environments, objects, and nonhuman life. Many participants described their relationships with nonhuman animals and plants as sustaining, particularly through sensory encounters with plants. Shaima observed (Figure 3), "Sometimes you forget about those beautiful plants and then you see them... These are beautiful things that we should stop and look at. Just like pain, I guess - we have to accept it too." Here, care transcends instrumental acts; it is rooted in attentiveness to one's surroundings and an acceptance of embodied vulnerability. Practices like bringing flowers indoors, cultivating herbs, or tending to gardens emerged as acts of care toward self, space, and nonhuman others - as shown in Romona's contribution (Figure 4). These findings underscore the situated, relational, and more-than-human dimensions of care, challenging conventional framing within strictly clinical or interpersonal domains.

Conclusion

This paper demonstrates how an EoC approach - centred on relationality, attentiveness, and responsiveness - can meaningfully reshape research on chronic pain by addressing systemic inequities and valuing lived experience. Through arts-informed, interdisciplinary collaborations, we created a research environment where participants were engaged as co-creators of knowledge rather than passive subjects, and where self-care practices, suffering, and thriving were explored within a more-than-human relational framework. *The Photovoice* approach, adapted to reflect participants' embodied realities and cultural contexts, enabled nuanced expressions of pain and care, foregrounding the environmental, social, and structural conditions that shape chronic pain experiences.

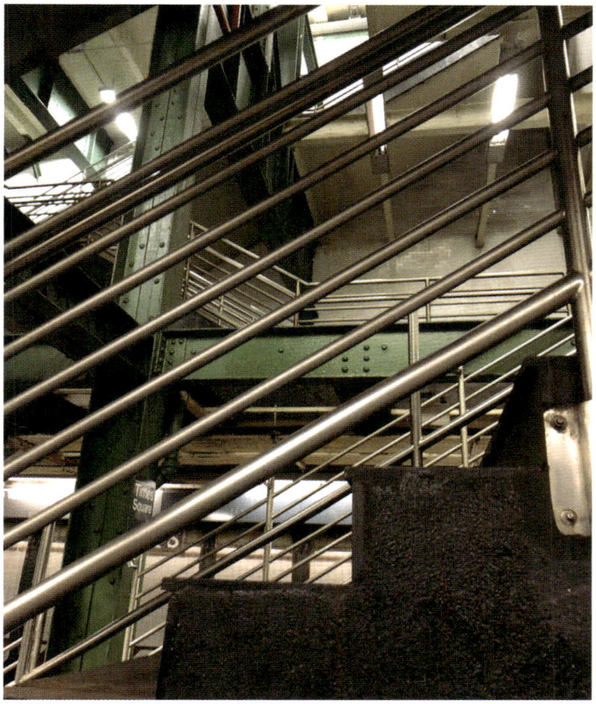

Figure 2: "This is a series of staircases that interlace through the middle of the station and feel never ending, especially if you are experiencing some kind of pain. I've seen plenty of people just stopped midway to catch their breath. My thoughts moved to how I would probably need to take the escalator. When you're catching the 2 train, you need to go up about three stories high which is broken up into half staircases, so there's really six levels of stairs which feel terrible, especially when you're in pain or it's too hot. So, I was actually at the bottom of that staircase and I took a photo as I was looking for the escalator. Just things that I didn't have to think about before. I'm not excited about the Michigan transportation system. It's made for cars, and so, if you have a car you're good to go, you can manage, you can get places sometimes that's the only way you can get places. So it makes me think about the infrastructure here, how that got put into place and who have the ability to own a car. It raised questions about managing transportation when you can't afford a car, or when you can't afford the gas for the car? All of those sort of considerations that you need to have, as you plot your life somewhere." (Doreen, *Photovoice* piece from the 2021 study). Reproduced with permission.

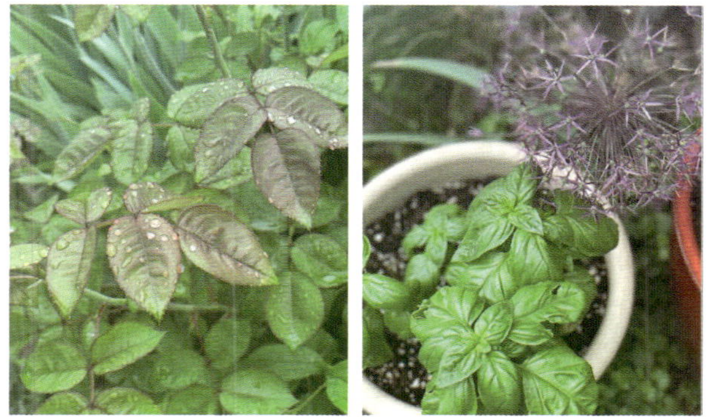

Figure 3: "And I was walking around it just poured rain and then stopped and the plants looked so fresh and so hydrated that I took my phone and I started taking pictures. Cause I really liked the moment, right after the rain. Just that pop of green and the smell, you know, earth. You're walking or just doing things, sometimes you forget about the pain. And sometimes you forget about those beautiful plants and then you see them, so I feel it's kind of the same thing, these are beautiful things that we should stop and look at. Just like pain, I guess, we have to accept it too. I used to paint and I know I see some purple in the left picture and you know the right, I feel both of them next to each other. Even though they're completely different plants but I feel both of them kind of complement each other." (Shaima, *Photovoice* piece from the 2021 study). Reproduced with permission.

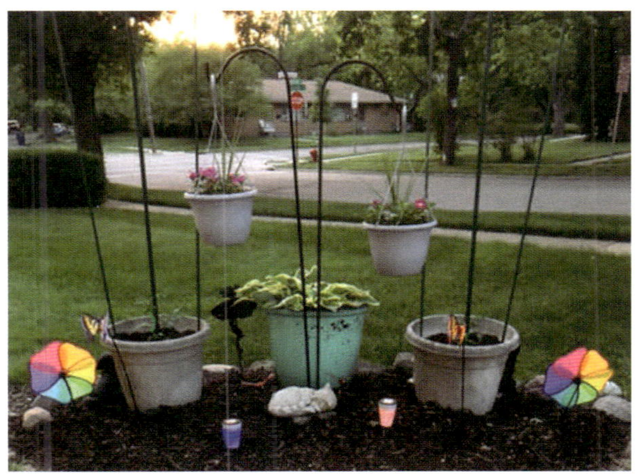

Figure 4: "My garden photo illustrates what I enjoy from taking care of my garden and the peace and tranquility I get from watching the colors change on my solar butterflies and stands." (Romona, *Photovoice* piece from the 2021 study). Reproduced with permission.

We argue for increased institutional support for interdisciplinary collaborations that draw on the strengths of art and design, STEMM, and social work to confront complex, "wicked" problems like chronic pain. Building research teams grounded in an EoC requires time, reflexivity, and sustained attention to power dynamics, disciplinary norms, and differential access to institutional resources. By addressing these differences, research teams can become more inclusive, ethically grounded, and deliver innovative research. By revaluing relational labour, designing equitable structures, and amplifying marginalised voices, this project illustrates how careful research practices can generate deeper understanding and new pathways for advocacy, healing, and institutional change.

Acknowledgements

This study was funded by the University of Michigan's Michigan Institute of Clinical Health Research, The Institute of Research into Women and Gender, and Stamps School of Art and Design. We are especially grateful to George Mashour for his advice and support of the larger project. *The Photovoice* study is one of six arts-informed translational research projects. We thank Dr. Shanna Kattari from UM's School of Social Work, who has experience designing and facilitating *Photovoice* studies and training facilitators, for advising us as we developed our draft design for this study. We also thank the team who worked hard to design the planned in-person study: Zahra Chevannes, Colleen Clark, Tricia Piechowski, Meghan Spiroff, and Ariel Mallett, who helped implement *The Virtual Photovoice.*

References

- Anonymous Participants, 2022. Journeying beyond Pain: Our Truth as Women of Color, and, The Invisible Struggle. Blurb Books. Available at: https://figshare.com/authors/Jane_Prophet/20964686 [Accessed 28 April 2025].
- Bacchi, C., 2024. 'Care Ethics: The Feminist Ethic of Care (FEC) and WPR'. Carol Bacchi (blog), 30 March. Available at: https://carolbacchi.com/2024/03/30/care-ethics-the-feminist-ethic-of-care-fec-and-wpr/ [Accessed 28 April 2025].
- Breivik, H., Collett, B., Ventafridda, V., Cohen, R. and Gallacher, D., 2006. 'Survey of Chronic Pain in Europe: Prevalence, Impact on Daily Life, and Treatment'. European Journal of Pain, 10(4), pp. 287-333.
- Chen, J., 2022. 'Digitally Dispersed, Remotely Engaged: Interrogating Participation in Virtual Photovoice'. Qualitative Research, p. 14687941221110175.
- Dahlhamer, J., Lucas, J., Zelaya, C., Nahin, R., Mackey, S., DeBar, L., Kerns, R., Von Korff, M., Porter, L. and Helmick, C., 2018. 'Prevalence of Chronic Pain and High-Impact Chronic Pain among Adults—United States, 2016'. Morbidity and Mortality Weekly Report, 67(36), p. 1001.
- Dittman Stanich, V. and LaPensee, E., 2022. 'Supporting Artists on STEMM Research Teams: Why and How'. Insights. Ann Arbor, Michigan, US: The Alliance for the Arts in Research Universities (a2ru). Available at: https://a2ru.org/research/supporting-artists-on-stemm-research-teams-why-and-how/ [Accessed 28 April 2025].
- Drew, S.E., Duncan, R.E. and Sawyer, S.M., 2010. 'Visual Storytelling: A Beneficial but Challenging Method for Health Research with Young People'. Qualitative Health Research, 20(12), pp. 1677-1688.
- eClinicalMedicine, 2024. 'Gendered Pain: A Call for Recognition and Health Equity'. eClinicalMedicine, 69 (March). Available at: https://doi.org/10.1016/j.eclinm.2024.102558 [Accessed 28 April 2025].
- Edwards, C.L., Fillingim, R.B. and Keefe, F., 2001. 'Race, Ethnicity and Pain'. Pain, 94(2), pp. 133-137.
- Gubrium, A.C., Hill, A.L. and Flicker, S., 2014. 'A Situated Practice of Ethics for Participatory Visual and Digital Methods in Public Health Research and Practice: A Focus on Digital Storytelling'. American Journal of Public Health, 104(9), pp. 1606-1614.
- Halpern, M.K. and Rogers, H.S., 2021. 'Art-Science Collaborations, Complexities and Challenges'. In: Routledge Handbook of Public Communication of Science and Technology, pp. 214-237. Routledge.
- Hassett, A.L., 2023. Chronic Pain Reset: 30 Days of Activities, Practices and Skills to Help You Thrive. Hachette UK.
- Haukenes, I., Hensing, G., Stålnacke, B.-M. and Hammarström, A., 2015. 'Does Pain Severity Guide Selection to Multimodal Pain Rehabilitation across Gender?' European Journal of Pain, 19(6), pp. 826-833.
- Hoffman, K.M., Trawalter, S., Axt, J.R. and Oliver, M.N., 2016. 'Racial Bias in Pain Assessment and Treatment

- Hassett, A.L. and Gevirtz, R.N., 2009. ‘Nonpharmacologic Treatment for Fibromyalgia: Patient Education, Cognitive-Behavioral Therapy, Relaxation Techniques, and Complementary and Alternative Medicine’. Rheumatic Disease Clinics, 35(2), pp. 393-407.
- Haukenes, I., Hensing, G., Stålnacke, B.-M. and Hammarström, A., 2015. ‘Does Pain Severity Guide Selection to Multimodal Pain Rehabilitation across Gender?’ European Journal of Pain, 19(6), pp. 826-833.
- Hoffman, K.M., Trawalter, S., Axt, J.R. and Oliver, M.N., 2016. ‘Racial Bias in Pain Assessment and Treatment Recommendations, and False Beliefs about Biological Differences between Blacks and Whites’. Proceedings of the National Academy of Sciences, 113(16), pp. 4296-4301.
- Johansson, E.E., Hamberg, K., Lindgren, G. and Westman, G., 1996. ‘“I’ve Been Crying My Way”—Qualitative Analysis of a Group of Female Patients’ Consultation Experiences’. Family Practice, 13(6), pp. 498-503.
- Kabo, F.W. and Mashour, G.A., 2019. ‘Measuring Team Science: Associations between a Clinical-Translational Science Institute and Investigator Ego Networks’. Journal of Clinical and Translational Science, 2(6), pp. 363-370.
- Kawa, N.C., Arceño, M.A., Goeckner, R., Hunter, C.E., Rhue, S.J., Scaggs, S.A., Biwer, M.E., Downey, S.S., Field, J.S. and Gremillion, K., 2021. ‘Training Wicked Scientists for a World of Wicked Problems’. Humanities and Social Sciences Communications, 8(1).
- Nicol, A.L., Sieberg, C.B., Clauw, D.J., Hassett, A.L., Moser, S.E. and Brummett, C.M., 2016. ‘The Association between a History of Lifetime Traumatic Events and Pain Severity, Physical Function, and Affective Distress in Patients with Chronic Pain’. The Journal of Pain, 17(12), pp. 1334-1348.
- Noddings, N., 1984. Caring: A Feminine Approach to Ethics and Moral Education.
- Padgett, D.K., Smith, B.T., Derejko, K.-S., Henwood, B.F. and Tiderington, E., 2013. ‘A Picture Is Worth…? Photo Elicitation Interviewing with Formerly Homeless Adults’. Qualitative Health Research, 23(11), pp. 1435-1444.
- Pinto, R.M., Rahman, R., Zanchetta, M.S. and Galhego-Garcia, W., 2021. ‘Brazil’s Community Health Workers Practicing Narrative Medicine: Patients’ Perspectives’. Journal of General Internal Medicine, pp. 1-9.
- Prophet, J., 2016. ‘Self-Portrait of the Artist Meditating on Death: A Feminist Technoscience Reading of the Apparatus of Contemporary Neuroscience Experiments’. In: The Routledge Companion to Biology in Art and Architecture, pp. 482-503. Milton Park, Abingdon, Oxon; New York, NY: Routledge.
- Prophet, J. and d’Inverno, M., 2004. ‘Creative Conflict in Interdisciplinary Collaboration: Interpretation, Scale and Emergence’. In: Interaction: Systems, Theory and Practice, pp. 251-270. Creativity and Cognition Studios.
- Prophet, J., Rahman, R. and Hassett, A.L., 2023. ‘An Online Photovoice Study Designed by Researchers from Art and Social Work to Better Understand the Experience of Chronic Pain by Women of Color’. AM Journal of Art and Media Studies, (32), pp. 69-89.
- Rahman, R., Azhar, S., Wernick, L.J., DeVylder, J.E., Maschi, T., Cohen, M. and Hopwood, S., 2023. ‘Mask Mandates, Race, and Protests of Summer 2020’. In: Dual Pandemics, pp. 154-165. Routledge.
- Rittel, H.W. and Webber, M.M., 1974. ‘Wicked Problems’. Man-Made Futures, 26(1), pp. 272-280.
- Siler, S., Borneman, T. and Ferrell, B., 2019. ‘Pain and Suffering’. In: 35. pp. 310-314. Elsevier.
- Team Science, 2016. Team Science. The Academy of Medical Sciences. Available at: https://acmedsci.ac.uk/policy/policy-projects/team-science [Accessed 28 April 2025].
- Tharp, B.M. and Tharp, S.M., 2019. Discursive Design: Critical, Speculative, and Alternative Things. MIT Press.
- The Ethics of Care, 2012. Transcript. Special Interest Group for Philosophy and Ethics. Ambleside, UK: The British Pain Society. Available at: https://www.britishpainsociety.org/static/uploads/resources/files/2012_The_Ethics_of_Care.pdf [Accessed 28 April 2025].
- Treede, R.D., Rief, W., Barke, A., Aziz, Q., Bennett, M.I., Benoliel, R., Cohen, M. et al., 2015. ‘A Classification of Chronic Pain for ICD-11’. Pain, 156(6), pp.1003-1007. Available at: https://doi.org/10.1097/j.pain.0000000000000160 [Accessed 28 April 2025].
- Tronto, J., 1993. Moral Boundaries: Towards a Political Ethic of Care.
- Wakefield, E.O., Pantaleao, A., Popp, J.M., Dale, L.P., Santanelli, J.P., Litt, M.D. and Zempsky, W.T., 2018. ‘Describing Perceived Racial Bias Among Youth with Sickle Cell Disease’. Journal of Pediatric Psychology, 43(7), pp. 779-788. Available at: https://doi.org/10.1093/jpepsy/jsy015 [Accessed 28 April 2025].
- Wallace, L.S., Wexler, R.K., McDougle, L., Miser, W.F. and Haddox, J.D., 2014. ‘Voices That May Not Otherwise Be Heard: A Qualitative Exploration into the Perspectives of Primary Care Patients Living with Chronic Pain’. Journal of Pain Research, 7, pp. 291-. Available at: http://link.galegroup.com/apps/doc/A400956167/HRCA?u=umuser&sid=HRCA&xid=4004ef1e [Accessed 28 April 2025].
- Wang, C., and Burris, M.A., 1997. ‘Photovoice: Concept, Methodology, and Use for Participatory Needs Assessment’. Health Education & Behavior, 24(3), pp. 369-387.
- Wang, C.C., Cash, J.L. and Powers, L.S., 2000. ‘Who Knows Streets as Well as the Homeless? Promoting Personal and Community Action through Photovoice’. Health Promotion Practice, 1(1), pp. 81-89.
- Ware, N.C., 1992. ‘Suffering and the Social Construction of Illness: The Delegitimation of Illness Experience in Chronic Fatigue Syndrome’. Medical Anthropology Quarterly, 6(4), pp. 347-361.
- Wilkin, A. and Liamputtong, P., 2010. ‘The Photovoice Method: Researching the Experiences of Aboriginal Health Workers through Photographs’. Australian Journal of Primary Health, 16(3), pp. 231-239.

SUPPLEMENT

CURRENT RESOURCES OF "HERSTORICAL" SIGNIFICANCE

Karen Ann Wong-Dorall

In recent years, numerous initiatives have emerged to support women – particularly those who have been historically marginalised – working at the intersection of art and science. These initiatives recognise the need for both online and in-person spaces where women can engage with the ethics of care and explore the transformative potential of transdisciplinary art and science practices. Rooted in the belief that feminist perspectives are essential for advancing equality, these efforts foster collaboration, experimentation, and dialogue, while addressing issues such as gender inequality, scientific representation, and the need for more inclusive narratives in both art and science. The following list features key organisations, platforms, and networks at the forefront of supporting women in these fields. Each entry highlights a unique initiative – ranging from community-building efforts to interviews with leading women in their interdisciplinary practice – that offers valuable resources, opportunities, and inspiration. While this chapter focuses primarily on women in art-science contexts, it also gestures towards wider feminist and rights-based movements in which women continue to play vital roles. These include global efforts to advance social justice, advocate for equity, and challenge structural barriers across multiple domains, including education, policy, and humanitarian work. Together, these initiatives foster inclusive environments where women can thrive, collaborate, and drive meaningful change.

Ars Electronica

http://ars.electronica.art/news/en/

Ars Electronica, founded in 1979 in Linz, Austria, is a renowned organisation that blends art, technology, and society. Its mission is to explore the intersection of these fields and promote innovation through interdisciplinary collaboration. Known for its annual Ars Electronica Festival, the organisation showcases cutting-edge digital art and fosters dialogue on topics like artificial intelligence, cybernetics, and environmental issues. Ars Electronicas' contributions to media art and its role in shaping the future of technology-driven creativity are globally recognised.

AWARE: Archives of Women Artists, Research & Exhibitions

http://awarewomenartists.com
Villa Vassilieff - 21, avenue du Maine 75015, Paris (France), info@aware-art.org

AWARE: Archives of Women Artists, Research & Exhibitions, founded in 2014 by curator Camille Morineau, is a non-profit dedicated to making women artists of the 18th to 20th centuries visible. The platform shares bilingual content, research, and interviews by over 500 global contributors. AWARE organises international events, symposiums, and awards, including the AWARE Prizes. It hosts a research centre in Paris, supports gender-sensitive research through initiatives like TEAM, AMIS, and NEST, and fosters global networks for women and non-binary artists.

Bioart Laboratories Foundation

http://bioartlab.com

BioArt Laboratories Foundation, founded in 2011 by Jalila Essaïdi, is a nonprofit fostering innovation at the intersection of science, technology, nature, and creativity. Based in Eindhoven, it attracts diverse professionals to collaborate on cutting-edge biotech and life sciences projects. Offering access to labs, biomaterials, and expert networks, it encourages entrepreneurship and creative exploration. The foundation supports emerging talents through events, exhibitions, and collaborations with universities and research centres, helping to develop new biomaterials, startups, and crossover innovations.

Bioartsociety

http://bioartsociety.fi

The Bioartsociety, based in Finland, is a platform for interdisciplinary projects at the intersection of art, technology, and biology. It supports artists and scientists working with biotechnology, offering resources to explore bioart practices. Established in 2008, the society has over 150 members in Finland and internationally. The association develops and facilitates activities that blend art and science, with a focus on biology, ecology, and life sciences. Ongoing collaborations include Ars Bioarctica, an art and science residency with the University of Helsinki, and a partnership with BioClub Tokyo and The Finnish Institute in Japan.

Faces

https://www.faces-l.net/

Faces is an international network for women in media arts, founded in 1997 by Diana McCarty, Kathy Rae Huffman, and Valie Djordjevic. It emerged from discussions at media culture events, addressing the lack of visibility for women in media. The main aim is to create a space for women to connect, share projects, and collaborate across various media fields. By 2025, the network had grown to include over 500 women, offering opportunities for information exchange and fostering a strong presence of women in digital and media arts.

Femeeting

https://femeeting.com/

Established in 2017 by artist Marta de Menezes and scholar Dalila Honorato, FEMeeting is a conference dedicated to promoting collaboration among women in art, science, and technology. Its aim is to disseminate projects, develop research methodologies, and foster collaboration strategies to enhance knowledge sharing. FEMeeting has facilitated numerous events, including conferences in Portugal, online gatherings during the pandemic, and collaborations with global nodes. Key achievements include the creation of *Teapot Chat and Sister Labs*, strengthening communication and support among women in the field.

Guerrilla Girls

https://www.guerrillagirls.com/

The Guerrilla Girls are anonymous artist activists using disruptive visuals, statistics, and headlines to expose gender and ethnic bias in art, film, politics, and pop culture. They champion intersectional feminism and human rights, revealing hidden stories and challenging mainstream narratives. Their projects, including posters, actions, and exhibitions at major museums, have spanned the globe. Notable works include interventions at the Whitney Museum and Tate Modern, with their book *Guerrilla Girls: The Art of Behaving Badly* named a top art book of 2020.

Nparadoxia – UK

http://www.katydeepwell.com/
Publisher: https://www.ktpress.co.uk/

n.paradoxa is an international feminist art journal focused on women, feminism, and contemporary art. Founded by Katy Deppwell in 1996, it started as a website and became a bi-annual print journal, publishing over 500 articles from women artists, curators, and writers in over 80 countries. Achievements include the Feminist-Art-Observatory and early cyberfeminist issues. Deppwell's work challenges dominant knowledge systems and promotes feminist knowledge through KT press, a not-for-profit publisher on feminism and contemporary art.

Women Eco Artists Dialogue (WEAD)

https://www.weadartists.org/

WEAD (Women Eco Artists Dialogue) is a pioneering network of feminist eco-artists, educators, curators, and writers working toward ecological and social justice. Founded to highlight women's unique perspectives, WEAD facilitates international networking, promotes ecofeminism, and supports environmental sustainability. By creating interdisciplinary platforms, WEAD fosters the growth of eco-art practices and amplifies the voices of women in the environmental movement. Members engage in exhibitions, publications, and educational outreach to challenge ecological degradation and promote eco-consciousness. *Art and Science Series:* A web series exploring intersections between art and science. Available at: https://www.weadartists.org/art-and-science-series

Institute Of Art Gender Nature (IAGN) – Switzerland

https://www.fhnw.ch/de

The Institute of Art Gender Nature (IAGN), led by Chus Martínez, explores art's connection to diversity, interspecies coexistence, social justice, and love. It promotes the coexistence of modern science, technology, and indigenous knowledge, emphasising diverse systems of thought for a post-colonial society. IAGN fosters collective learning, creating trust between artists and art, which transfers to society. Key initiatives include *The Womxn's Factor, Promise No Promises!* podcast series, *Art is Ocean seminars, Phenomenal Ocean* podcast, and the *ACT: Performance Festival* for Swiss art students.

Wins ETHZ Society for Women in the Natural Sciences – Switzerland

https://wins.ethz.ch/

WiNS (Women in Natural Sciences) is a student and alumni organisation at ETH Zurich that supports women in the natural sciences. WiNS promotes gender equality and fosters an inclusive community for women pursuing science and engineering fields. The organisation offers networking events, career advice, and mentorship opportunities, helping women connect with professionals and researchers. By creating a platform for women in STEM, WiNS works to overcome the challenges faced by women in male-dominated fields and contribute to a more balanced scientific community.

LASERZURICH – Switzerland

https://www.laserzurich.com/
Director: Jill Scott, info@laserzurich.com

LASERZURICH is a creative incubator that bridges the arts and sciences, aiming to foster public dialogue and mutual understanding. It provides a platform for discussions on new inventions, scientific discoveries, and challenging ideas across disciplines. In partnership with Life Science Zurich, *LASERZURICH* has developed an experiential, gender-equal, and educational research approach. Their initiatives include publications and community events, promoting equal opportunities, equal representation, human rights, and environmental justice. Upcoming talks include: *Biodiversity, Water, Us and Soil and Resilience, Climate Extremes and Microorganisms.*

Mz. Baltazar's Laboratory – Austria

https://www.mzbaltazarslaboratory.org/de/
orga@lists.mzbaltazarslaboratory.org

Mz.* Baltazar's Laboratory, founded in 2008 by Stefanie Wuschitz and Patricia J. Reis, is a creative space that bridges art, technology, and activism, promoting fearless making and provocative thinking. Rooted in open-source technology, it offers an inclusive, accessible, and radical environment, especially for those traditionally excluded from scientific and tech spaces, such as women and transgender individuals. The lab fosters intersectional feminist values, supporting empowerment, and challenging patriarchy through workshops, exhibitions, and events. Its collective, composed of diverse members, is flexible and collaborative, coming from various cultural, linguistic, and educational backgrounds.

STEAM

https://brilliantlabs.medium.com/why-steam-education-matters-for-girls-in-canada-88a757518f39

STEAM integrates art into traditional STEM education, creating a transdisciplinary approach that fosters creativity and collaboration. Its aim is to empower girls by building confidence, challenging stereotypes, and providing equal opportunities in science and technology. STEAM has successfully engaged young girls, particularly through initiatives like bio-making, while promoting gender equality and encouraging problem-solving and analytical thinking. This approach has also led to a positive shift in science museums, where art is increasingly recognised as an essential part of science education for driving positive change. See Article: Fostering Future Innovators - The Role of STEAM Education for Girls in Canada

Stemettes – UK

https://stemettes.org/

Stemettes is an award-winning social enterprise that inspires and supports girls, young women, and non-binary individuals to pursue careers in Science, Technology, Engineering, Arts, and Maths (STEAM) across the UK, Ireland, and beyond. Their mission is to engage, inform, and connect the next generation by showcasing diverse role models in STEAM. By providing resources and opportunities, Stemettes aims to ensure that women and non-binary people are proportionally represented in these fields and can make informed career decisions.

Girls who Code

https://girlswhocode.com/

Girls Who Code is a global non-profit founded in 2012 by Reshma Saujani to close the gender gap in technology. The organisation offers free coding education through programs like Summer Immersion, Clubs, and College Loops, reaching over 670,000 girls, women, and non-binary individuals. In 2024, it introduced AI and Data Science courses, teaching students to apply these skills in areas such as financial literacy and music production. Girls Who Code aims to empower young women to lead in the tech industry and beyond.

Association for Women in Science (AWIS)

https://awis.org/

The Association for Women in Science (AWIS) advocates for equitable access to opportunities, mentorship, and resources for all women in STEM, especially those historically excluded. AWIS promotes diversity as a catalyst for scientific innovation, fosters work/life integration, and celebrates scientific contributions. It works to remove structural barriers, provides professional development, educates on bias, and supports women's career growth. AWIS is committed to creating inclusive spaces and fostering a sense of belonging within STEM fields.

The Marie Skłodowska-Curie Actions (MSCA)

https://marie-sklodowska-curie-actions.ec.europa.eu/

The Marie Skłodowska-Curie Actions (MSCA) program is committed to gender equality in research, with 44% female researchers. It promotes equal pay, work-life balance, and career development opportunities for women. MSCA fosters role models and inspires young women in STEM. By supporting mobility, excellence, and inclusiveness, MSCA encourages international cooperation, open science, and responsible research. It contributes to Europe's research and innovation capacity, supports the European Green Deal, and strengthens higher education institutions, research centres, and non-academic organisations globally.

Women In Science And Engineering (Wise) – UK

https://www.wisecampaign.org.uk/

WISE is a UK-based nonprofit that champions diversity in STEM, empowering women to enter, thrive, and lead in science and engineering fields. It aims to increase the participation of women in STEM careers through advocacy, education, and networking. WISE supports women in achieving leadership positions and helps organisations develop inclusive cultures. WISE runs mentoring programs, provides career development resources, and promotes female role models to help overcome the barriers women face in STEM industries.

Rightstech Women (RTW) – Switzerland

https://rightstech.org/

RightsTech Women (RTW) is a Geneva-based nonprofit founded in 2018 to advance the human rights of women and girls in STEM (Science, Technology, Engineering, and Mathematics). RTW aims to achieve gender parity in STEM education and employment by 2030 through advocacy, human rights education, and capacity-building initiatives. Notably, RTW was recognised as a champion in the 2021 WSIS Prizes for its innovative hybrid training programs that integrate STEM skills with human rights education.

Women In Tech® Global

https://women-in-tech.org/

Women in Tech® Global, founded in 2018 by Ayumi Moore Aoki and headquartered in Paris, is a leading organisation dedicated to closing the gender gap and empowering women in technology. With chapters in 54 countries and over 250,000 members, it aims to impact 5 million women and girls in STEAM by 2030. Its mission focuses on education, business, digital inclusion, and advocacy, driving systemic change and fostering international co-operation to create a more inclusive digital world.

Journal of Open Innovation: Technology, Market and Complexity

https://www.sciencedirect.com/journal/journal-of-open-innovation-technology-market-and-complexity

The Journal of Open Innovation: Technology, Market, and Complexity (JOItmC), established to explore open innovation, is a peer-reviewed, open access journal that covers multi-disciplinary research. The journal's mission is to address the limitations of capitalism and promote the sustainability of human economic life. It publishes research across various fields, including economics, management, public policy, and natural sciences.
Article: An Organisational Perspective on ArtScience Collaboration: Opportunities and Challenges of Platforms to Collaborate with Artists. Available at: https://www.sciencedirect.com/science/article/pii/S2199853122002591

Creative Resilience: Art by Women in Science – a Unesco Publication (2021)

https://www.unesco.org/en/creative-resilience

Creative Resilience is a UNESCO initiative launched in July 2021, inviting women in STEM worldwide to submit artworks reflecting their experiences during the COVID-19 pandemic. The exhibition features over 100 pieces by 54 women scientists from 31 countries, including neuroscientists, microbiologists, doctors, nurses, medical students, researchers, science communicators, engineers, and mathematicians. Through various art forms such as painting, photography, digital drawing, block print, sculpture, crocheting, and film, these «sci-artists» provide testimony of how the global health pandemic has transformed the way we interact and how we are slowly emerging from it into new, transformed societies. The exhibition aims to give visibility to women scientists, highlighting their unique scientific perspectives, personal journeys, creations, and resilience throughout the pandemic. It was inaugurated at UNESCO Headquarters in Paris on 27 October 2021 and featured at Expo Dubai in 2022. A 360° virtual tour is also available online, allowing global audiences to explore the exhibition.

The Feminist Arts Project – US

https://thefeministartproject.org/

The Feminist Art Project is an international collaborative initiative recognising the Feminist Art Movement and the aesthetic, intellectual and political impact of women on the visual arts, art history and art practice, past and present. The project is a strategic intervention against the ongoing erasure of women from the cultural record. The Feminist Art Project promotes diverse feminist art events and publications through its website calendar/archive and facilitates networking and regional program development worldwide.

National Museum of Women in the Arts (Nmwa) – US

https://nmwa.org/

The National Museum of Women in the Arts (NMWA) is the first museum dedicated exclusively to celebrating women in the arts. Founded in 1981, it promotes the representation of women artists through exhibitions, programs, and advocacy. NMWA highlights historical and contemporary women artists, aiming to address gender imbalances in the art world. Located in Washington, D.C., the museum's collection was built from the Holladay Collection and serves as a centre for education, social change, and cultural engagement.

Women's Art Library – UK

https://www.gold.ac.uk/make/

Located in the UK, the Women's Art Library (WAL) is a comprehensive research collection that explores women's contributions to the visual arts. It holds archival materials from women artists and creators, providing valuable resources for students, researchers, and anyone interested in learning about women's art history. WAL offers an online catalogue and exhibitions, fostering greater visibility for women artists and promoting awareness of their pivotal role in shaping art movements.

National Endowment For The Arts – US

https://www.arts.gov/

Established in 1965, the National Endowment for the Arts (NEA) is a federal agency that is the largest funder of arts and arts education in the U.S. It supports arts participation and fosters an environment where the arts benefit all Americans. The NEA provides grants to nonprofit organisations, public agencies, educational institutions, tribal communities, and individual writers and translators. Grants are reviewed by panels of arts experts and require matching nonfederal funding, with annual appropriations from Congress.
From their blog post (2023): At the Intersection of Art and Science: A Conversation with Rebecca Rutstein.
Available at: https://www.arts.gov/stories/blog/2023/intersection-art-and-science-conversation-rebecca-rutstein

Artconnect

https://www.magazine.artconnect.com/

ArtConnect's mission is to empower international artists by providing a platform that helps them access opportunities to advance their careers. Founded in 2012, ArtConnect is driven by an artist's first mindset and a commitment to making the art world more accessible. The platform fosters innovation and supports artists in thriving. With a focus on creating tools that enable success, ArtConnect has become the leading database of opportunities for artists worldwide, and continues to evolve its resources for future growth.
Interview with Artists: https://www.magazine.artconnect.com/interviews/collaborating-with-nature
Collaborating with Nature: Art and Sustainability: A look at some artistic practices working at the intersection of art and science, nature and technology.

The Royal Society – UK

https://royalsociety.org/news-resources/women-in-stem/

The Royal Society, founded in the 1660s, is an independent scientific academy of the UK, which aims to recognise, promote, and support excellence in science, while using science for the benefit of humanity. Its mission is to advance economic, social, and cultural well-being through scientific research and innovation. The Society plays three key roles: acting as a charity to support scientists, maintaining a Fellowship of eminent scientists, and serving as the UK's national academy to advocate for science and provide independent advice on scientific matters that benefit the public. In 2025, The Royal Society commemorated the 80th anniversary of the election of its first female Fellows with new documentaries, celebrating the achievements of women in STEM and honouring the pioneering scientists who were the first women elected to the Royal Society.

Technoetic Arts

https://intellectdiscover.com/content/journals/ta

Technoetic Arts is a platform for transdisciplinary research in art and technology. Technoetic Arts focuses upon the juncture between art, technology and the mind. Divisions between academic areas of study, once rigidly fixed, are gradually dissolving due to developments in science and cultural practice. This fusion has had a dramatic effect upon the scope of various disciplines. Women's Agency in Art and Science (Editorial, Oct 2023). Technoetic Arts. Available at: https://www.researchgate.net/publication/377676069_Editorial_Women's_agency_in_art_and_science

Human Rights Careers

https://www.humanrightscareers.com/?s=women%27s+rights

Human Rights Careers provides well-researched information on human rights career opportunities and creating accessible educational content. Their mission is to inspire young professionals and career changers to pursue human rights careers, educate through engaging content, and equip job seekers with the necessary skills. Run by a team of human rights professionals, the platform aims to make human rights careers more accessible to people from all backgrounds, serving as a launchpad for global human rights impact.

Association for Women's Rights in Development (Awid)

https://www.awid.org/

The Association for Women's Rights in Development (AWID) is a global feminist membership organisation founded over 40 years ago to advance gender justice and women's human rights. AWID supports feminist movements by challenging systems of oppression and co-creating feminist futures. Its key strategies include advocacy, solidarity, convening, and creative expression. AWID also leads initiatives to build feminist economies, strengthen movement resourcing, and uphold universal rights and justice. Through collaborative efforts, AWID fosters inclusive power-sharing and transformative, intersectional change worldwide.

The Revolutionary Association of the Women of Afghanistan (Rawa)

http://www.rawa.org/index.php

The Revolutionary Association of the Women of Afghanistan (RAWA) was founded in 1977 to fight for women's rights, social justice, and secular democracy in Afghanistan. It became involved in resistance against Soviet occupation and later fundamentalist groups like the Taliban. RAWA has established schools, hospitals, and training programs for refugee women. Despite facing violent opposition, including the assassination of its founder, RAWA continues its struggle for women's rights and political freedoms, advocating for a free, democratic, and secular Afghanistan.

Endnote

The above list of resources is incomplete and we hope you can add many more resources to it, to do so please write to SciArt, https://sciart.ch/contact/

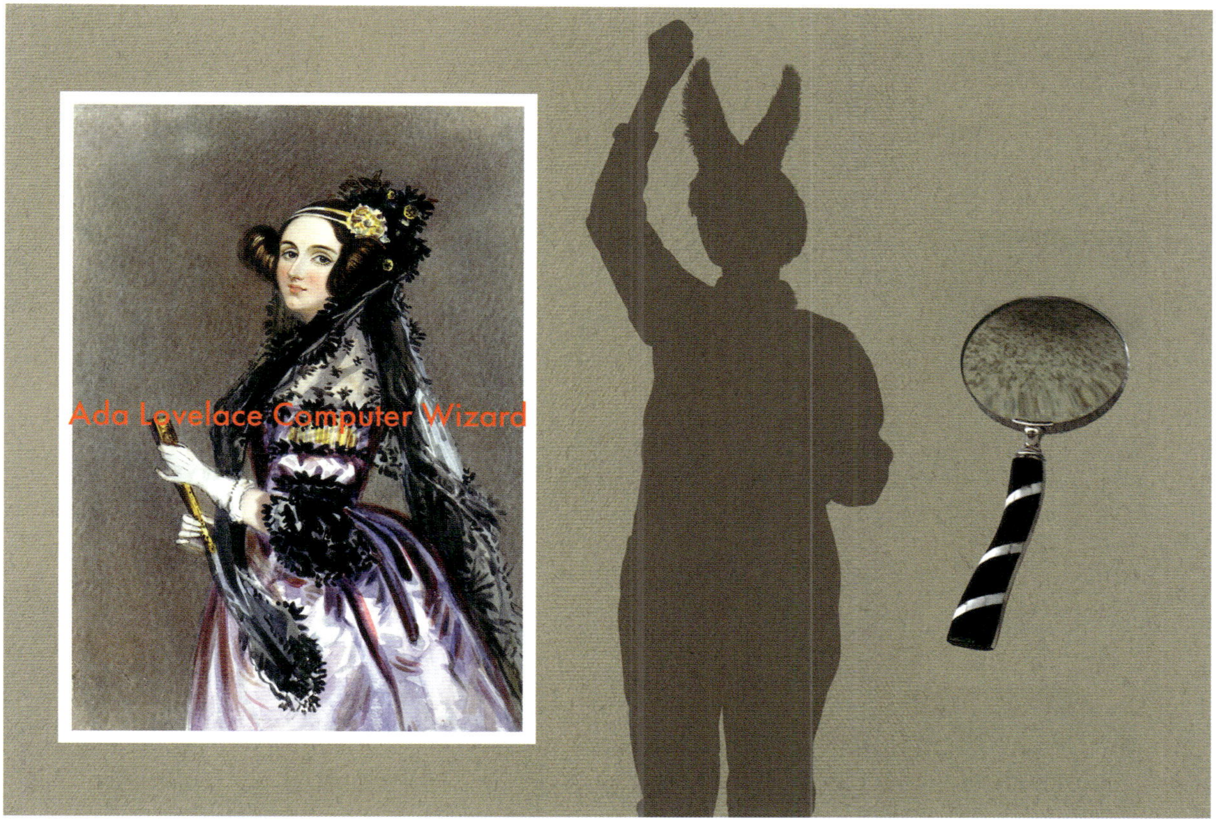

Are we all donkey? - the working of a survival kit. Rust, D. (2025).
This performance is a mesh-up of a lecture, workshop, experiment, improvisation and a dance and it asks again and again: What do donkeys, springtails, microorganisms in the soil and shee-dadas have in common? What stands for the feminine and for the other, or for the often stigmatised, the unknown and marginalised? What do they have to do with each other and with us? Performance Festival 2025, in Płocku Poland. https://dorothearust.ch (See page 95, related to the exhibition *Femel_Fissions*).

BIOGRAPHIES

Trish Adams

Trish Adams's research and artworks explore what it means to be human in the twenty-first century, particularly in relation to biotechnical and ecological developments. In 2003, she pioneered the creation of beating cardiac cells from her own adult stem cells at the University of Queensland, which informed her interactive artwork *machina carnis*. In 2007, as a visiting artist at the Queensland Brain Institute, Adams worked on cognitive and navigation experiments with European honeybees, leading to works like *HOST* (2008). Her ongoing honeybee research explores ecological issues such as the endangerment of bees and urban overcrowding, seen in works like *Urban Swarming* (2013) and *Disordered Swarming* (2014). Adams has also collaborated on projects focusing on deafness, including the Disconnections series, which received an Australia Council grant. She is currently an Adjunct Professor at QUT and a Visiting Research Fellow at RMIT University.

www.trishadams.tv

Tarsh Bates

Tarsh Bates was born in Mununjali/Beaudesert, Yugambeh/Queensland, grew up in Matamata, Aotearoa/New Zealand, and has lived for the last 35 years in Boorloo/Perth, Nyungar Boodja/South-Western Australia. They recently moved to Ubmeje, Sápmi, the lands of the Sámi people in northern Sweden. They have worked as a pizza delivery driver, fruit and vegetable stacker, toilet-paper packer, compost researcher, honeybee ejaculator, gallery invigilator, raspberry picker, academic, editor, bookkeeper, car detailer, and life drawing model. They have a background in biotechnology and contemporary art, and hold a Master and PhD in Biological Art from SymbioticA, the University of Western Australia. They have been a Seedbox postdoctoral research fellow at SymbioticA and an UmArts postdoctoral research fellow in Design and Molecular Biology at Umeå University. They are enamoured with *Candida albicans* and smell as ecological orientation.

http://tarshbates.tumblr.com/

Daniela Brill

Daniela Brill has been working as a university assistant with a diploma/master's degree at the Institute of Entrepreneurship at Johannes Kepler University since October 2024. Previously, she was a research assistant at the Communications Engineering department at Johannes Kepler University (January 2022–December 2023). Daniela is a visual artist from Bogotá, Colombia. She studied Transdisciplinary Art for her bachelor's degree and Art & Science for her master's degree at the University of Applied Arts Vienna. Her research focuses on the intersection between art-science, protest, and entrepreneurship, and the possible influences of aesthetic elements and artistic research on aesthetics and entrepreneurship. Daniela works artistically in collaboration with scientific institutions worldwide, including Art at CMS at CERN, the HEPHY institute in Vienna, the ORIGIN network of high energy physics, and the ArtSci Center + Lab UCLA. Brill is the creator and co-organiser of Suratómica. She has been awarded art-science residencies at ISTA, Coalesce BioArt, and others.

https://www.danielabrillestrada.com/

Kathleen Ditzig

Kathleen Ditzig is a Singaporean art historian and curator. As a curator at the National Gallery Singapore, she researches art histories of technology from a Southeast Asian perspective and works on projects related to advanced technologies. She received her PhD from Nanyang Technological University in 2023 with a dissertation titled *Exhibiting Southeast Asia in the Cultural Cold War: Geopolitics of Regional Art Exhibitions* (1940s–1980s). She obtained an MA from the Centre for Curatorial Studies, Bard College, in 2015. Beyond exhibitions, her research and writing have been published by *Southeast of Now* (NUS Press), *Journal of Social Issues in Southeast Asia* (NUS Press), *Afterall* (University of the Arts London), post: *Notes on Art in a Global Context* (MoMA), *Finance and Society* (Cambridge), *Artforum, OSMOS magazine, Art Agenda, Art Review Asia, and Flash Art*, and in books including *Perhaps It is High Time for a Xeno-Architecture to Match* (Sternberg, 2018).

https://www.artoutreachsingapore.org/bio/kathleen-ditzig

María Fernández

María Fernández is Associate Professor of Art History and Visual Studies at Cornell University. Her research interests include the history and theory of digital art, gender studies, Latin American art, and the intersections of these fields. She is the author of *Cosmopolitanism in Mexican Visual Culture* (University of Texas Press, 2014), for which she was awarded the Arvey Prize by the Association for Latin American Art in 2015. She edited *Latin American Modernisms and Technology* (Cornell Institute of Comparative Modernities and Africa World Press, 2018). With Faith Wilding and Michelle Wright, she co-edited Domain Errors: *Cyberfeminist* Practices (Autonomedia, 2002). Her essays have been published in journals and edited volumes, most recently in *Latin American and Latinx Visual Culture*, 5(2), 2023, and *A Companion to Feminist Art*, edited by Hilary Robinson and Maria Elena Buzek (Wiley, 2019). She is currently writing a book on the work of the British cybernetician Gordon Speedie Pask.

https://arthistory.cornell.edu/maria-fernandez

Afton Hassett

Hassett is a licensed clinical psychologist who is an associate professor and Director of Pain and Opioid Research in the Department of Anaesthesiology at the University of Michigan. As a principal investigator at the renowned Chronic Pain & Fatigue Research Center at UM, she conducts interdisciplinary research exploring the role of cognitive, affective, and behavioural factors in chronic pain, as well as scalable behavioural interventions. She has published over 120 peer-reviewed articles and is a leader in the field of resilience and pain. Dr Hassett is a past president of the Association of Rheumatology Professionals – a division of the American College of Rheumatology. She is also the author of *Chronic Pain Reset: 30 Days of Activities, Practices and Skills to Help You Thrive*, an innovative pain self-management book for patients and their clinicians.

https://aftonhassett.com/

Svenja Kratz

Svenja Kratz is an artist and researcher working at the intersection of art, science, and technology. She holds a PhD in Biotechnology and Contemporary Art from the Queensland University of Technology (QUT), with expertise in cell and tissue culture and interdisciplinary arts practice. Since 2008, she has collaborated with researchers across music, design, architecture, artificial intelligence, genetic engineering, molecular biology, and biomanufacturing to produce both collaborative and solo works that explore the complexity of living systems and highlight the philosophical and ethical implications of engineered life. She was a 2021 Australian Network for Art and Technology (ANAT) Synapse art-science recipient, and her creative works have been exhibited at local, national, and international venues, including the Sydney Powerhouse Museum (2013), Contemporary Art Tasmania (2016), the Science Gallery London (2019), and World Science Festival Brisbane (2024).

https://www.svenjakratz.com/

Alexandra Krawiec

Alexandra Krawiec is a Fellow of the Royal Society of Arts (RSA), the RSA's representative in Poland, and a member of the RSA's Responsible AI Steering Committee. She holds an MA in English philology and a PhD in economics. Her interests encompass decision-making, data management, organisational culture, and women's leadership. She currently serves as Head of Data Acquisition, a role that enables her to closely follow the development of artificial intelligence and its impact on science and daily life. Dr Krawiec began her career as a journalist at the BBC and has since worked as an academic, CEO of an art foundation, and documentary filmmaker. She has interviewed public figures, leading scientists, and Nobel Prize laureates. She has led or collaborated on projects with institutions including the European Research Council, the Massachusetts Institute of Technology, the 92nd Street Y, the Austrian Space Forum, the Polish Academy of Sciences, and others.

https://scholar.google.com/citations?user=tuy_rnAAAAAJ&hl=en

Bigna Lenggenhager

Bigna Lenggenhager is a cognitive neuropsychologist specialising in multisensory integration, the bodily self, interoception, and embodied cognition in both normative and clinically or experimentally altered states of consciousness. She has conducted research across academic and clinical institutions in Switzerland, Italy, and Germany, and frequently participates in interdisciplinary projects that bridge the domains of science, art, and medicine. Dr Lenggenhager is particularly interested in investigating phenomena that extend beyond conventional cognitive neuroscience – such as out-of-body experiences – which are often associated with parascience or mysticism. She maintains rigorous scientific standards, combining a range of psychological and neuroscientific methodologies, including virtual and augmented reality, and increasingly incorporates phenomenological and qualitative approaches. She has received interdisciplinary project grants from the Swiss National Science Foundation, the European Commission, the Universities of Zurich and Konstanz, and various private foundations. Her internationally recognised research has been published in over 100 peer-reviewed journal articles, reviews, and book chapters.

https://linktr.ee/inesmontalvao

Inês Montalvão

Inês Montalvão (Portugal, 1984) is a multidisciplinary creative with demonstrated experience in the museum field, exhibition design, and curation. She focuses her practice on art-science, exploring cross-disciplinary approaches, storytelling, illustration, and innovative ways to create meaningful experiences. Inês has been based in Helsinki, Finland, since 2017, where she co-founded Mandarina Collective, a group focused on art and science with a multicultural, diverse, and inclusive approach to their performances, workshops, and exhibitions. She is also co-founder of the Lingua Plantae project, which aims to develop a shared language between humans and plants through biodata sonification and sound curation. In May 2023, Inês began her role as Program Director for Artists with Evidence, an international organisation with a programme that fosters dialogue and innovation within the art-science field.

https://linktr.ee/inesmontalvao

Rachael Parsons

Rachael Parsons is an Australian curator, educator and academic, currently serving as Art Museum Director at the New England Regional Art Museum (NERAM). With over 12 years of experience, she has worked across independent and institutional contexts within university, commercial, public and artist-run spaces. Most recently, she held the position of Manager, Exhibitions and Curatorial at NERAM, where she delivered a range of public programmes and curated *HINTON: Treasures of Australian Art* - a permanent salon display drawn from NERAM's Howard Hinton Collection. Prior to her role at NERAM, Rachael was Curator for Digital Media at QUT Precincts (Queensland University of Technology), where she developed and managed an ambitious exhibition programme focused on contemporary digital, new media and technology-based creative practice. Her curatorial work at QUT showcased groundbreaking digital art by both local and international artists, with an emphasis on accessibility and public engagement with creative technologies.

https://www.neram.com.au/neram-announces-new-director/

Jane Prophet

Jane Prophet is a professor of Transforming Lives at Sheffield Hallam University, UK. She is an interdisciplinary visual artist and critical theorist of art, science, and new media whose work combines contemporary art, technology, and health studies. Her research explores how creative practices intersect with climate change, sustainability, and health challenges. She uses digital tools such as AI and projection mapping to address ecological change and human-environment interactions and collaborates with scientists to create art that bridges art and science. Her research on arts-informed approaches to health includes studies on chronic pain and public art's impact on reducing youth firearm injuries. Prophet employs creative practice and community-based participatory research methods informed by concepts from feminist science and technology studies. She co-edited *Plants By Numbers*, an open-access anthology exploring plant ecologies, art, design, and computation.

https://www.janeprophet.com/

Helen Pynor

Helen Pynor is an interdisciplinary artist and researcher whose practice explores philosophically and experientially ambiguous zones - such as the life-death boundary, the intersubjective nature of organ transplantation, and the animate-inanimate boundary in relation to prosthetics. She works across installation, sculpture, photography, video, media art, wet biology, microscopy, and performance. Pynor frequently undertakes in-depth residencies and collaborations in scientific and clinical institutions, including the Max Planck Institute of Molecular Cell Biology and Genetics, Dresden. Her work has been exhibited widely internationally, including at Tekniska Museet, Stockholm; ZKM | Centre for Art and Media, Karlsruhe; Beijing Media Art Biennale; National Taiwan Museum of Fine Arts; Experimenta International Triennial of Media Art, Australia; FACT (Foundation for Art and Creative Technology), Liverpool; Science Gallery Dublin; Museum of Applied Arts and Sciences, Sydney; and ISEA. She has received an Honourable Mention at Prix Ars Electronica, Linz, and national awards in Australia.

www.helenpynor.com

Rahbel Rahman-Tahir

Rahman studies organisational and provider-level factors influencing the community health worker workforce across Pakistan, Brazil, and the United States. She has expanded her focus to include providers with similar lived experiences as the clients they serve, namely peer educators and peer workers, using the umbrella term *community-based providers* in her research. She examines the structural, contextual, and provider-level factors that impact the community-based provider workforce's delivery of integrated services, including mental health, maternal health, sexual health, interpersonal violence, substance abuse, and disease prevention. Her research includes predictors of maternal mental health in the Pakistani community and explores how the COVID-19 pandemic exacerbated racism and stigma in the lives of both community-based providers and the clients they serve. She intentionally uses community-based participatory research (CBPR) approaches, reflecting her commitment to advancing health equity and healthcare delivery systems - specifically by shifting ownership of the research process to those impacted.

https://gss.news.fordham.edu/faculty/study-reveals-how-we-can-empower-community-health-workers/

Clarissa Ribeiro

Clarissa Ribeiro is an assistant professor in the Fine Arts Department, School of Communication and Arts at the University of São Paulo, and a former programme director of the Roy Ascott Studio's Technoetic Arts (TA) SIVA/DeTao Advanced Program in Shanghai. She holds a PhD in Arts (ECA USP/

Planetary Collegium, UK) and was awarded a Fulbright postdoctoral grant at UCLA's Art|Sci Center and Lab. Her work explores the intersection of art, science, and technology, focusing on cross-scale information dynamics, the exploration of ecologies-as-cosmologies, and metaphysical aspects of information visualisation. She holds the Pete Townshend Endowed Senior Lecturership in Performative Technoetics (2022–2024), serves on the editorial board of *Technoetic Arts* journal, and is an ad hoc reviewer for *Leonardo* journal. Since 2017, she has chaired the Leonardo/ISAST *LASER Talks* in Brazil and China. Her work has been widely published and exhibited internationally, and she also contributes to major international art and science platforms, including ISEA and SIGGRAPH.

https://www.clarissaribeiro.com/

Claudia Schnugg

Claudia Schnugg is a curator and art-science scholar based in Austria. She has been a researcher and visiting researcher at UCLA Art|Sci Center, JKU Linz, Copenhagen Business School, and the European Southern Observatory. Her 2019 book *Creating ArtScience Collaborations* was published by Palgrave Macmillan. Claudia curates residency programmes and art-science projects, resulting in more than 60 artworks over the past 10 years. She is the founding curator of the Universe Pavilion, Venice. Curated residencies include ARTcib SciArt Residency at acib Vienna, MASE at ESA/ESTEC, and Resonances IV at the JRC of the European Commission. Recent exhibitions include *NaturArchy* (iMAL, Brussels, 2024), *Intersecting Realities* (Palatul Stefania, Cultural Capital Timișoara, 2023), *Cosmic Elements* (Times Art Museum Beijing, 2023; China Resources Tower Arts Center, Shenzhen, 2023; Times Art Museum Chengdu, 2024), and *Cosmological Elements* (Fosun Foundation, Shanghai, 2022). Claudia is a member of international juries for art prizes, residency projects, and scientific boards for art-science projects.

https://www.claudiaschnugg.com

Jill Scott

Jill Scott is a media artist and a trans-disciplinary researcher. Currently, she curates the *LASER-ZURICH* for Leonardo Society USA. She is professor emerita at the Institute for Cultural Studies, at the University of the Arts (ZHdK) in Zurich and founded their Artists-in-Labs Program in 2000. Her own artwork spans 44 years of production about the human body, behaviour, and body politics, but in the last 24 years, she has focused on creative media art experiments about neuroscience, ecology, and sensory perception, presented in international conferences, festivals, and museums. Her works can be found in the collections of German Museums and Art Centers (ZKM), in Australian and US Museums. She has published six books on art and science research, including *Neuromedia: Art and Science Research* (Springer, 2018), *Transdiscourse 1: Mediated Environments* (2011), *Transdiscourse 2: Turbulence and Reconstruction* (2015) and *Transdiscourse 3: Women in Art Science and Body Politics* (2025) all with De Gruyter Press.

https://www.jillscott.org/

Christa Sommerer

Christa Sommerer is an internationally renowned media artist, researcher, and pioneer of interactive art. She has worked at the IAMAS Academy in Gifu, the ATR Research Labs in Kyoto, and the NCSA in Champaign-Urbana, USA. In 2004, together with Laurent Mignonneau, she established the Department of Interface Cultures in Linz, Austria. Sommerer has held visiting professorships at the Central Academy of Fine Arts (CAFA), Beijing; Tsukuba University; and Aalborg University, Denmark. Together with Laurent Mignonneau, she has created around 50 interactive artworks that have been exhibited in approximately 380 international exhibitions. Between 2021 and 2024, their 30-year retrospective exhibition toured from the ZKM in Karlsruhe to the OK Center Linz, iMAL Brussels, and Azkuna Zentroa in Bilbao (Ohlenschläger, Weibel & Weidinger, 2022). This exhibition is accompanied by a comprehensive overview of their artworks in the book *The Artwork as a Living System* (Ohlenschläger, Weibel & Weidinger, 2022).

https://interface.ufg.ac.at/christa-laurent/

Christian Stary

Christian Stary is currently a full professor of Business Informatics and heads the Communications Engineering department and the Knowledge Management Competence Centre at Johannes Kepler University Linz, Austria. He received his diploma in computer science in 1984, his PhD in usability engineering, and his Habilitation degree from the Vienna University of Technology, Austria, in 1988 and 1993, respectively. He has held visiting professorships in the USA and several European countries. His research interests include interactive distributed learning support systems that incorporate knowledge-based and organisational development techniques. His projects aim at intelligent design based on the needs of those involved. Process management plays a crucial role alongside the development of methods grounded in epistemology. His work is visible at international conferences and workshops on interdisciplinary research in stakeholder-centred development. He is involved in several international associations, for example as chairman of the International Council on Knowledge Management.

https://www.jku.at/kompetenzzentrum-wissensmanagement/ueber-uns/team/christian-stary/?utm_source=chatgpt.com

Margaret Tan

Margaret Tan was Senior Lecturer and Director of Programmes at Tembusu College, National University of Singapore (NUS), as well as Co-director of the NUS Art/Science Residency Programme. As a practising artist, she was one of the first artists-in-residence at The Cyberarts and Cyberculture Research Initiative at NUS (2001), and the Artist-in-Labs programme at the University of Applied Science and Arts in Zurich (2004). Her artworks investigate the intersections of body with space, technology, and culture from a feminist perspective, and have been showcased both locally and internationally. Margaret holds a BFA from RMIT/LASALLE College of the Arts, an MA in Interactive Media and Critical Theory from Goldsmiths College, University of London, and a PhD from the

Department of Communications and New Media, NUS, researching the topic of pervasive computing and Singapore's IT Masterplan called Intelligent Nation 2015 (Tan, 2015).

www.margaret-tan.com

Lubi Thomas

Lubi Thomas is a curator with extensive experience in digital and new media arts, working across exhibitions, festivals, residencies, mentorships and transdisciplinary projects. Her practice bridges the creative fields of art, technology, science and society – a curatorial intersection she has explored through a wide range of national and international projects. Lubi has developed cultural policy models and site-specific engagements with organisations including LEGO Education, ARS Electronica, the European Media Art Platform, the Royal Institution, Wellcome Trust and the Australia Council for the Arts. Over two decades, she has collaborated with artists whose work integrates scientific tools, technological innovation and research-based methods to produce compelling contemporary art. A hallmark of her curatorial approach is a commitment to site-responsive, audience-centred curation, whether within traditional galleries or non-traditional environments.

https://www.seditionart.com/users/lubi-thomas

Victoria Vesna

Victoria Vesna is an artist and professor at UCLA's Department of Design Media Arts and director of the Art|Sci Center, bridging the School of the Arts and the California NanoSystems Institute. Initially trained as a painter at the University of Belgrade (1984), her interdisciplinary work has evolved into experimental research exploring the impact of communication technologies on identity and behaviour, particularly in relation to scientific innovation. She earned her PhD from CAiiA-STAR, University of Wales (2000), and collaborates with scientists across disciplines – from neuroscience to nanotechnology. Vesna has exhibited in over 20 solo and 70 group shows, published more than 20 academic papers, and delivered over 100 invited talks. She is the North American editor of AI & Society and editor of *Database Aesthetics* (2007) and *Context Providers* (2011). Currently, she is developing a series on art, science and technology based on her UCLA online course.

https://victoriavesna.com

Karen Ann Wong-Dorall

Karen is an English Language Arts and Drama educator and professional actress working internationally across film, television, stage, and commercials. Raised in multicultural Singapore, she holds a BA (First Class Hons) in English Language and Drama and Performance, a Diploma in Education, and an MA in Professional Acting from Mountview Academy of Theatre Arts, London. Her creative practice blends performance and pedagogy. Equally at home in the classroom and on set, Karen teaches learners of all ages and collaborates with emerging theatre and filmmakers on imaginative, socially engaged projects. Known for portraying complex, assertive women, she recently appeared as Joyce Bayani in *Die Beschatter* (SRF/Netflix), *Neumatt* (SRF/Netflix), and *Game Over - The Fall of Credit Suisse* (Ascot Elite). She has taught in Singapore's public schools and IB programmes in Vienna, Zurich, and Basel. In 2022, she collaborated with Jill Scott on *The GMO Debate - Then and Now*, playing an NGO figure, and now takes on her latest role as researcher and copy editor in *Transdiscourse 3* (De Gruyter Press, 2025).

https://app.spotlight.com/3018-5646-7283

Rewa Wright

Rewa Wright is a senior lecturer in Creative Practice (Film, Screen & Animation) at Queensland University of Technology, Australia, and a media arts and computational design researcher whose work encompasses exhibition, performance, publication, presentation, and Indigenous justice. Wright's work has been included in SIGGRAPH 2023 (Los Angeles and Sydney), SIGGRAPH 2019 (Brisbane), Ars Electronica: In *Kepler's Gardens* 2020 (online), the Aotearoa Digital Arts Symposium 2022, The Wrong Biennale, and six iterations of the International Symposium of Electronic Arts (ISEA). She has over 20 years of experience in various aspects of motion-based and sonic media, including live performance, music, digital design, and virtual image creation. Her projects weave together emerging technologies, clean blockchains, and digital healthcare. Wright is an ecologically conscious researcher, and her Māori heritage (Ngāi Tawake/Te Kaimaroke/Te Uri o Hau hapu of Aotearoa/New Zealand) enables her to combine Indigenous knowledge systems from both embodied and scholarly perspectives.

https://rewawright.com/about/

Links for the CVs of the other featured artists or writers can be found in the relevant sections of this book.

The four guest artists in this book are:
Julie Rrap, https://www.julierrap.com
Dorothea Rust, https://dorothearust.ch/en/
VNS Matrix, https://vnsmatrix.net
Ulrike Rosenbach, https://ulrike-rosenbach.de

Editor
Jill Scott

Copyediting
Karen Ann Wong-Dorall
Marille Hahne

Cover Illustrations
Habitation. Helen Pynor. (2021).
The Artwork as a Living System. Christa Sommerer & Laurent Mignonneau. (2022).
Rhizopolis. Joanna Rajkowska. (2021).
Eskin. Jill Scott. (2018).
Flaps: *SOMOS Standing On My Own Shoulders.* Julie Rrap. (2024).

Graphic Design
Karin Schiesser, Zurich

This publication was generously supported by
SciArt: The Fusion of Discovery and Creativity Zurich Switzerland, https://sciart.ch
Cassinelli-Vogel-Stiftung, Zurich
LifeScience Zurich

Printing
Gerin Druck GmbH, A-Wolkersdorf

ISBN 978-3-68924-141-4
e-ISBN (PDF) 978-3-68924-148-3

Library of Congress Control Number: 2025943855

Bibliographic information published by the Deutsche Nationalbibliothek
The Deutsche Nationalbibliothek lists this publication in the Deutsche Nationalbibliografie; detailed bibliographic data are available on the Internet at http://dnb.dnb.de.

www.degruyterbrill.com
Questions about General Product Safety Regulation:
productsafety@degruyterbrill.com